FLORIDA'S CIVIL WAR

MERCER UNIVERSITY PRESS

Endowed by

TOM WATSON BROWN

and

THE WATSON-BROWN FOUNDATION, INC.

FLORIDA'S CIVIL WAR

Terrible Sacrifices

Tracy J. Revels

MERCER UNIVERSITY PRESS | *Macon, Georgia*

2016

MUP/ H923

© 2016 by Mercer University Press
Published by Mercer University Press
1501 Mercer University Drive
Macon, Georgia 31207
All rights reserved

9 8 7 6 5 4 3 2 1

Books published by Mercer University Press are printed on acid-free paper
that meets the requirements of the American National Standard for
Information Sciences—Permanence of Paper for Printed Library Materials.

ISBN   978-0-88146-589-1
Cataloging-in-Publication Data is available from the Library of Congress

For Dr. William Warren Rogers

Beloved professor, mentor, and friend

Contents

Preface

During the Civil War, a newspaper correspondent wrote that St. Augustine "is a part of another planet, having no special part or connection with the rest of the world."[1] He might as well have been writing about the entire state. No one, except perhaps the slightly more than 140,000 residents of the "Land of Flowers," seemed to think Florida had much of a connection to the Confederacy, to the war effort, or to life in general. Ignored and abandoned by the Confederate government, Florida struggled to craft its own defenses and provide provisions for the army, to which it had contributed a disproportionate number of its residents. Jefferson Davis's only interest in the state was in how much Florida could give, not in what Florida needed. Florida's governor, one of the few chief executives capable of pushing aside the doctrine of states' rights in favor of Confederate nationalism, protested such treatment, yet never refused Richmond's demands. For this willingness to meet the needs of the Confederacy, to yield to the calls for more men, money, and supplies, Florida received no great accolades or special recognition. Florida was lost even to the Lost Cause.

Florida is still a fascinating Confederate state. It was a region of great diversity of thought and experience. Though one-third of its white families owned slaves in 1860 and its most settled counties were part of the cotton plantation belt, Unionism (or at least a wait-and-see attitude) was so strong in Florida that the secession convention dared not put the ordinance of secession to a popular referendum. Planters were a minority of the Florida population. Most people were small farmers, and a surprising number made their living in professions not generally associated with enthusiasm for secession: real estate dealers, lumbermen, fishermen, wreckers, salt makers, wagon drivers, steamboat captains, and tourism entrepreneurs. While most rural Floridians were born in Southern states, Florida's port cities had a significant number of Yankee residents, many

---

[1] P. J Staudenraus, ed., "A War Correspondent's View of St. Augustine and Fernandina: 1863," *Florida Historical Quarterly* 41 (July 1962): 60.

of them recent immigrants with little attachment to the "peculiar institution" of slavery. Still, Florida was the third state to secede from the Union, a move that may be less surprising when one considers the regional connections of Florida's political leadership and the strange and unreasonable fear that gripped the state's white Southern population upon the election of Lincoln. Florida entered the Confederacy in the throes of Southern peer pressure, but over the course of four devastating years, a very different kind of pressure—that of a struggle to survive—shaped the state. Floridians of all varieties and loyalties found themselves asked to make many terrible sacrifices. This is their story.

* * *

I wrote *Florida's Civil War: Terrible Sacrifices* to provide a narrative of life in Florida during the Civil War, a story of men and women, free and slave, who worked, fought, lived and died in a place far from the famous fields of battle. I do not attempt to trace all military events within the state or to provide a comprehensive examination of the economic and political aspects of the war. This book is, hopefully, a consideration of the social factors that shaped the state and its role within the Confederacy. Readers who wish to dive deeper into the story will find suggestions for further reading in the footnotes and in the epilogue. The sources consulted in this work include many notable monographs and articles, all of which are readily accessible. In general, I avoided manuscripts and archival materials, except when necessary to allow ordinary Floridians to speak across time. In these cases, the spelling and punctuation of the period have been maintained.

As always, I would like to thank the many institutions and individuals who have made this book possible, beginning with the amazing editors and staff of Mercer University Press. I am deeply indebted to Wofford College for its continued support via research grants and constant, enthusiastic encouragement. My colleagues are wonderful, and my students are inspiring. The professional staff of the Sandor Tesler Library is superb and made research a joyful process. I am grateful to Dr. Phillip Stone (Wofford Archivist), Meghan Cathey, and Phillip Jones for their always superior assistance. I am also grateful to the staff of the State Library and Archives of Florida for their help, and to Dr. Joe Knetsch for his insight. Dr. Dwain Pruitt of the University of Louisville and Dr. Brian Rucker of Pensacola State College provided essential editing and constant friendship. I would like to also recognize the staff and volunteers of the North Florida Community College Library and the Treasures of Madison County. My mother, LaNora Zipperer, endured an early edit of this project and has been an inspiration to me in all aspects of my life.

My greatest gratitude is extended to my husband, Dr. John Moeller, who shared this project with me in the first year of our marriage, for which I love him all the more.

Finally, this book is dedicated with enduring affection to my dissertation director, Dr. William Warren Rogers, Professor Emeritus at Florida State University. Someone once told me that I "sounded like Bill Rogers." I have known no higher compliment.

This 1859 map of the state shows the clustering of settlements in the region known as Middle Florida, which stretched from Jackson County to Alachua County. This was Florida's plantation belt. Vast regions of the state were still largely uninhabited, and port cities such as Key West, Jacksonville, and Tampa held more diverse populations and divided opinions. *State Archives of Florida*

A Georgia native and the owner of a sizeable plantation, John Milton was a hardworking chief executive who cooperated with the Confederate government while remaining a strong advocate for his state. His tragic death only days before the end of the war deprived Florida of a dedicated public servant.
State Archives of Florida

Photographed around 1855, Mauma Mollie was the nurse and cook for the Partridge family of Jefferson County. Like many other slaves, she had migrated with her owner's family from South Carolina. Florida's frontier conditions meant that female slaves not only cooked and cleaned, but also drove livestock, chopped down trees, hunted, and worked in the fields. *State Archives of Florida*

Ordinary Floridians, especially those engaged in the cattle trade, were often referred to as "crackers." Tough and quick to anger, they were an independent and opportunistic segment of the population. During the war, some cracker cowmen joined the Cow Cavalry while others enlisted in Federal units. Providing for their families was generally more important than political allegiance to these Florida pioneers. This 1895 Frederic Remington sketch captures not only the look but also the attitude crackers maintained after the war. *State Archives of Florida*

Florida's Confederate women organized sewing circles, aid societies, and other charitable groups to support the war effort. They made uniforms and flags, raised funds, and provided assistance to indigent families. This 1861 composite portrait of the Ladies Soldiers Friend Sewing Society of Tallahassee includes many elite women who viewed themselves as "fighting" the war with their domestic skills. *State Archives of Florida*

A former senator from Florida, Stephen Russell Mallory served as Confederate Secretary of the Navy. Imaginative and innovative, he devised strategies to help the Confederacy overcome its scarcity of ships and sailors. Embracing new technology, Mallory backed the building of ironclads and the experiments which led to the first effective submarine. Briefly imprisoned after the war, he returned to his Florida law practice. Mallory died in 1873. *State Archives of Florida*

Salt-making was a vital enterprise in which Floridians excelled during the war. Very little expertise or technology was required, and Floridians were adept at repurposing old equipment. As this 1862 *Harper's Weekly* illustration shows, saltworks were frequently targeted by Union vessels. Workers were forced to flee and property was destroyed, but often within days of the attack a new establishment was operational. *State Archives of Florida*

This Madison County youth sat for his portrait before departing for the battlefield. His haphazard and nonregulation uniform was probably fashioned by family members. Perhaps he had not yet acquired a gun; if so, his condition was a reflection of many other Florida soldiers, who had a great deal of militant spirit but little beyond words to express it. *State Archives of Florida*

On February 20, 1864, the only major battle fought in Florida found Union and Confederate forces almost evenly matched. The staunch Confederate defense prevented Federals from marching into Middle Florida. While Union black troops showed their mettle, many of those who fell behind met horrific fates. The Confederate victory gave Floridians hope, though the Yankees maintained their stronghold in Northeast Florida. *State Archives of Florida*

Chapter 1

The Gates of Hell

Antebellum Florida and Secession

It was an "excitement that threw even the horse races in the shade." At precisely 12:22 p.m. on January 10, 1861, after days of impassioned speeches absorbed by "gloriously happy" Tallahassee spectators, the Florida convention voted 62–7 in favor of secession, declaring Florida a "Sovereign and Independent Republic."[1] As hats flew, handkerchiefs waved, and onlookers cheered, the delegates congratulated themselves on having launched a third Southern state from its Union mooring. Amid the revelry, a bold individual voiced a contrary opinion. Confronted the next day by rejoicing Secessionists who crowed that they had "done it," former territorial governor Richard Keith Call, once a companion of Andrew Jackson, fired back: "Yes, you have done it! You have opened the gates of Hell, from which shall flow the curses of the damned which shall sink you to perdition."[2]

Four years later, Florida and her sisters in rebellion would lie broken and helpless, their economies wrecked, their land shattered, and thousands of their sons committed to the grave. Their slaves would be freed, their political power smashed, and their families reduced to a cycle of poverty that would take generations to overcome. Florida and the other

---

[1]Susan Bradford Eppes, *Through Some Eventful Years*, 1926 facsimile ed. (Gainesville: University of Florida Press, 1968) 142; "Notes on Secession in Tallahassee and Leon County," *Florida Historical Quarterly* 4 (October 1925): 63–64; Donald R. Hadd, "The Irony of Secession," *Florida Historical Quarterly* 41 (July 1962): 27–28.

[2]Ellen Call Long, *Florida Breezes; or, Florida, New and Old*, 1883 facsimile ed. (Gainesville: University of Florida Press, 1962) 306–308.

Southern states would pay a high price for voiding the great compact of the Union via their secession.[3]

It is likely that none of these outcomes occurred to the people in Tallahassee, with exception of Richard Keith Call.

* * *

Northern newspapers were quick to dub Florida the "smallest tadpole in the dirty pool of secession," and with good reason. Florida was a large state in terms of territory, with some 54,000 square miles of land and almost 1,200 miles of coastline, but it was the smallest state of the Confederacy in population. The 1860 census records 140,424 individuals, almost evenly divided between white and black, free and slave. Florida had 41,128 white males and 36,319 white females to 31,348 slave males and 30,397 slave females. The free black population of Florida was miniscule, with only 454 males and 478 females. Florida was also a youthful state: 99,056 Florida residents were under the age of thirty, and the average white Floridian was just 21.2 years old. In the all-important category of white men aged 18 to 45, the age of military service, Florida could offer roughly 16,000.[4]

Florida became an American territory in 1821, after three centuries of being a kind of semi-tropical football kicked from one empire to another. It was a troublesome territory, difficult to govern, a haven for pirates, rebels, and renegades of all varieties. The Seminole Indians, who incorporated dispossessed Native Americans as well as escaped African slaves, also proved to be a powerful barrier to white American settlement.

---

[3]For a detailed and scholarly yet immensely readable study of the entire conflict, see James M. McPherson, *Battle Cry of Freedom: The Civil War Era* (New York: Oxford University Press, 1988). For a shorter but equally compelling narrative of events and outcomes, consult Louis P. Masur, *The Civil War: A Concise History* (New York: Oxford University Press, 2011).

[4]*Philadelphia Inquirer*, 2 February 1861; Canter Brown, Jr., "The Civil War, 1861–1865," in Michael Gannon, ed., *The New History of Florida* (Gainesville: University Press of Florida, 1996) 231; *Eighth Census, 1860; Population*, 50–53; Roland M. Harper, "Ante-Bellum Census Enumerations in Florida," *Florida Historical Quarterly* 6 (July 1927): 50–52.

A series of especially bloody wars was waged against the tribe. To encourage Americans to take up residence in the territory, in 1842 Congress passed the Armed Occupation Act, which offered 160-acre homesteads to adult males willing to risk their lives for Florida soil. By 1845, the year Florida entered the Union, most of the Seminoles had been forcibly removed, but enough Seminoles remained in the Everglades to fight a third brief war (the Billy Bowlegs War, 1856–1858) and to remain a lingering threat to settlers bold enough to plunge into the southern portion of the peninsula. Very little seemed to deter Florida's American pioneers, especially during the 1850s.[5]

In 1860 only about 36,000 of Florida's free residents were native to the state. Most of the non-natives had been born in other areas of the South. The majority of all Floridians were residents of the region known as Middle Florida, which stretched from Jackson County in the west to Alachua County in the East. The boom years of the 1850s had drawn people from other cotton-planting regions, with Middle Florida heavily infused by South Carolina and Georgia clans. They brought their slaves with them, establishing farms and plantations, committing Florida to the slaveholding mindset and regime. They also brought their politics, including the philosophy of states' rights and a virtual deification of John C. Calhoun. Even in the beginning of her statehood, Florida was thoroughly Old South.[6]

Florida's planters differed from their South Carolina and Georgia cousins in that they lived in frontier conditions, frequently lacking the refinements that characterized the aristocrats of the cotton kingdom. An observer noted that the average Florida planter "lived in a low, badly-built, wind-cracked, fenceless, vineless, paintless mansion in the Pine Lands," while Sarah Jones, the English governess of Governor John Mil-

[5]Charlton W. Tebeau, *A History of Florida* (Coral Gables: University of Miami Press, 1971) 149. For an overview of Florida's territorial and early statehood era, see Daniel L. Schafer, "U.S. Territory and State," and for a consideration of the Seminoles, see Brent R. Weisman, "Florida's Seminoles and Miccosukee Peoples," both in Michael Gannon, ed., *The New History of Florida*.

[6]Harper, "Ante-Bellum Census Enumerations in Florida," 55; Dorothy Dodd, *Florida in the War, 1861–1865* (Tallahassee: Peninsular Publishing, 1959) 11–13.

ton's children, characterized the Florida elite as a class that bragged of horses and carriages, but tolerated "slovenliness, disorder, incompleteness, and discomfort" in most other aspects of their lives.[7]

Though planters had status and were often community leaders, the majority of the state's white residents were not slaveholders. The typical white Floridian was a "cracker," a small farmer who lived a life of rude plenty. The term "cracker" may have come from the sound of a cattle whip, or from the cracking of corn, or even from the pastime of "cracking" a joke or tall tale. A cracker's "sole ambition was satisfied by the ownership of a few cattle that fed, winter and summer, on grass that cost nothing, and of hogs, which cost less, and of a few acres of corn requiring but little labor to ripen, and last, but most essential of all things, with a gun and ammunition for the hunt." Most crackers of this era possessed strong kinship ties, a belief in popular democracy, a tenacious connection to the land, and a firm sense of racial superiority over blacks, whom they believed were fit only for slavery. Borrowing a phrase from historian Frank L. Owsley, crackers were Florida's "plain folks." Though never a peasant class, before the war crackers tended to respect and follow the political leadership of the planters, hoping to prosper and join them as slaveholders.[8]

The African-American population of the state was largely enslaved. Most slaves labored in the fields of Middle Florida, but bondsmen and women could be found across the state. Approximately 7,000 slaves lived

---

[7]Julia Floyd Smith, *Slavery and Plantation Growth in Antebellum Florida, 1821–1860* (Gainesville: University of Florida Press, 1973) 4; Catherine Cooper Hopley {Sarah L. Jones}, *Life in the South* (London: Chapman and Hall, 1863) 2:252. An observer of life behind Confederate lines, the British author published her memoir under the name "Hopley," but historian Dorothy Dodd and Ellen Call Long stated that she used the name "Sarah Jones" while in Florida, and I have retained "Jones" throughout this text.

[8]James M. Denham, "The Florida Cracker before the Civil War as Seen through Travelers' Accounts," *Florida Historical Quarterly* 72 (April 1994): 456–57; George H. Gordon, *A War Diary of Events in the War of the Great Rebellion, 1863–1865* (Boston: James R. Osgood, 1882) 298. For the classic study of ordinary white Southerners, see Frank L. Owsley, *Plain Folk of the Old South* (Baton Rouge: Louisiana State University Press, 1949).

and worked in Florida's cities and small towns.[9] The rawness of settlement meant that slaves were required to perform a variety of tasks ranging from planting, plowing and harvesting to cutting lumber, draining swamps, and hauling goods. Slaves worked aboard riverboats and on trains and served in more specialized positions as cooks and teamsters in larger towns. There was little division of tasks by gender, and the frontier conditions of the state sometimes made for lapses in the severity of regulations, or led to owners assigning immense responsibility to trusted individuals.[10] But Florida was in no way an easier place to be enslaved. The heavy workloads and unsettled conditions took their toll, and with every year the institution became more important to the Florida economy. By the start of the Civil War approximately one-third of Florida's white families owned at least one slave, and even those Floridians without slaves saw the institution as foundational to the South's prosperity.[11]

Florida's free black population was clustered mainly in the state's coastal towns. Free blacks inhabited a netherworld between true freedom and complete bondage.[12] Some were descendants of free peoples of color who achieved their status during the Spanish and English occupations while others were immigrants from the Caribbean or, in rare cases, liberated slaves. Their very presence undermined the idea that blacks were inferior because many free blacks demonstrated solid work ethics and achieved modest financial success. During the 1850s, fear and jealousy led to a tightening of regulations on what many white Floridians perceived as "the most dangerous incendiary element" in their society. Free

---

[9]*Eighth Census, 1860: Population*, 50–53.

[10]Edwin L. Williams, Jr., "Negro Slavery in Florida: Part II," *Florida Historical Quarterly* 28 (January 1950): 187; Larry Eugene Rivers, "Dignity and Importance': Slavery in Jefferson County, Florida 1827–1860," *Florida Historical Quarterly* 61 (April 1983): 423–25; Smith, *Slavery and Plantation Growth*, 27. For the best monograph on slavery in the state, see Larry Eugene Rivers, *Slavery in Florida: Territorial Days to Emancipation* (Gainesville: University Press of Florida, 2000).

[11]Kenneth M Stampp, *The Peculiar Institution: Slavery in the Ante-Bellum South* (New York: Alfred A. Knopf, 1956) 30; Smith, *Slavery and Plantation Growth*, 10–11; Rivers, "Dignity and Importance,'" 404–405.

[12]*Eighth Census, 1860, Population*, 50–53.

persons of color were required to register in their communities, to maintain white guardians, and to pay exorbitant taxes and fees for even the smallest gatherings or entertainments. Oppressive ordinances in Pensacola caused a group of free blacks to abandon the city for Tampico, Mexico, in 1857. Most free persons of color in Florida lived simply and quietly, avoiding attention, being all too aware of how easily they could be enslaved in a mockery of due process.[13]

Florida's social and economic diversity historically resided in the port cities. St. Augustine, Fernandina, and Pensacola had known multiple European masters. Pensacola and Jacksonville were boomtowns in 1860, thriving with native Southern ambition and Yankee enterprise. Key West was home to sailors, wreckers, and scavengers of many nationalities, a salty city in all ways, where saloons outnumbered churches. Though only "a little village," Tampa welcomed schooners from New York and New Orleans, and counted Cuban fishermen, Irish laborers, and Yankee merchants among its residents. Almost every port along the coast made some claim to healthfulness and the advantages of consuming sea air in a tubercular age. This created the first waves of Florida tourists, who arrived to spend lonely winters in rickety boarding houses, often cursing both their illness and their innkeepers. While tiny by the standards of Savannah or New Orleans, the Florida port towns hummed with the activity of a new region coming to life and being incorporated into both national and international economies.[14] Florida's capital likewise

[13]Much work remains to be done on Florida's free persons of color. See Smith, *Slavery and Plantation Growth*, 93, 11–12, 119–20; David Y. Thomas, "The Free Negro in Florida before 1865," *South Atlantic Quarterly* (10 October 1911): 337–41; Ray Granade, "Slave Unrest in Florida," *Florida Historical Quarterly* 55 (July 1976): 23; John Hope Franklin and Allred A. Moss, Jr., *From Slavery to Freedom: A History of Negro Americans* 6th ed. (New York: Alfred A Knopf, 1988) 141.

[14]Otis L. Keene, "Jacksonville, Fifty-Three Years Ago: Recollections of a Veteran," *Florida Historical Quarterly* 1 (January 1909): 9–15; Herbert J. Doherty, Jr., "Florida in 1856," *Florida Historical Quarterly* 35 (July 1956): 61; Karl H. Grismer, *Tampa: A History of the City of Tampa and the Tampa Bay Region of Florida* (St. Petersburg: St. Petersburg Publishing, 1950) 131–35; John Solomon Otto, "Hillsborough County (1850): A Community in the South Florida Flatwoods," *Florida Historical Quarterly* 62 (October 1983): 193; Stan

was on the rise. Tallahassee's residents enjoyed horse races, circuses, theatrical performances, and May fetes. A mere village in a county of only 12,343 people, by 1860 Tallahassee also boasted fifty merchants, two newspapers, five churches, and twenty lawyers.[15]

Besides frequent outbreaks of tropical diseases such as yellow fever, Florida's greatest obstacle to growth and prosperity was poor transportation. The only comfortable mode of travel was via an ocean-going vessel or on a steamer along the St. Johns River. Roads were nothing more than old Indian trails. An overland journey from Gainesville to Tallahassee could take more than a week. The state possessed only six railroads, including the just-completed Florida Railroad (from Jacksonville to Cedar Key), and none was designed to link Florida to the north. Combined, the Florida railroads had a mere 401.5 miles of track and very little in the way of rolling stock. Even the newest and best line, the Florida, had only two passenger cars.[16]

Vast tracts of central and southern Florida were uninhabited, at least by law-abiding citizens. Fewer than 300 people lived along the Atlantic Coast south of Cape Canaveral, most of them clustered into what were called the Indian River settlements. The region of modern Miami was home to fewer than thirty people, and the entire area was considered nothing more than a refuge for pirates. Much of Florida was still, in many ways, a "rogue's paradise" despite its decade and a half of statehood. Anyone unfortunate enough to have to travel across the state took his chances with outlaws, who were generally more aggressive than panthers and bears. Cracker wives did chores with shotguns at the ready, and

Windhorn and Wright Langley, *Yesterday's Key West* (Miami: E. A. Seeman, 1973) 22.

[15]Mary Louise Ellis and William Warren Rogers, *Tallahassee and Leon County: A History and Bibliography* (Tallahassee: Historic Tallahassee Preservation Board, 1986) 12; William Warren Rogers, "A Great Stirring in the Land: Tallahassee and Leon County in 1860," *Florida Historical Quarterly* 64 (October 1985): 154; Clifton Paisley, *The Red Hills of Florida, 1528–1865* (Tuscaloosa: University of Alabama Press, 1989) 187–90.

[16]Tebeau, *A History of Florida*, 191–92; John E. Johns, *Florida during the Civil War* (Gainesville: University of Florida Press, 1963) 134. Johns's work remains a milepost in the study of Civil War Florida.

Florida's children grew up with tales of bloody Indian massacres. Even Tallahassee had its share of gore, as politically motivated duels had achieved legendary proportions.[17]

Despite its hazards as the nation's southernmost frontier, Floridians were proud of their young state and felt a deep connection to their fellow Southerners, to whom they were bound by blood.[18] Secession was a topic around Florida's porches and dinner tables during the turbulent 1850s. Increasingly, Floridians and other Southerners believed that arguments for halting the spread of slavery in the territories were actually battle cries for ending slavery in the South.[19] Susan Bradford Eppes of Tallahassee recalled how her family freely discussed the political issues of the day, but started locking all their doors after John Brown's 1859 raid on Harper's Ferry. Fear was replacing faith in the Union, and Floridians increasingly turned toward a more radical position as the decade waned.[20]

The 1850s was a decade of economic growth but political calcification in Florida. The Whig party was dying in both the nation and the state. In 1852, Floridians elected Democrats to the governor's chair and

[17]Rodney E. Dillon, Jr., "South Florida in 1860," *Florida Historical Quarterly* 60 (April 1982): 440–43; Grismer, *Tampa*, 131–35; Rodney E. Dillon, Jr., "'A Gang of Pirates': Confederate Lighthouse Raids in Southeast Florida, 1861," *Florida Historical Quarterly* 67 (April 1989): 441–42; Herbert J. Doherty, Jr., "Code Duello in Florida," *Florida Historical Quarterly* 29 (April 1951): 244–52. For a thorough discussion of antebellum Florida's violent past, see James M. Denham, *"A Rogue's Paradise": Crime and Punishment in Antebellum Florida, 1821–1861* (Tuscaloosa: University of Alabama Press, 1997).

[18]Edward E. Baptist, "The Migration of Planters to Antebellum Florida: Kinship and Power," *Journal of Southern History* 62 (August 1996): 527–55. For an enlarged perspective, see Baptist's monograph, *Creating an Old South: Middle Florida's Plantation Frontier before the Civil War* (Chapel Hill: University of North Carolina Press, 2002).

[19]Dorothy Dodd, "The Secession Movement in Florida, 1850–1861, Part I," *Florida Historical Quarterly* 12 (July 1933) 1–24; McPherson, *Battle Cry of Freedom*, 159–60.

[20] "A Child's Recollection of Secession and the Causes Leading Thereto," United Daughters of the Confederacy Scrapbooks, vol. 2, State Archives of Florida, Tallahassee. Though anonymous, details within the essay confirm that Susan Bradford Eppes, the author of *Through Some Eventful Years*, composed it.

the General Assembly. Though the margins of Democratic victory were notably slim, 1852 was the last year the Whigs mustered candidates.[21] Meanwhile, Florida radicals watched the birth of the Republican party with suspicion and alarm. In 1854 Governor James E. Broome warned Floridians of "fanatical organizations" that were "pure and wickedly sectional in character." While the Republican party failed to spread in the South, two party politics lingered in Florida, as some Whigs were absorbed into the Democratic party while other conservative stalwarts aligned themselves with the newly-formed American party. Also called the "Know-Nothing" party for its origins in secret societies, the American party appealed to both wealthy planters and small farmers by playing on their anti-foreign and anti-Catholic prejudices. The party organized in Florida and offered a slate of candidates in 1856 but was disappointed and soon disappeared. Democrats splintered on a national level in 1860, torn asunder by the issue of slavery's expansion. Floridians looking for conservative options could vote for the hastily organized Constitutional Union party, a desperate coalition of old Whigs and survivors of the American party. Its leaders meekly conceded the "wrongs inflicted on the South" but advocated "pacific, rational, and judicial methods" for righting them. While challengers to Democratic hegemony had consistently failed in the 1850s, the elections of 1860 were hard-fought. Democratic victories, though solid, were never seismic. Floridians were falling into the radical camp, but they did not go meekly or dumbly, and opposition to the ideals of the rabid secessionists remained strong in certain enclaves.[22]

Madison Starke Perry, an Alachua County planter, was elected governor in 1856. Born in South Carolina, the Democratic standard bearer typified the party's states'-rights heritage and strong Carolina connections. In 1858 he warned the state of the "largely increased strength and influence of the abolition element" in national affairs. When John

---

[21]Johns, *Florida during the Civil War*, 2–3.

[22]Dorothy Dodd, "The Secession Movement in Florida, 1850–1861, Part II," *Florida Historical Quarterly* 12 (October 1933): 45, 49; Johns, *Florida during the Civil War*, 3–9; John F. Reiger, "Secession of Florida from the Union: A Minority Decision?" *Florida Historical Quarterly* 46 (April 1968): 358.

Brown's raid set Southern nerves on edge, Perry blamed the Republicans for the outrage and called for the re-organization of Florida's militia. Advocating "eternal separation from those whose wickedness and fanaticism forbid us longer to live with them in peace and safety," Perry stoked the flames of secession in his adopted state.[23]

These flames spread rapidly and burned brightly as Floridians anticipated the 1860 presidential election. Florida's fiercely partisan newspapers, which had over 15,000 subscribers and also passed hand to hand, did their part to inflame the debate. Religious leaders gave Southern assurance from the pulpit. Reverend W. J. Ellis's pro-secession message, reprinted in Florida newspapers, told the state's worshippers that "the Lord of Hosts is with us—that our cause is in truth the cause of humanity."[24] Across the state, volunteer military units organized and began to drill. Public meetings were called and attracted a wide spectrum of Floridians. The number of women at a Tampa gathering impressed a reporter, who noted the blue cockades in their hats: "a token of resistance to abolitionist rule." Even children were caught up in the excitement. Cora Mitchell, the daughter of a Unionist family, recalled attending a mass meeting in Apalachicola: "I felt the thrill of it all, and though too young to enter into the merits of the question, was carried along by the general excitement and influence." In St. Augustine, Frances Kirby Smith, mother of future Confederate general Edmund Kirby Smith, kept her Colorado-stationed son updated on community preparations, asserting that "Southern men and Southern women will not sit down with folded hands if the masses elect a Black Republican President."[25]

---

[23]Dodd, "The Secession Movement, Part II," 45–46; W. Buck Yearns, "Florida" in W. Buck Yearns, ed., *The Confederate Governors* (Athens: University of Georgia Press, 1985) 58–59.

[24]William Warren Rogers, "Newspaper Mottoes in Ante-Bellum Florida," *Florida Historical Quarterly* 42 (October 1963): 154; Lee L. Willis III, "Secession Sanctified: Bishop Francis Huger Rutledge and the Coming of the Civil War in Florida," *Florida Historical Quarterly* 82 (Spring 2004): 421–37.

[25]Grismer, *Tampa*, 137; Cora Mitchell, *Reminiscences of the Civil War* (Providence: Snow & Farnham Co., Printers, 1916) 3–4; Thomas Graham, *The Awakening of St. Augustine: The Anderson Family and the Oldest City, 1821–1924* (St. Augustine: St. Augustine Historical Society, 1978) 86.

Not everyone agreed with the growing enthusiasm for secession. Florida's senators Stephen Mallory and David Yulee were lukewarm at best though they would yield to public opinion and assist in Florida's departure from the Union. Residents of port cities were more divided than their fellows in Middle Florida. Pragmatic souls expressed concern over what secession and a possible war would do to the shipping and tourism industries. In Tallahassee, Richard Keith Call minced no words, calling secession treason, and his daughter Ellen Call Long turned a jaundiced eye on the fashion for fire-eating.[26] But Unionists were overwhelmed and outgunned, especially by the media. Of Florida's twenty-four newspapers, only five endorsed the Constitutional Union party in 1860, one supported Douglas, and none recommended Lincoln. Moderates were denounced as "Submissionists" and "Union Shriekers." Across the state Unionists were assaulted, and violence erupted as partisans fought with fists, knives, guns, and whips. Even if the Republican party had attracted supporters in Florida, to speak in favor of "Old Abe" would have been suicidal in late 1860.[27]

The elections of 1860 found Florida controlled by the Democrats. In October, Democrat John Milton was elected governor, defeating his Constitutional Union opponent Edward A. Hopkins by 1,746 votes. Democrats maintained a safe majority in the General Assembly as well. On November 6, in a record turn-out, Floridians cast 8,543 votes for John C. Breckinridge (representing the Southern Democrats), 5,437 votes for John Bell (Constitutional Union), and 376 votes for Stephen Douglas (Northern Democrats). Though not on the ballot in Florida and many other Southern states, Lincoln and the Republicans prevailed in the national drama. His election sent Floridians into a well-orchestrated

---

[26]C. Wicliffe Yulee, "Senator Yulee," *Florida Historical Quarterly* 2 (April 1909): 38; Dodd, "The Secession Movement, Part II," 52–53; William Burr Jones to father, 28 September 1860, William Burr Jones Biographical File, St. Augustine Historical Society; Long, *Florida Breezes*, 282.

[27]Johns, *Florida during the Civil War*, 10; Reiger, "Secession of Florida from the Union," 359–360; Daniel L. Schafer, *Thunder on the River: The Civil War in Northeast Florida* (Gainesville: University Press of Florida, 2010) 23. It should be noted that Unionism did not necessarily imply support for abolition. Many Florida Unionists, including some of Northern birth, owned slaves.

frenzy, despite Richard Keith Call's plea for calm deliberation. "WHAT IS TO BE DONE?" one Tallahassee newspaper asked. "We say *Resist.*" Public meetings demanded action, and Secessionists burned Lincoln in effigy.[28] Two days after the election, Governor Perry wrote to his South Carolina counterpart, William H. Gist, assuring him that "Florida is ready to wheel into line with the gallant Palmetto State, or any other Cotton State or States," though he modestly demurred from encouraging his state to take the lead. Florida would shy away from immediate action, but eagerly anticipated the developments to follow.[29]

Timing greatly favored the Secessionists. Florida's General Assembly met in regular session on November 26, negating the need for any special session, and the next day Governor Perry delivered his annual message, which called for immediate secession and raised the specter of Florida's sharing the bloody fate of Santo Domingo if she failed to act with alacrity. Perry asked the General Assembly to call a convention of the people of the state, to revise militia laws, and to appropriate $100,000 for military expenditures. The lawmakers responded obediently. Perry rushed to South Carolina, both to buy arms and to confer with other Southern leaders.[30]

Florida's convention was scheduled to begin on January 3, 1861. Delegates were elected on December 22, 1860, under the same laws that governed election to the statehouse. Extraordinary measures were taken to ensure that all of Florida's counties would be able to participate, including special certifications for the delegates from South Florida, who would need to quickly board a steamer in Key West in order to reach the convention before it assembled. The only true issue at stake in the election was whether Florida should secede immediately or wait until after Georgia and Alabama had acted. News of South Carolina's secession two days before Florida's vote certainly influenced electors at the polls. Popu-

---

[28]Herbert J. Doherty, Jr., *Richard Keith Call: Southern Unionist* (Gainesville: University of Florida Press, 1961) 156; Thomas S. Graham, "Florida Politics and the Tallahassee Press, 1845–1861," *Florida Historical Quarterly* 46 (January 1968): 242; Dodd, "The Secession Movement, Part II," 50–52.

[29]Johns, *Florida during the Civil War*, 11.

[30]Hadd, "The Irony of Secession," 22–23; Johns, *Florida during the Civil War*, 12.

lar opinion and the usual political chicanery guaranteed that the convention would be in the hands of delegates favoring immediate secession.[31]

The sixty-nine men who assembled in Tallahassee were local leaders representing a cross-section of Florida's professions. Their median age was forty-three, with only seven delegates under the age of thirty and five over the age of sixty. Sixteen states of birth were represented, as well as the Bahamas and Ireland. Only seven men were natives of Florida, and three members' birthplaces went unrecorded. Twenty-five delegates considered themselves farmers. Ten were listed in the 1860 census as merchants, seven as lawyers, seven as planters, and four as physicians. While the average median amount of real property was $11,224.70 per delegate, the figure is distorted by the presence of a few extraordinary wealthy individuals, including E. E. Simpson of Santa Rosa, whose total 1860 wealth was listed at $2,530,000. Most of the attendees were financially comfortable men, but thirty delegates held less than $5,000 in real property, and several had less than $1,000 in real property, indicating fortunes yet to be made. Perhaps a more important signal of opinion than personal wealth was the fact that fifty-one of the sixty-nine men held slaves.[32]

A festive air surrounded the convention, as onlookers, journalists, and states'-rights celebrities crowded into town. After a short delay to allow all delegates to arrive, the first essential action of the convention on January 5 was the election of its president. John C. McGehee of Madison was a large slaveholder and had been an advocate of secession throughout much of the past decade. In his acceptance speech, McGehee noted the primary reason for secession: the Republican party, which now controlled the nation, "must inevitably destroy every vestige of right growing out of property in slaves." Without resistance, McGehee warned, "our doom is decreed."[33] On January 7 the convention was treated to speeches from three leading spokesmen for secession, E. C. Bullock

---

[31]Johns, *Florida during the Civil War*, 13–14; Ralph A. Wooster, "The Florida Secession Convention," *Florida Historical Quarterly* 36 (April 1958): 374; Dodd, "The Secession Movement, Part II," 55; Reiger, "Secession of Florida from the Union," 362–63.

[32]Wooster, "The Florida Secession Convention," 374–76.

[33]Ralph A. Wooster, *The Secession Conventions of the South* (Princeton: Princeton University Press, 1962) 71–72; Hadd, "The Irony of Secession," 24.

of Alabama, Leonidas W. Spratt of South Carolina, and Edmund Ruffin of Virginia.[34] A proposal requiring the ordinance of secession to be subjected to a popular vote was rejected. The final vote came on January 10, and was 62–7 in favor of immediate secession, which cast Florida in the wake of South Carolina (December 20) and Mississippi (January 9). Eager to link their actions to the inspirational nobility of the founding fathers, the convention requested that Tallahassee resident Elizabeth Eppes, a descendant of Thomas Jefferson, decorate the ordinance of secession with a blue ribbon.[35]

Florida was already acting like a sovereign republic. Confiscating federal property would mean obtaining arms and supplies as well as neutralizing military threats within the state's borders. On January 5, with the blessing of the radical leaders of the convention, Governor Perry ordered the seizure of the arsenal near Chattahoochee as well as Fort Marion (the former Castillo de San Marcos) in St. Augustine. Discretion was encouraged, but force was endorsed if resistance was offered. The next day, the ordnance sergeant in charge of the arsenal found himself squared off against the Quincy Guards. He had no choice but to surrender, as he had only three men under his command. In the early morning of January 7, the solitary, elderly sergeant in charge of Fort Marion found 125 state artillerymen at his gate, demanding the keys. Grumbling with displeasure, he handed them over, but not before demanding a receipt for the historic garrison. The next day the unfinished Fort Clinch on Amelia Island also tumbled into state hands.[36]

Grabbing guns and a fort from weary old men was one thing; conquering active federal military installations was another. Canny officers were ahead of the game. Captain John M. Brannan, commanding at Key West Barracks, had already written to the War Department on Decem-

---

[34]Wooster, "The Florida Secession Convention," 376; Edmund Ruffin, "Edmund Ruffin's Account of the Florida Secession Convention: A Diary," *Florida Historical Quarterly* 12 (October 1933): 76.

[35]Reiger, "Secession of Florida from the Union," 366; Wooster, "The Florida Secession Convention," 377–78; "Notes on Secession in Tallahassee and Leon County," 64.

[36]Johns, *Florida during the Civil War*, 23–24; Samuel Proctor, "Jacksonville during the Civil War," *Florida Historical Quarterly* 41 (April 1963): 345.

ber 11, 1860, warning his superiors that secession was imminent in Florida and, when it happened, the state would surely attempt to take Fort Taylor, just outside of Key West. He requested orders, but events moved faster than replies. When word of the seizures at Chattahoochee and St. Augustine reached him, Brannan shifted his entire command into Fort Taylor, joining his men with those under the leadership of Captain Edward B. Hunt. His next message informed Washington of his unsanctioned but astute act and revealed the precarious circumstances the captains faced: the fort had only a four months' supply of food and was virtually helpless without immediate reinforcement. Recognizing their strategic importance, the Buchanan administration had decided to hold the forts at Key West and Dry Tortugas, and orders authorizing Brannan's movements were sent out on January 4, arriving as a belated sanction of the captain's wise actions. On January 10, Major Lewis Arnold and a small force of sixty-two enlisted men and four officers was dispatched to reinforce Fort Jefferson on Dry Tortugas, arriving on January 18 to begin cooperating with the troops at Fort Taylor. Supply ships with food and building materials followed, and by February 6 Brannan felt confident that the newly reinforced and armed forts could not be taken. No attempt was ever made on them, and Florida had, unknowingly, lost a major advantage it might have offered to the Confederacy. Without control of the forts at the peninsula's tip, the South could never hope to establish any security in the Gulf of Mexico.[37]

Pensacola presented a more complex problem for both sides. Floridians knew the importance of the region, which encompassed not only a fine natural harbor in Pensacola Bay, but five military installations as well: Fort Pickens, Fort McRee, Fort Barrancas, Barrancas Barracks, and the Pensacola Navy Yard. In the absence of senior officers away on leave, 1st Lieutenant Adam J. Slemmer commanded Barrancas Barracks. With his forty-six artillerymen, Slemmer was attentive to the swirling rumors. On January 8 he requested orders from Washington, while attempting to arrange temporary defenses with Commodore James Armstrong at the navy yard. But Armstrong was old and cautious, reluctant to cooperate with the army without direct orders from the navy. The entire naval yard

---

[37]Johns, *Florida during the Civil War*, 24–26.

was divided. Many senior officers were Southerners, and many of the junior officers were Unionists. Even husbands and wives espoused opposite sides of the "infernal session" issue. It was confusion on a small but historic scale.[38]

Sensing trouble, Slemmer began to fortify Fort Barrancas and took the precaution of placing a guard against intruders. An attempt to seize the fort failed without violence, and, on January 9, Slemmer received the orders he had been waiting for: consult with Commodore Armstrong and prevent the seizure of the forts at Pensacola.[39]

Together, Slemmer and Armstrong faced a critical dilemma. Lacking adequate troops to man the mainland forts, the only sensible action was to transfer all their men to Fort Pickens. From its position on Santa Rosa Island, Pickens commanded the harbor and the other installations on the bay and was easily re-enforceable. Armstrong agreed to make the *Wyandotte* and the storeship *Supply* available to ferry men and materials across the bay.[40] On January 10, as the secession vote was being taken in Tallahassee, Slemmer and his command began crossing to Santa Rosa Island, but disharmony between the commanders remained a potent factor. Armstrong stubbornly refused to take necessary defensive measures, including removing the men under his command to Fort Pickens or destroying munitions that could fall into enemy hands. Other officers clashed over appropriate actions. Lieutenant Henry Erban attempted (without orders) to blow up the ammunition stored at Fort McRee but was stymied by the Secessionist wife of the fort's absent caretaker. She refused to give up the keys, forcing Erban and his men to break down the door and begin tossing munitions into the water. The incensed lady summoned a posse of Southern sympathizers, who fired Florida's first shots of the Civil War, driving the Federals away without injury. Before

---

[38]Edwin C. Bearss, "Civil War Operation in and around Pensacola, Part I," *Florida Historical Quarterly* 36 (October 1957): 125–27; Johns, *Florida during the Civil War*, 26–27; George F. Pearce, *Pensacola during the Civil War: A Thorn in the Side of the Confederacy* (Gainesville: University Press of Florida, 2000) 8–9.

[39]Pearce, *Pensacola during the Civil War*, 10–11.

[40]Bearss, "Civil War Operations, Part I," 127–28.

the day of miscues and accusations of treason was over, Erban observed elderly Commodore Armstrong "crying like a child."[41]

January 11 found the city of Tallahassee euphoric. The elegantly decorated ordinance of secession was ready for signatures. On the east portico of the capitol, in the presence of governor-elect John Milton, the General Assembly, flocks of dignitaries, and hundreds of ordinary citizens, sixty-four of the sixty-nine delegates signed their names. Cheers erupted, loud and lusty, as the last man put down his pen. Milton unfurled a new flag, a white silk banner with three stars—one each for South Carolina, Mississippi, and Florida. Princess Catherine Murat, a grand-niece of George Washington and the widow of a nephew of Napoleon, pulled the lanyard for the first cannon salute to the new Republic of Florida.[42]

Lost in the crowd, Richard Keith Call bowed his head. Tears streamed down his face.[43]

---

[41]Johns, *Florida during the Civil War*, 27–28.

[42]Ellen Call Long, "Princesses Achille Murat: A Biographical Sketch," *Florida Historical Quarterly* 2 (April 1909): 27–28, 33–34; *Charleston Daily Courier*, 17 January 1861; Samuel Proctor, ed., *Florida a Hundred Years Ago* (Tallahassee: Florida Civil War Centennial Committee, 1963), n.p. Governor Perry was unable to attend the event due to illness.

[43]Johns, *Florida during the Civil War*, 21; Susan Bradford Eppes, *Through Some Eventful Years*, 144–45.

Chapter 2

In the Midst of a Hostile Country

West Florida, 1861–1862

"Streets were lighted up with bonfires, bells were rung and cannon fired. Stirring speeches were made and Southern songs were sung." Madison, the hometown of John C. McGehee, president of the Florida convention, erupted in celebration when its most famous resident telegraphed the news of secession from Tallahassee. As in other communities across Florida and the South, prominent men boasted that they would drink all the blood that was spilled should there be a war over secession. Few believed that the North would be foolish enough to resist Southern independence. Those who did expect a war proclaimed that Southerners would meet the foe with "stout hearts and armed nerves," certain to prevail. Floridians were generally enthusiastic about secession, but tragically naïve about its consequences.[1]

Secession was celebrated as "the most glorious event in the history of Florida" in the plantation belt, but in underpopulated South Florida it was essentially a non-event. People in the deep reaches of the peninsula could shrug and assume any conflict resulting from secession would have very little impact on their lives. In regions like the Peace River Valley, even slaveholders were far more interested in community matters, such as local politics and marketing of cattle to Cuba, than in declaring Southern independence. Other Floridians were aware that a war over secession would divide families and friends and therefore was best avoided. From Pennsylvania on January 15, 1861, John Scott wrote to his brother George Washington Scott in Tallahassee: "Is there no remedy for this seeming madness?" The Scott brothers would eventually fight for oppo-

---

[1]Caroline Mays Brevard, *A History of Florida*, vol. 2, *Florida as a State* (Deland: Florida State Historical Society, 1925) 51; *St. Augustine Examiner*, 29 December 1860.

site sides, an appallingly common tragedy of the next four years, and South Florida's citizens who had initially assumed a calm nonchalance would find their lives brutally upended when the war eventually pitted neighbor against neighbor.[2]

* * *

Immediate preparations for possible war were more symbolic and ceremonial than practical. Young men hurried to join local units, fearful of missing out on glory. Women stitched flags rich with emblems of defiance: eagles, stars, sunbursts, cotton boles, and palmettos that celebrated Florida's ties to South Carolina. Volunteers basked in community attention. In Quincy, the Young Guards feasted on a dinner cooked by local women. A belle served each man his meal with sisterly attention. "Every man who was at the supper will consider that it is his duty to *fight and die*, if necessary, in defense of our country's rights and the honor of the ladies of Quincy," a representative proclaimed.[3] Young women were especially essential to the rituals of flag presentations and leave-takings. These halcyon days before real fighting began became treasured memories to many veterans. "I well remember the presentation of company colors by the sister of our captain," a soldier of the 1st Florida Infantry later wrote. "I have seen many flags since, but that was the most beautiful to me."[4]

Somber notes were sounded, but only very softly, and almost always in private. Not everyone in Florida was eager for war. Ellen Call Long, a cynic to the core, doubted that the Tallahassee matrons so eager to buckle on their husbands' swords would be willing to accord the same honor to their sons. In Tampa, Dr. Robert Jackson and his wife, Nancy, were survivors of brutal encounters with the Seminoles; the older couple was

---

[2]Dodd, *Florida in the War*, 11; Canter Brown, Jr., *Florida's Peace River Frontier* (Orlando: University of Central Florida Press, 1991) 153–55; Marion B. Lucas, "Civil War Career of Colonel George Washington Scott," *Florida Historical Quarterly* 58 (October 1979): 129.

[3]*Quincy Republic*, 6 April 1861.

[4]William Watson Davis, *The Civil War and Reconstruction in Florida*, 1913 facsimile ed. (Gainesville: University of Florida Press, 1964) 93.

"not in sympathy with secession" as they "had seen enough of war." Despite their objections, their sons hurried to enlist.[5] Watching men parade with their militia company in Jacksonville, Octavia Stephens was terrified. She dashed off a letter to her husband, Winston, a planter on the St. Johns River: "I declare it made me feel dreadfully to think what they were drilling for, you know how glad I feel when I think you are not in any company, and I hope and pray you may never be in any." By the time the letter reached Winston, he had been elected 1st Lieutenant of the St. John Rangers.[6] The objections of worried wives and mothers were largely useless. Whether they felt true dedication to the Southern cause or simply succumbed to peer pressure, Florida's young men were eager, in the first flush of rebellion, to volunteer for military duty. Most of them undoubtedly expected the war (if there even was one) to be short, no more than a year at most. To fail to sign up would be to miss out on making history.

Units organized in late 1860 and the first months of 1861 were haphazard, untrained, and full of bluster. As historian William H. Nulty observes, these local companies "were poorly armed at best and probably had more effect on the development of a militant political attitude than they did on the organization of an effective militia."[7] Governor Perry had long been requesting a significant re-organization of the state's military, and finally the General Assembly was willing to take action. Approximately a month after secession, Florida's Civil War Militia was created. Current captains and lieutenants received recruitment lists. Individuals who signed were liable to six months' service, and no one under the age of fifteen or unfit for military duty was to be enrolled. Rules for the composition of companies, regiments, and brigades were established, and April 1 was set as the election date of officers. Surgeons, chaplains, and other noncombatants were to be appointed. The governor was charged

---

[5]Long, *Florida Breezes*, 282;

[6]Cynthia Farr, *A Sketch from the Life of Mrs. Nancy Jackson* (Tampa, 1900) 16; Arch Fredric Blakey, Ann Smith Lainhart, and Winston Bryant Stephens, Jr., *Rose Cottage Chronicles: Civil War Letters of the Bryant-Stephens Families of North Florida* (Gainesville: University Press of Florida, 1998) 62–63.

[7]William H. Nulty, *Confederate Florida: The Road to Olustee* (Tuscaloosa: University of Alabama Press, 1990) 5.

with raising two regiments of infantry and one of cavalry. For the first year of the war, this Florida army remained a separate organization from the Confederate army.[8]

The Confederate government was organizing even as Florida's men were rushing to enlist and train. Representatives from the seven states that had seceded convened in Montgomery and adopted a provisional constitution that was ratified on March 11. Jackson Morton, James Patton Anderson, and James B. Owens spoke for Florida. All had previously been members of Florida's convention. The Montgomery body also selected Jefferson Davis as provisional president, and he gave his inaugural speech a week later. Florida officially joined the Confederate States of America on February 28, 1861, by act of the reassembled Florida convention. The Confederate States Army was created on March 6, 1861, and the first requisition for Florida troops came from the Confederate War Department on March 9. These soldiers were to hasten to Pensacola, which was a focal point, possibly the arena where the war's first shots would be fired. Governor Perry was asked to supply 500 state troops for duty in the city, where they would be joined by thousands of soldiers from Georgia, Louisiana, Alabama, and Mississippi. More calls to Confederate service would follow. By the end of 1861, the War Department levied Florida for 5,000 men, leaving the state defended by only 762 militia troops in January 1862. This would remain a persistent problem for the state: Florida would never have enough men to defend her vast territory. But remaining behind to guard a region so far from the real action was a fate most would-be Florida heroes sought to avoid in the first year of the war.[9]

Enthusiasm for a fight was the only thing Florida had an ample supply of in 1861. Volunteers were expected to furnish their own uniforms and equipment, with reimbursement promised if the volunteers were called into actual service of the Confederacy. The $100,000 the General Assembly had voted for the purchase of arms was soon spent, with little to show for it. Lacking any type of munitions factories, Florida

[8]Johns, *Florida during the Civil War*, 34–35.
[9]Masur, *The Civil War*, 21–22; Dodd, *Florida in the War*, 13; Johns, *Florida during the Civil War*, 37.

was forced to buy its firearms out of state. Tents, canteens, hats, and uniforms were also in short supply.[10] Civic-minded men banded together to raise money for local companies. A representative example comes from Pensacola, where approximately seventy-five men pledged from $1 to $300 each "for the purpose of equipping and supplying the families of two companies of twelve month volunteers to be raised in the County of Escambia for the Confederate Army."[11] Ladies' "thimble brigades" worked day and night to create uniforms, but the best efforts of civilians could offer only patchwork, irregular assistance completely inadequate to meet the state's military needs. In November 1861, Governor Milton informed the legislature of the "humiliating fact" that there was not a completely equipped company in the entire militia.[12] Direct taxation might have provided some consistency of support, but only Alachua County even attempted this option. Unfortunately for the state, Alachua Country's solution to the problem of supply failed miserably in a morass of misunderstandings and wounded pride after collecting less than $2,000 for local troops.[13]

As men assembled into camps, the lack of arms and equipment soon led to complaints and recriminations, as well as embarrassment. Cavalry units had been especially popular, leading Governor Milton to famously grumble, "Almost every man who has a pony wishes to mount himself at the expense of the Confederate Government." These companies were expensive to outfit and maintain. One Florida cavalry company mocked their lack of horses by practicing charges on piggy-back, half of the men playing the roles of cavaliers and the other half gaining experience as their steeds. By December 1861 the governor had enough of horse-less cavalrymen, and Confederate Secretary of War Judah P. Benjamin ordered no further cavalry troops were to be accepted from Florida.[14]

---

[10]Johns, *Florida during the Civil War*, 35–37.

[11]Julien C. Yonge, "Pensacola in the War for Southern Independence," *Florida Historical Quarterly* 37 (January 1959) 367–69.

[12]George C. Bittle, "Florida Prepares for War, 1860–1861," *Florida Historical Quarterly* 51 (October 1972): 145.

[13]Johns, *Florida during the Civil War*, 39–40.

[14]Ibid., 37–38; Bittle, "Florida Prepares for War," 150.

In summer 1861, the Confederate government took over the recruitment of troops in the South. In June, Florida was divided into military districts commanded by Confederate officers who were empowered to requisition troops from the governor. Though still only governor-elect at the time, Milton protested this action as undermining the organization of the state militia, insisting that Floridians wanted their governor, not the Confederate government, in control of their defense. But Milton was failing to grasp the importance of unifying the Confederate military. Florida's dual military system finally ended in January 1862. The state convention reconvened and blithely abolished the state militia, effective March 10, as an economy measure. Shortly thereafter, the famous Confederate Conscription Act of April 16, 1862, completely changed the way men were drawn into military service.[15] Private military charities and enterprise continued in Florida, especially the actions of the many ladies aid societies, which remained important in boosting local morale and attempting to meet the needs of the men on the battlefields and their dependents at home. But it was already a case of too little, too late.

In the meantime, however, Pensacola seemed poised to fire the opening salvo of the Civil War.

* * *

History is sometimes written in hours. On January 10, Lieutenant Slemmer, believing Fort Pickens to be the most important and defensible of the installations on Pensacola Bay, began transferring men and supplies there. That evening, William H. Chase, the retired army engineer who had constructed the fortifications at Pensacola, arrived in the city from a covert trip to Alabama, where he had consulted with that state's governor, Andrew B. Moore. With Florida's militias still small, poorly organized and technically extralegal, forces from Alabama would be necessary to seize Pensacola. Moore had already begun a correspondence on the subject, and by January 6 the governors of Florida, Alabama, Geor-

---

[15]Bittle, "Florida Prepares for War," 145; Reiger, "Florida after Secession: Abandonment by the Confederacy and Its Consequences," *Florida Historical Quarterly* 50 (October 1971): 130, Johns, *Florida during the Civil War*, 40–41.

gia, and Mississippi were in agreement that military action could not wait upon secession and that the fortifications at Pensacola should be seized. Chase received authorization from Governor Perry to capture the forts at Pensacola if there was "assurance of success," and Senator Stephen Mallory would also shortly send word that he expected Pickens and McRee to be captured. January 8 found Chase in Mobile, recruiting the services of Colonel F. B. Shepard and local volunteers to proceed to Santa Rosa Island and seize Fort Pickens. Ahead of his troops but behind the Union forces' move to Fort Pickens, Chase's plan was foiled, and he was forced to wire to Colonel Shepard, canceling his order. Fort Pickens would not fall so easily.[16]

Beginning the next evening, January 11, Pensacola started to fill with romantically named companies from Alabama, among them the Montgomery True Blues, the Tuskegee Light Infantry, the Metropolitan Guards, the Wetumpka Guards, and the Independent Rifles. Along with Florida volunteers from the region, they enjoyed the hospitality of the city, consuming fried oysters and playing tourist until roll calls were sounded. At the navy yard, Commodore Armstrong dithered, unwilling to make the final commitment to remove all his men to Fort Pickens or to destroy his materials of war. Armstrong claimed to have been unaware of the number of volunteers in the city and their serious intentions. It was an emergency, but not one that he felt justified acting upon—until it was too late.[17]

On January 12, at midday, two state commissioners, backed by the Alabama Volunteers and the Pensacola Rifle Volunteers, arrived at the gates of the navy yard and demanded its surrender. A rowdy crowd of townsfolk came along as well to watch the fun. Armstrong conferred with the commissioners and with Colonel Tennent Lomax, the commander of the Alabama troops. Then, in an action that would lead to his court-martial, Armstrong meekly surrendered the navy yard and ordered

---

[16]Pearce, *Pensacola during the Civil War*, 12–13; Samuel Proctor, *Florida a Hundred Years Ago*, n.p.; Ernest F. Dibble, "War Averters: Seward, Mallory, and Fort Pickens," *Florida Historical Quarterly* 49 (January 1971): 232.

[17]Bearss, "Civil War Operations, Part I," 125–65, 132; Pearce, *Pensacola during the Civil War*, 18.

the flag hauled down.[18] The victor's spoils from forts Barrancas and McRee included cannon, howitzers, mortars, and thousands of pounds of powder and projectiles. Armstrong later defended his actions, arguing,

> to all practical purposes I was in the midst of a hostile country. Thus situated with a handful of men in a defenseless yard, surrounded by ex-cited and hostile people, and opposed by so large a hostile body of well-armed and well-disciplined troops, whose number was capable of hour-ly increase, and without means of augmenting my own, I was suddenly called upon to decide the momentous question of whether to capitulate or fight.

Armstrong truly faced an unenviable dilemma, one exacerbated by the Secessionist leanings of a number of his senior officers and the dis-graceful treatment the U.S. Navy had doled out to the 200 laborers and mechanics working at the yard, many of whom had not been paid in two months. Surrounded by a population he felt he could not trust to fight (military and civilian Secessionists), near retirement (he was sixty-six years old and had been in the navy since 1809), and relatively unfamiliar with his surroundings (he had taken command of the yard on October 30, 1860), Armstrong made his decision based on delusion and caution rather than cowardice or corruption. It did him little good. Found guilty on multiple charges, including conduct unbecoming to an officer, Arm-strong was suspended from duty for five years. He died in disgrace in 1868.[19]

Lieutenant Slemmer was made of sterner stuff. Luckily for him, the *Wyandotte* and the *Supply* were commanded by loyal men and had been moved out into the harbor beyond Confederate reach. A series of en-counters took place between Slemmer and his Secessionist counterparts after the surrender of the Pensacola installations. On January 12, Captain V. M. Randolph, in charge of the navy yard, was rowed out to Fort Pick-ens with a written order from William Chase (now a colonel and the commander of all Florida forces in the area) demanding the fort's surren-der. Slemmer's answer was immediate: he would not surrender Fort

---

[18]Reiger, "Florida after Secession," 128; Johns, *Florida during the Civil War*, 28–31.

[19]Pearce, *Pensacola during the War*, 20–24.

Pickens "so long as he was able to defend it." It was a bold reply, as Slemmer had only eighty men and the fort was rather dilapidated, a "bad damp dirty looking place" that had not been occupied since the Mexican War.[20] Three days later, Chase went across the bay, informing Slemmer that he had "full powers from the governor of Florida" to take control of all the city's installations, and warning that he had between 800 and 900 men. If Slemmer held out, the blood would be on his hands when superior forces overwhelmed him. Slemmer's reply, after a consultation with the captain of the *Wyandotte*, was that they would hold their positions and any guilt for spilled blood would be Chase's to bear as the aggressor. On January 18, the Secessionists tried again with another note warning of the dire consequences of intransience, especially as reinforcements from Alabama and Mississippi were arriving daily. Slemmer refused to change his answer, and Chase sent no more requests.[21] The situation in Pensacola Bay now mirrored the one in Charleston harbor.

Southern troops continued to pour into Pensacola. Eight companies from Mississippi and three more from Alabama—Guards, Riflemen, and Dragoons by the score—embarked from Mobile and arrived in Pensacola via steamer, making for some tense moments as their vessels passed beneath the guns of Pickens. Slemmer kept his word not to fire his weapons unless provoked, and the men landed safely. Though many among the new arrivals longed to attack the fort, Chase held them off. Some felt he had too great an affection for the fort he had built, but others argued he knew it to be impregnable. Politics played the deciding role in the delay, however. Senator Mallory telegraphed Chase on January 16 informing him that "no blood must be shed in present state of affairs…we must first organize Southern Confederacy." The Buchanan administration still sought compromise, and delegates were meeting in the Willard Hotel in Washington on the same day that the Confederate constitutional convention was convening in Montgomery. Hopes of preventing

---

[20]Bearss, "Civil War Operations, Part I," 133; Pearce, *Pensacola during the Civil War*, 20, 24; John E. MacKenty, "The Battle for Fort Pickens," in Virginia Parks and Sandra Johnson, eds., *Civil War Views of Pensacola* (Pensacola: Pensacola Historical Society, 1993) 27.

[21]Pearce, *Pensacola during the Civil War*, 24–26.

war kept the Pensacola forces in check.[22] The Fort Pickens truce, as it came to be known, gave Slemmer time to make basic repairs to his island citadel. Meanwhile, supporting the militia companies in Pensacola became too expensive, and the Mississippi troops were withdrawn on February 6. The Alabama companies that remained at Barrancas Barracks and Fort Barrancas were organized into the 1st Regiment, Alabama Volunteers and became the first regiment transferred into Confederate service following the creation of the Confederate army. For these Southern volunteers, the Fort Pickens truce meant long days of doing little but drilling on the white sand beaches, eating oysters, watching the horizon and pondering whether they would ever go to war.[23]

Lincoln's inauguration on March 4 heightened the tension. On March 7, Confederate President Jefferson Davis assigned Brigadier General Braxton Bragg command of all troops in and around Pensacola. The stern general was displeased with the ragtag bunch of volunteers and the pathetically inadequate defenses. He moved quickly to improve discipline and batteries while preserving the fragile truce and forbidding citizens to provide wood, food, or other provisions to the Federal ships near the harbor. By late March he had erected better batteries, and by mid-April he had shaped something like an army out of the nearly 5,000 troops that had arrived from points across the Deep South. Meanwhile, in Washington, the fate of Fort Pickens was tangled in knots of executive decision-making, as Lincoln began his great power struggle with Secretary of State William Seward. Lincoln finally ordered Fort Pickens reinforced and Fort Sumter re-supplied. By a quirk of timing, Captain Israel Vogdes, an artillery company, and 110 marines landed at Fort Pickens on the night of April 12, only hours after the guns of Charleston had begun to batter the walls of Fort Sumter. The war was on and the truce was broken.[24]

---

[22]Ibid., 27–31; Yonge, "Pensacola in the War for Southern Independence," 359.

[23]Pearce, *Pensacola during the Civil War*, 40–44.

[24]Edwin C. Bearss, "Civil War Operations in and around Pensacola, Part II," *Florida Historical Quarterly* 39 (January 1966): 241; Pearce, *Pensacola during the Civil War*, 41, 48–67.

Within days, Pickens received more men and a new commander, Colonel Harvey Brown. By the end of April, the fort held some 850 officers and men along with significant supplies of tents, lumber, ordnance and horses. Improvements were made on the Confederate side as well. By May the Alabama and Florida Railroad was completed, linking Pensacola to Montgomery, and telegraph lines were also strung. President Jefferson Davis paid a brief visit to the city on May 15, causing "hilarious excitement" among the troops, who assumed offensive action was imminent. The opposite was true. Davis's visit likely convinced him that Bragg's well-trained men would be more useful elsewhere, and in a short time Bragg was sending 2,800 of his best drilled and equipped soldiers off to Virginia, where they would meet the enemy at Bull Run.[25] For those left behind, summer 1861 seemed endless, with little to do except drill and bake in the sun. Most of the citizens of Pensacola were leaving the area, and the city's records and government were relocated to Greenville, Alabama. Provisions ran low and disease ran rampant. "All hands are becoming monstrously tired of this hot climate, fleas, flies & mosquitoes," a teenaged Alabama volunteer wrote to his father. Less than a month later the boy succumbed to typhoid fever.[26]

For the men on Santa Rosa Island, the days were equally monotonous. On June 25, the 6th Regiment, New York Volunteers (famously known as Wilson's Zouaves) arrived on the island. These raw troops from the slums of New York City camped one mile east of Pickens, on the area of the island most exposed to possible Confederate attack. Desperate to avoid sun blindness, the men covered the white sand with pine boughs and erected arbors of branches. This would prove to be a picturesque—but ultimately fatal—bit of decorating. For the moment, however, life in Pensacola continued its humdrum pace, each side overestimating the other's numbers. As historian George F. Pearce observes, "leaders of both governments wanted to prevent the outbreak of hostilities in this

---

[25]Pearce, *Pensacola during the Civil War*, 69–82.

[26]Mary Dawkins, "North against South in Pensacola," in Parks and Johnson, eds., *Civil War Views of Pensacola*, 4; Henry Eugene Sterkx and Brooks Thompson, "Letters of a Teenage Confederate," *Florida Historical Quarterly* 38 (April 1960): 343–45.

rather remote theater of war." Pensacola's guns rumbled only for the Fourth of July celebrations, with both sides offering salutes.[27]

Finally, on September 2, action began when Brown ordered the destruction of a stranded Confederate dry dock, followed twelve days later by the capture and burning of the schooner *Judah*, which was being outfitted as a privateer at the navy yard. In the struggle for the vessel, each side lost three men, marking the first Civil War military encounter in Florida with the loss of life.[28] By October, Bragg decided that "daring, almost desperate" action was necessary to reassure both the public and his men that such Federal insults would not be tolerated. A thousand volunteers were recruited for a secret mission under the leadership of Brigadier General Richard H. Anderson. They arrived on Santa Rosa Island in the early morning hours of October 9, overrunning the Zouave camp and putting it to the torch. The dried branches that had provided comfort made excellent kindling, and most of the regiment's provisions and equipment were destroyed. The Confederates had the satisfaction of watching their enemies scramble for the safety of the fort in various states of panic and undress, but their amusement was short-lived. By daybreak well-disciplined troops marched out of Fort Pickens and the attackers were forced to retreat. Still untutored in the ways of war, many Southerners were lost or wounded as they straggled in disorder to their boats. Anderson listed his casualties as eighteen killed, thirty-nine wounded, and thirty taken prisoner. Brown's losses were fourteen killed, twenty-nine wounded, and twenty-four taken prisoner. Though the numbers indicated a virtual tie and the Federals were not dislodged from Fort Pickens, the Confederates proclaimed the Battle of Santa Rosa Island a victory, and it lifted morale within the city.[29]

Union retaliation was inevitable and came in the form of a massive two-day bombardment. Beginning on the morning of November 22, Union guns from Fort Pickens, the *Niagara*, and the *Richmond* poured their fire on a line of Confederate defenses, including Fort McRee, Fort Barrancas, and fourteen sand batteries. The startled Confederates hurried to

---

[27]Pearce, *Pensacola during the Civil War*, 85, 107–11.

[28]Bearss, "Civil War Operations, Part I," 146.

[29]Pearce, *Pensacola during the Civil War*, 114–18.

answer the challenge though they were often forced to reduce their rate of fire in order to conserve ammunition. On the second day the bombardment resulted in the destruction of the villages of Warrington and Woolsey. Fort Pickens emerged relatively undamaged. The artillery battle effectively silenced the Confederate guns, and Brown reported, "the insults to our glorious flag have been fully and fearfully avenged." Neither side was prepared to move after the artillery duel, however, so another stalemate began.[30]

A sporadic bombardment on January 1, 1862—perhaps ordered by an intoxicated Confederate officer while General Bragg was absent—did little damage to Fort Pickens while costing the Confederates several valuable structures in the navy yard. Just weeks later, in what would become a familiar pattern, military events outside of the state had a greater impact on Florida than any warlike action inside it. Confederate losses on the Kentucky-Tennessee border (Fort Henry on February 6 and Fort Donelson on February 16) led to orders withdrawing the troops from Pensacola. The men would go Corinth, Mississippi, to strengthen depleted Confederate armies.[31] This withdrawal was to be accomplished stealthily. All materials that might aid the enemy, including public and private property, were to be destroyed. On March 10 the burning began, an operation that cost many loyal Confederate civilians their livelihoods as sawmills, machine shops, and vessels were torched.[32] Evacuation was a slow, piecemeal, and tiresome process, made more difficult by the lack of good transportation facilities. Pensacola became even less important on May 2, when Union forces under Major General Benjamin Butler occupied New Orleans. On May 9, the last Confederate soldiers marched out of Pensacola. That night, cavalry companies set to work burning the remains of the military installations, igniting everything from the navy yard

---

[30]Bearss, "Civil War Operations, Part I," 158–64.

[31]Pearce, *Pensacola during the Civil War*, 136–39; Edwin C. Bearss, "Civil War Operations in and around Pensacola, Part III," *Florida Historical Quarterly* 39 (April 1961): 338–39.

[32]For a detailed examination of the destruction Confederates brought to the area, see Brian R. Rucker, "Bad Day at Blackwater: Confederate Scorched Earth Policy in West Florida" *Pensacola History Illustrated* 6 (Summer 2002): 3–13.

to Fort McRee, but mercifully sparing the civilian dwellings. Early in the morning of May 10, Union Lieutenant Richard H. Jackson went ashore to accept the surrender of the city from her acting mayor and civil officials. By May 12 Union troops were parading in the town square to the tune of "Yankee Doodle." The Federals who had waited so long beneath the merciless Florida sun found little to welcome them besides the grateful hurrahs of Pensacola's slaves and the "sour looks and downcast faces" of the few remaining white residents.[33]

Florida missed its opportunity for Civil War immortality when war erupted at Charleston rather than Pensacola. Events in Pensacola were inconsequential to the rest of the war, but they taught important lessons to the commanders and soldiers on both sides. The Battle of Santa Rosa Island had revealed "the vices and virtues" of volunteer forces, demonstrating the need for more drill and discipline. Bragg would be effective in this role, and the soldiers that he trained in Pensacola would acquit themselves honorably on the field at Shiloh. Union artillerymen received valuable practice over the bay, and the Federal advantage in terms of powder and equipment was made apparent. Perhaps the most memorable lesson for all the men who survived their time at Fort Pickens and in the installations around Pensacola was the strange nature of war in Florida. Boredom, heat, and mosquitoes led to dissatisfaction, disease, and death.[34]

The city of Pensacola would remain under Union control until it was abandoned again in March 1863. Campaigns along the Mississippi required a concentration of Federal forces, and an evacuation was ordered. Some units were transferred to New Orleans, and the remainder withdrew to Fort Pickens and Fort Barrancas. By continuing to hold these forts, the Federals effectively controlled Pensacola Bay, keeping blockade runners out and utilizing the navy yard as a repair station. Fearful of Confederate retaliation once the city was abandoned, "nearly the entire population" loaded up on carts and followed the departing soldiers. Fires

---

[33]Bearss, "Civil War Operations, Part III," 352; Pearce, *Pensacola during the Civil War*, 142–63.

[34]Bearss, "Civil War Operations, Part III," 347, 353; Pearce, *Pensacola during the Civil War*, 67, 157.

broke out in the city, and individuals took small measures of revenge. Private Melvan Tibbetts and his buddies from the 15th Maine ransacked Dr. John Brosnaham's apothecary, taking away hair oil, china plates, mattresses, chairs, and sheet music. It was a fate they felt the doctor deserved for being one of "the greatest seceshes in the world."[35] Before they departed, the Yankees took a census and found only ten men, thirty women, and thirty children in what had once been Florida's largest and proudest city. Pensacola was now a ghost town, with most of its houses lacking doors and weeds growing tall in the streets. Though they occasionally conducted raids and skirmishes in the area, neither side attempted to reclaim the city during the war. A few residents would drift back in 1864, but it would be another decade before a lumber boom helped revitalize the historic town. In the meantime, the entire region became, in the memorable phrase of historian Brian Rucker, a place of "uprooted families, disrupted lives, deprivations, bitterness and violence."[36]

[35]Pearce, *Pensacola during the Civil War*, 184–88.

[36]Dawkins, "North against South in Pensacola," 4–5; Brian R. Rucker, "Blackwater and Yellow Pine: The Development of Santa Rosa County, 1821–1865," PhD diss. (Florida State University, 1990) 2:681–82, 712–14.

Chapter 3

Florida May Be Lost

Confederate Abandonment, 1862

As the Civil War began, Florida was in political flux, having elected a new chief executive in October 1860, but being bound to a lame duck governor through October 1861. Madison Starke Perry's leadership had been crucial in preparing Florida's departure from the Union, but his actions following secession created a state of military havoc. This late-term work would challenge and haunt his successor, John Milton.[1]

Perry was over-eager and impractical. Equipping and arming the hundreds of men who answered Florida's call of duty was impossible, but Perry worked tirelessly to locate and purchase supplies, sent personal representatives to Savannah and Charleston, and attempted to negotiate a special shipment of arms from North Carolina. He prompted and publically commended individual donations and paid for cargos brought in by blockade runners in the early months of the war. Despite these efforts, many companies were little more than assemblies of unarmed men. Determined to meet the levies from the Confederate command, Perry refused to wait until proper regiments were formed and armed, but he instead permitted unattached companies and individuals to volunteer for Confederate service as soon as they were decently equipped. This benefited the Confederacy while it deprived Florida of her defenders. Perry garnered a reputation as a supreme Confederate nationalist, rarely contradicting the War Department or making demands for his state. But he never recognized the problems of communication, transportation, and lack of materiel that Florida faced. In his pride and delusion, he was close kin to other Southern leaders. Remaining true to his beliefs, he served as

---

[1]Bittle, "Florida Prepares for War," 149.

a colonel in the 7th Florida Regiment until illness forced his retirement. He died at his Alachua County plantation in March 1865.[2]

* * *

John Milton, Florida's Civil War governor, inherited a plethora of misfortunes. Born in Louisville, Georgia, in 1807, he was a graduate of the University of Georgia. After practicing law in Georgia and Louisiana, Milton fought against the Seminoles and settled in Florida in 1845. By 1860 he was a Middle Florida success story, the owner of Sylvania, a 7,000-acre plantation in Jackson County, the master of fifty-two slaves, and the father of eleven children. Sarah Jones, the English tutor who lived with Milton's family in the first year of the war, described him as a well-dressed man, brusque upon meeting her, with "a great press of business on hand," but ultimately kind and thoughtful, indulgent to his wife, children, and new employee.[3]

Following an abortive run for Congress in 1833 on a Georgia nullification ticket, Milton entered Florida politics in 1850 when he was elected to the lower house of the Florida legislature. He established a reputation for being hard-working and fair-minded, and he was appointed to the chair of several important committees. He retired from public life after one term, not emerging until he fought a battle for the Democratic nomination for governor in 1860. In many ways Milton was a product of his frontier heritage and planter class, a fervent believer in individualism and states' rights with little fondness for Indians. But he was no fire-eater, despite having achieved his office on a wave of Secessionist emotion.[4]

---

[2]Yearns, "Florida," 58–61.

[3]Daisy Parker, "John Milton, Governor of Florida: A Loyal Confederate," *Florida Historical Quarterly* 20 (April 1942): 348–55; Yearns, "Florida," 61–62; Sarah L. Jones, "Governor Milton and His Family: A Contemporary Picture of Life in Florida during the War," *Florida Historical Quarterly* 2 (July 1909) 42–44.

[4]Daisy Parker, "John Milton, Governor of Florida: A Loyal Confederate," 348–55; Yearns, "Florida," 61–62.

Like the other Southern governors, Milton faced the unique task of determining the nature of the relationship between his state and the Confederate government, as well as administering a "sovereign republic" plunged into war. Unlike his peers, Milton was able to tell the difference between theory and practice, and could, in the assessment of historian Daisy Parker, "keep the ultimate aim in view." He understood that cooperation with the central government was a necessary evil; without it, the positive good of Southern independence would never be achieved. He gave sound advice to his fellow governors: "It is best where it can be honorably done to avoid all conflicts and competition between the State and Confederate authorities for political power, or commercial privileges, at all events during the war."[5]

Throughout the conflict, Milton was notable for his patience and perseverance. He disliked and disapproved of many measures ordered by Richmond, yet he always acquiesced to them in a timely manner. He doubted the constitutionally of conscription, but he insisted that it was a judicial matter to be decided at a more precipitous time and urged Floridians to volunteer rather than be drafted. While he frequently pleaded for more draft exemptions, he would not indiscriminately grant them. He took other governors, such as Georgia's Joseph E. Brown, to task for trying to impose their will on the central government for their own selfish measures. Milton believed that at war's end, "the rights of the States and the constitutional powers of the Confederate Government will be adjusted by an intelligent, brave, and free people, to secure the enjoyment of civil liberty to themselves and their posterity." In many ways, Milton "set a fine example for all." Unfortunately for the South, Milton's pragmatic approach was virtually unknown among the other chief executives.[6]

Milton was far from passive, however, and on the impressment of private property issue he took extreme umbrage with Richmond. For Milton it was perhaps more than a legal abstraction. He was all too aware of Florida's frontier conditions and of how the loss of livestock and

---

[5]Parker, "John Milton," 355–56; Albert Burton Moore, *Conscription and Conflict in the Confederacy* (New York: The MacMillan Company, 1924) 235–36.

[6]Parker, "John Milton," 357–60; Moore, *Conscription and Conflict*, 235.

provisions could condemn an already impoverished family to complete destitution, driving them into the arms of the enemy. Though Milton eventually yielded to pressure to submit, the outrage clearly bled with the ink on the letters he sent to Jefferson Davis and other officials.[7]

Milton faced an equally difficult challenge on the domestic political front. Governor Perry had left behind great disorganization in the state's defenses, and Milton resented Perry's political meddling in the military leadership of the state's regiments. Then within months of Milton assuming office, radical Democrat opponents decided to make a bid for limiting the governor's authority. They had the Florida convention reassemble on January 14, 1862, and used it to create an executive council composed of four members elected by the convention. This council was to share fully in the governor's power. Fortunately for Milton, the convention's efforts were largely wasted. The executive council met only five times and rubber-stamped Milton's actions in prosecuting the war, then its individuals stopped attending meetings. By November 1862 Milton could state that he had not even seen a council member since May. The legislature quietly voided the plural executive, leaving Milton in political control of the state. Though his authority was finally accepted, many of the problems he faced were beyond his ability to control.[8]

* * *

"I have been down the coast to visit Amelia Island and examine the defenses," Robert E. Lee wrote to his daughters on November 22, 1861. "They are poor indeed. I hope the enemy will be polite enough to wait for us." As Lee was sadly aware, any Federal incursion on the eastern coast of Florida could be met with only token resistance. Guns were antiquated or uninstalled, and the most significant fortress seized by the Confederacy, Fort Clinch, which guarded the entrance to the Cumberland Sound, was unfinished. Just two months before Lee's visit, Brigadier

---

[7]Parker, "John Milton," 360.

[8]Bittle, "Florida Prepares for War," 149–50; William C. Havard, "The Florida Executive Council: An Experiment in Civil War Administration," *Florida Historical Quarterly* 33 (October 1954): 82–95; Yearns, "Florida," 63.

General John B. Grayson had toured the same area, and wrote to his superiors that the state was in a deplorable condition, destined to fall easily into the hands of the North unless ordnance and officers were sent immediately to her aid. From Fernandina all the way around the state to Pensacola, the defensive story was the same: outdated cannons lacked powder, shot, and men capable of aiming and firing them. Only eight companies were assigned to guard the entire Gulf Coast. Citizens of Apalachicola and Tampa trembled, protested, and considered relocation. But despite their eloquence and astute assessments, neither Grayson nor Lee was able to convince Richmond of Florida's distress.[9]

Governor Milton did his best, telegraphing Secretary of War Benjamin that "Florida wants arms. She has never received a musket from the Confederate States.... Can I get some?" When three weeks passed without a reply, Milton corresponded with President Davis. "We need troops and munitions of war, and officers of military education, experience, and ability," Milton insisted, warning that "if not properly aided, Florida may be lost to the Southern Confederacy. Her citizens have almost despaired of protection from the Confederate Government."[10] The governor's frantic pleas went unanswered. Following the Confederate defeats in Tennessee in February 1862, the state's troops were needed in other theaters of war. Less than a thousand troops remained behind to defend Florida's vast territory, with Lee advising that the few available Confederate troops in the state should concentrate on protecting the Apalachicola River, "by which the enemy's gunboats may penetrate far into the State of Georgia." Governor Milton was apoplectic, writing to Secretary Benjamin that

> the effect of the order is to abandon Middle, East, and South Florida to the mercy or abuse of the Lincoln Government.... I cannot...believe that an order to that effect would have been issued without previous notice to the executive of the State, that proper measures might have been advised for the protection of the lives, liberty, and property of the citizens of...Florida.

---

[9]Karl A. Bickel, "Robert E. Lee in Florida," *Florida Historical Quarterly* 27 (July 1948): 62.

[10]Reiger, "Florida after Secession," 129.

Despite Milton's eloquent protest, no orders were countermanded; Florida had been essentially surrendered by the Confederacy.[11]

This abandonment was a bitter pill to Floridians, who felt betrayed and forsaken. From Pensacola, Brigadier General Samuel Jones reported great alarm throughout the region. At Rose Cottage plantation on the St. Johns River, Octavia Stephens wrote to her husband Winston, "I suppose you heard that the Government has abandoned this State and the Governor has ordered all the regiments that are mustered into the Confederate service away from east Fla. What is to become of us. I think we will have to leave or be made Lincolns subjects...." Writing to his wife at almost the same time as she was penning her fears to him, Winston expressed similar concerns and gave her a promise of action. Winston believed if the state was "abandoned to the enemy...we will have a rebellion in this State, as the people are determined not to go out of State and leave their families to the mercies of the enemy and fight for others and your good for nothing *old Man* is one of that number. I will not abandon my family for any cause." Most East Floridians, however, reluctantly began to accept the idea of occupation by Federal forces.[12]

It did not take long for the Union to recognize Florida's weakness and the advantage of having outposts on its Atlantic Coast. One of Lincoln's first wartime orders was the blockade of Southern ports. A key component of Winfield Scott's much-derided "Anaconda Plan," the blockade, which tightened with each passing month, would slowly strangle the South. Though Union blockade duty held the promise of sudden riches when vessels filled with valuable contraband were captured (all crewmen shared in these prizes), generally life aboard a blockade enforcer was uncomfortable and monotonous. Walter K. Scofield, the assistant surgeon aboard the *Sagamore*, recorded long days with little to break up the weary routine besides occasional raids along the coast. These forays gave the men their chance to act like pirates, stealing honey and cattle or whatever loot they could find. Scofield held little affection for the region he guarded and wrote that the worst punishment for any blockade runner would be to seize his vessel and maroon him in Florida amid the swamps,

---

[11]Ibid., 131.
[12]Ibid.; Blakey, et al., *Rose Cottage Chronicles*, 105–106.

mosquitoes, and sand fleas. Acting Master's Mate John F. Van Nest described the misery of being posted off Indian River in July 1864: "The weather is very warm and makes me feel very uncomfortable and millions of Mosquitoes, and they almost eat me up and I can scarcely sleep at night for them." For Van Nest, the "dull lazy life" on the blockade came to an end with an epidemic of yellow fever aboard his vessel. Unnerved by the relentless decimation of the crew, the young man jumped overboard and drowned.[13]

Though one of the war's most famous activities, blockade running in Florida had relatively little impact on the Confederate war effort. Though Florida has many rivers and secluded inlets, the state's lack of transportation meant the cost outweighed the benefits. When the steamer *Florida* brought some 64,000 pounds of powder and nearly 2,000 rifles in through St. Andrew Bay, local citizens needed five days to haul the ordnance to the Chattahoochee arsenal. Cargo brought up the Indian River had to be transferred to a wagon for a trip to the St. Johns River, taken on the St. Johns to the Ocklawaha, and transferred again to a wagon to be driven to the railroad at Waldo. Once the major ports were closed early in the war, Florida's importance as a center for blockade running was vastly reduced. At the same time, blockade enforcement vessels stirred trouble for Florida Confederates as Unionist refugees and runaway slaves eagerly sought the safety of Union ships and provided vital intelligence about conditions within the state to their rescuers.[14]

Fort Taylor and Fort Jefferson in the Florida Keys had been in Union hands from the start of the war, but more stations to provide places for refueling, repairs, and rest for weary blockading vessels would have been welcome. Fernandina and St. Augustine would serve these purposes exquisitely. Port Royal, South Carolina, and islands off the Carolina and

---

[13]Masur, *The Civil War*, 25–27; Dodd, *Florida in the War*, 27–28; John F. Van Nest, "Yellow Fever on the Blockade of Indian River: A Tragedy of 1864, Letters of Acting Master's Mate John F. Van Best," *Florida Historical Quarterly* 21 (April 1943): 352, 357.

[14]Dodd, *Florida in the War*, 30–32. For a thorough consideration of how blockade enforcement affected the state, see George E. Buker, *Blockaders, Refugees, and Contrabands: Civil War on Florida's Gulf Coast, 1861–1865* (Tuscaloosa: University of Alabama Press, 1993).

Georgia coasts fell to the Federals in November 1861, making the conquest of Florida's east coast "only a question of ships."[15]

On February 28, 1862, a Union expedition consisting of twenty-six vessels left Port Royal under the command of Flag Officer Samuel F. DuPont. Aboard were a battalion of marines and an army brigade. On March 2 they arrived off Fernandina, a city already on the run, as Brigadier General James H. Trapier was evacuating both Amelia and Cumberland islands in obedience to Richmond's orders to shift troops from the Florida coast to the Confederate interior. Informed of the evacuation by a runaway slave, DuPont tried to halt it, but the tricky navigation of the sound prevented the gunboat *Ottawa* from reaching the town until the next day. In a duel of desperate minutes, the *Ottawa* spotted what proved to be the final train from Fernandina hurdling across the trestle toward the mainland. Shots rang out from the train windows and from a party of Confederate cavalry. The *Ottawa* answered with shells, exploding a flatcar loaded with furniture and killing two young men who were riding on a sofa. But the train made it to safety, with former Senator David Yulee aboard.[16] Less fortunate was the steamer *Darlington*, which was nearly blasted to smithereens when it refused the order to stop. Finally halted, it was found, in the words of DuPont, "*crammed* with women and children" who had almost been sacrificed to the captain's determination not to "show the white feather."[17] Fort Clinch and Fernandina were rapidly occupied by the expedition. The Confederates had lost twenty of their thirty-three artillery pieces and a small amount of stores; Confederate civilian losses were more dramatic as citizens lacked time to gather their property before taking flight. Fernandina was a divided town, however, and the invading Yankees found a small party of "Union men" and delighted slaves to welcome them, as well as whites who had "a half-frightened, half hang-dog look, as if they feared some injury."[18] Though described by one Yankee visitor as resembling "a second rate

---

[15]Proctor, "Jacksonville during the Civil War," 347.

[16]*New York Times*, 15 March 1862; Johns, *Florida during the Civil War*, 62.

[17]John D. Hayes, *Samuel Francis DuPont: A Selection from His Civil War Letters*, 3 vols. (Ithaca: Cornell University press, 1969) 1:352.

[18]*New York Times*, 15 March 1862.

New England factory village, minus the factory," the little settlement thrived in Union hands for the rest of the war, becoming a sanctuary for runaway slaves, a rest station for troops, and a base for other operations along the coast.[19]

With the Federals comfortably settled in Fernandina, Major General George B. McClellan ordered Major General Thomas W. Sherman to occupy St. Augustine. The nation's oldest city offered refuge to blockade runners beneath the protection of Fort Marion. To take St. Augustine, it was strategic to temporarily seize Jacksonville, opening the St. Johns River as a pathway to the interior. The expedition broke into two halves, and one headed immediately for the gateway city.

Jacksonville was already in a state of panic. Soldiers straggling in from Fernandina warned that gunboats capable of running "anywhere there was a heavy dew" were on their way to town. Some families packed up and fled to Lake City. On March 11, Federal gunboats appeared at the mouth of the St. Johns, and late that afternoon Confederate troops commanded by Major Charles Hopkins arrived in the town, not to fight for the city but to destroy property that could be useful to the enemy.[20] The troopers assured the citizens that no harm would come to them. Mayor Halstead H. Hoeg likewise counseled citizens to remain in their homes, where they would be unmolested. These proved to be false promises.

Like Fernandina, Jacksonville was a town with staunch partisans. Confederates lived next to Unionists, and both parties feared the worst, the Confederates from possible Union occupation and the Unionists from inevitable Confederate retaliation. By midnight, as sawmills, an iron foundry, and a gunboat burned, ruffians called Regulators arrived in the shadow of Confederate troops. Consisting of Confederate refugees from the area, the Regulators intended to intimidate and punish Union

---

[19]Sarah Whitmer Foster and John T. Foster, Jr., "Historic Notes and Documents: Harriet Ward Foote Hawley: Civil War Journalist," *Florida Historical Quarterly* 83 (Spring 2005): 455–56.

[20]Johns, *Florida during the Civil War*, 64; Richard A. Martin, "Defeat in Victory: Yankee Experience in Early Civil War Jacksonville," *Florida Historical Quarterly* (July 1974): 10.

sympathizers. The worst aspects of civil war reigned during the night. Private homes as well as the Judson Hotel, the city's premiere hostelry, were indiscriminately torched. Three Unionist men were killed, one in the street and two more as they tried to escape on a boat. Even women were fired upon, and Jacksonville's shaken inhabitants spent a miserable night outdoors, guarding their possessions as an early morning downpour finally extinguished the blazes. As daylight came, many residents fled, but by noon the Union forces had landed. Navy officers took Unionist leaders aboard the *Isaac Smith* and toasted their escape with crackers, cake, and wine.[21]

Union troops resided in Jacksonville for approximately a month. Businesses reopened, and even some Secessionists now saluted the "old flag." Many of the people who had remained in Jacksonville were recent immigrants from the North. They professed their loyalty to the Union and insisted that a strong Federal presence in the city should be maintained. Federal officers encouraged these citizens to organize a loyal state government and begin the process of returning Florida to the Union. Meanwhile, Confederate forces gathered at Baldwin and began a series of raids, attacking pickets and foraging parties. With requests for reinforcements denied by the Union War Department, the Federals had no choice but to abandon the wrecked city. The Jacksonville Unionists were terrified. Everyone knew what would happen if they were left behind at the army's departure. Arrangements were made to take many families from Jacksonville to Fernandina or New York. Even though some Confederate residents returned to Jacksonville after the Federal evacuation, the city was not again a Confederate stronghold.[22]

The second portion of the Federal expedition had St. Augustine as its destination, and when the flotilla arrived on March 11, the gunboats found a defenseless city. Robert E. Lee had opined that the small garrison at St. Augustine "serves only as an invitation to attack," and so the two Confederate companies and about twenty percent of the city's popu-

---

[21]Proctor, "Jacksonville during the Civil War," 348–49; Martin, "Defeat in Victory," 13–18.

[22]Proctor, "Jacksonville during the Civil War," 349–50; Martin, "Defeat in Victory," 19–28.

lation had fled to New Smyrna in the hours before the Federal arrival.[23] Acting Mayor Christobal Bravo ran up the white flag at Fort Marion and met Commander C. R. P. Rodgers at the wharf, eagerly escorting him to a meeting of the city council, where the town was promptly surrendered. The only salvos fired were verbal ones from the city's loyal women, including one widow who announced to Rodgers that the "men had behaved like cowards but there were stout hearts in other bosoms" as she struck her own for emphasis. While a demolished flagpole (also a feminine effort) greeted the Yankee occupiers, Rodgers reported that many citizens were "earnestly attached to the Union" and more cared "very little about the matter." Cooperation rather than hostility would initially characterize the city, which remained under Union control for the rest of the war.[24]

On the Gulf Coast, things were no better for Florida's safety. On January 15, 1862, troops from the blockading vessel *Hatteras* landed at Cedar Key. The tiny town held an importance that belied its size. The Gulf terminus of the Florida Railroad, it was also a prime blockade runner sanctuary. The Union party quickly destroyed the railroad depot and wharf, several railroad cars, the telegraph office, a warehouse, a handful of vessels, and the abandoned Confederate defenses. "We were extremely successful, with the expenditure of very little powder and no one killed," the commander reported. No resistance had been offered. In an extremely embarrassing incident, the Confederate lieutenant in charge of the defenses, along with fourteen of his men, miscalculated the length of their flatboat poles and were swept directly into the hands of the enemy by a strong current. Four of them escaped imprisonment: they had the good fortune to be suffering from measles and the physician of the *Hatteras* would not risk an outbreak aboard his vessel.[25]

---

[23]Omega G. East and H. B. Jenckes, "St. Augustine during the Civil War," *Florida Historical Quarterly* 31 (October 1952): 78–79.
[24]Thomas Graham, "The Home Front: Civil War Times in St. Augustine" in Jacqueline K. Fretwell, ed., *Civil War Times in St. Augustine* (St. Augustine: St. Augustine Historical Society, 1988) 26–27.
[25]E. A. Mueller, "Suwannee River Steamboating," *Florida Historical Quarterly* 45 (January 1967): 277; Thomas Graham, "Letters from a Journey through

Apalachicola was also a city far more important than its tiny size would suggest. Though possessing less than 2,000 residents, the port town did a flourishing trade with the Apalachicola, Flint, and Chattahoochee River valleys. It was the third most important cotton port on the Gulf, with more than a million dollars worth of snowy bales from three states tucked away in its warehouses. Easily accessible to blockade runners, it was worth protecting. In 1861, some 1,200 men were on duty in and around the town, enjoying fried oysters, brass bands, and strong liquor. But with the disbanding of the militia and the withdrawal of Confederate troops, the city was left completely helpless. Most of its residents fled, scattering to inland Florida towns, or to Georgia and Alabama, leaving only the poorest whites, a few Unionists, and a number of slaves behind. Cora Mitchel remembered wandering through a "dead city" where grass, rather than "high piles of cotton bales," grew in the streets.

Unchallenged, a detachment of sailors and marines from the *Mercedita* and the *Sagamore* entered the town and raised the Union flag on the morning of April 3, 1862. Federal Commander Henry S. Stellwagen assembled the populace—a ragged, surly lot of fewer than 500—and lectured them on the evils of secession. "We had no part in it," someone shouted. "We are almost starving," a woman wailed. Stellwagen gave them permission to continue fishing in the bay and abandoned the town after thirty-six hours. Apalachicola would remain in limbo during the war, the property of neither side, a miserable hamlet whose stranded residents were emaciated and demoralized.[26]

Key West was the city Florida abandoned before the Confederacy did. The Union forces at Fort Taylor and Fort Jefferson were never challenged. Despite the virulence of some of its leading citizens, Key West was not a Secessionist bastion. Former residents of New York, Connecticut, and Massachusetts made up nearly half the population, and foreign-

---

the Federal Blockade, 1861–1862," *Florida Historical Quarterly* 55 (April 1977): 439–47.

[26]Joseph D. Cushman, Jr. "The Blockade and Fall of Apalachicola, 1861–1862," *Florida Historical Quarterly* 41 (July 1962): 38–46; Mitchel, *Reminiscences of the Civil War*, 24–25; William Warren Rogers, *Outposts on the Gulf: Saint George Island and Apalachicola from Early Exploration to World War II* (Pensacola: University of West Florida Press, 1986) 65–69.

born individuals outnumbered Americans. In early 1861, strict Federal discipline was established in the polyglot town. Dissenters were sent packing, the display of Rebel flags was banned, and the Confederate partisan newspaper *Key of the Gulf* became the Unionist *Key West New Era.* Many Union regiments were rotated through the forts, and officers frequently imported their wives. The women of Key West engaged in many of the same activities as those in Confederate Florida: they presented flags, raised money, and established hospitals. The *New Era* even called upon the ladies to nag reluctant males into service: "Union women cannot go into the army, but they can shame their men into going."[27]

On October 5, 1862, the Federals returned to Jacksonville on a mission to dislodge guns on the St. Johns Bluff and scan the St. Johns River for Confederate steamers. Upon reaching the town, Union soldiers fought a brief skirmish with Rebel cavaliers. "How the Seceshes did yell," Captain Valentine Chamberlin of the 7th Connecticut Volunteers chuckled in a letter home, noting that a fellow captain had fainted upon hearing the famous war cry. In his comrade's defense, Chamberlin conceded, he "had never been in any muss before." With the Rebels swatted away from the city, the Union soldiers had a "gala time" plundering a drug store. Chamberlin discovered a printing press with an issue of the *Southern Rights* newspaper nearly set. Calling in the printers in his ranks, Chamberlin had a satiric pastiche copy of the paper printed and distributed. Otherwise the Yankees found only empty shops and shuttered churches. Jacksonville was a desolate hull of a town, with just a few women and blacks in residence. The Federal expedition captured the steamer *Governor Milton* and burned a number of farms and plantations on the St. Johns River before departing on October 9, 1862.[28]

---

[27]Reiger, "Florida after Secession," 134–35; Johns, *Florida during the Civil War,* 25–26, 155; Dillon, "South Florida in 1860," 443–44; Jefferson B. Browne, *Key West: The Old and the New* (St. Augustine: Record Company, 1912) 93; *Key West New Era,* 20 September, 8 November 1862.

[28]Valentine Chamberlain, "A Letter of Captain V. Chamberlain, 7th Connecticut Volunteers," *Florida Historical Quarterly* 15 (October 1936): 90–92; Proctor, "Jacksonville during the Civil War," 351–52. For a detailed look at what might have been Florida's Civil War version of "The Onion," see Valentine B. Chamberlain, "'Southern Rights' and Yankee Humor: A Confederate-

By the end of 1862, Florida had lost more than she could afford. Ringed by blockading vessels, her most significant coastal cities under complete Union control or cowering in its shadow, the state had been written off by Richmond as collateral damage. Yankee observers would mock the state's weakness. One war correspondent noted that if Fernandina had been properly garrisoned, the "little railroad town" could have become "the impregnable entrepot for the Secesh State of Florida."[29] Governor Milton was infuriated, but there was little he could do. In an October letter to President Davis, Florida's beleaguered governor summarized his state's woes. "Disaster after disaster has occurred, until the State is exposed to and threatened with immediate subjugation, and many of our citizens have become indignant and almost reckless as to the fearful results." Milton believed (erroneously) that Floridian women and children had been taken captive, and he fretted that a slave insurrection was imminent.[30]

Florida's only consolation was her size: it seemed unlikely that Union forces would ever penetrate the interior. Refugees from both coasts made their way to inland communities, which did their best to welcome them. As a result, Middle Florida, the state's safest region, remained devoted to the Confederate cause and maintained its faith in state and Confederate leadership.[31] Florida's citizens were asked to continue to make sacrifices, even as Florida's welfare was coolly ignored by the Confederacy. While her troops took to the battlefields, much would be expected of Floridians at home.

Federal Jacksonville Newspaper," *Florida Historical Quarterly* 34 (July 1955): 30–35, which contains a photocopy of the pastiche issue.

[29] Staudenraus, ed., "A War Correspondent's View of St. Augustine and Fernandina: 1863," 64–65.

[30] Yearns, "Florida," 64; Reiger, "Florida after Secession," 132–33.

[31] Reiger, "Florida after Secession," 133.

Chapter 4

Florida Will Not Be Ashamed of Her Sons

Floridians in the Confederate Service

At the beginning of the Civil War, it seemed that Florida could make only the smallest of contributions to the Confederacy. Her manpower was limited, but as the war lengthened, the age cohort for drafting soldiers expanded. Eventually, men from the ages of seventeen to fifty were eligible for conscription, and virtually all white males were tapped in some way for home front defense. Before the war's conclusion, Florida would send somewhere between 14,000 to 15,000 men to the Confederate forces. The exact number is impossible to compute and always controversial because of re-enlistments, desertion, duplication of names, loss of records, and the Southern soldier's habit of simply abandoning one unit for another whenever the mood struck him. But whatever the exact count, Florida gave a staggering proportion of its white men to the Confederate struggle.[1]

* * *

Reasons Florida's men fought for the Confederacy varied. Many, in the early months, enlisted for the excitement, the adventure, and the camaraderie of serving beside friends. Most companies were organized out of the same communities, so peer pressure was intense. Young men rallied around local celebrities and heroes. Several young men from the Waukeenah Academy even followed their beloved headmaster into the

---

[1]Charles P. Summerall, "Soldiers Connected with Florida History Since 1812," *Florida Historical Quarterly* 9 (April 1931): 248; Dodd, *Florida in the War*, 45; Masur, *The Civil War*, 62–63.

ranks.[2] Other soldiers, like Michael Raysor of Jefferson County, felt a sense of duty to Florida. However the state went, they went. Some fought to protect their right to own slaves. But most were swept away by the tide of Southern pride and nationalism and never analyzed the feelings and motivations that propelled them to the conflict. Initial enlistments were brief, only a year, reflecting the naïve optimism of the Confederacy.[3]

Florida's soldiers of the eastern theater missed the opening act of the Civil War, as no Florida units were present at the Battle of Bull Run on July 16, 1861. Three days before the conflict, the 2nd Florida Infantry Regiment, under the command of Colonel George T. Ward of Leon County, was mustered into service. Organized near Jacksonville, the troops departed for Virginia but failed to reach the Old Dominion in time to participate in the action. Instead, the 2nd Florida was assigned to duty with the theatrical Major General John B. Magruder's Division, and spent much of fall 1861 building fortifications and preparing for the inevitable springtime assault.[4]

---

[2]Johnathan C. Sheppard, "'This Seems To Be Our Darkest Times': The Florida Brigade in Mississippi, June–July, 1863," *Florida Historical Quarterly* 85 (Summer 2006): 64–65; Zack C. Waters and James C. Edmonds, *A Small but Spartan Band: The Florida Brigade in Lee's Army of Northern Virginia* (Tuscaloosa: University of Alabama Press, 2010) 7–8.

[3]Aaron Sheehan-Dean, "'If It Was Not For You I Would Be Willing To Die': The Civil War Correspondence of Michael and Sallie Raysor," *Florida Historical Quarterly* 86 (Winter 2008): 392; Knox Mellon, Jr., "A Florida Soldier in the Army of Northern Virginia: The Hosford Letters," *Florida Historical Quarterly* 46 (January 1968): 244; Waters and Edmonds, *A Small but Spartan Band*, 7–8.

[4]Board of State Institutions, *Soldiers of Florida in the Seminole Indian, Civil, and Spanish-American War* (1903; repr., Macclenny, FL: Richard J. Ferry, 1983) 77–78; J. J. Dickison, "Military History of Florida" in Clement A. Evans, ed., *Confederate Military History*, vol. 11 (Atlanta: Confederate Publishing Company, 1899) 19–20; Sigsbee C. Prince, Jr., "Edward A. Perry, Yankee General of the Florida Brigade," *Florida Historical Quarterly* 29 (January 1951): 199; Lewis N. Wynne and Robert Taylor, *Florida in the Civil War* (Charleston: Arcadia Publishing, 2002) 38.

During early sparring of the 1862 Peninsula Campaign, Magruder applauded the 2nd Florida for fighting "in the most brilliant manner." The 2nd Florida would take great pride in its elite status and its reputation as the "Old Guard" of the Florida Brigade. Answering Richmond's urgent need for more defenders, the state organized the 5th Infantry Regiment on April 8 and the 8th Infantry Regiment on July 5. They joined the veteran 2nd Regiment in the newly named Army of Northern Virginia and, reassigned to Brigadier General Roger A. Pryor's Brigade, saw action at Second Bull Run. Pryor was especially pleased by their performance, writing that the fresh Florida troops "exhibited the cool and collected courage of veterans."[5]

Florida troops fought with Stonewall Jackson and arrived as part of his reinforcements of Lee at the Battle of Antietam. Heavy losses led to reorganization that winter, and the Florida troops were consolidated into a single brigade under the command of newly promoted Brigadier General Edward A. Perry. The Army of Northern Virginia solidly repulsed Major General Ambrose Burnside's ill-conceived offensive at Fredericksburg on December 13, 1862, and Florida's men fought in the "Furnace" during the Battle of Chancellorsville on May 3, 1863, with surprisingly light casualties.[6]

Florida's good luck would not hold. The dramatic Battle of Gettysburg, on July 1–3, 1863, cost General Robert E. Lee a third of his army. The 8th and the 2nd Florida lost their regimental colors as well as a substantial number of their men. "No troops could have fought better than our Floridians," future governor Francis P. Fleming told his family, but its name was virtually all that the Florida Brigade retained after Gettysburg.[7]

---

[5]Board of State Institutions, *Soldiers of Florida*, 78–79, 187; Waters and Edmonds, *A Small but Spartan Band*, 8–9; Wynne and Taylor, *Florida in the Civil War*, 36–39.

[6]Board of State Institutions, *Soldiers of Florida*, 187; Wynne and Taylor, *Florida in the Civil War*, 40–45.

[7]Wynne and Taylor, *Florida in the Civil War*, 48–49; Edward C. Williamson, ed., "Francis P. Fleming in the War for Southern Independence: Letters from the Front, Part II," *Florida Historical Quarterly* 28 (October 1949): 148;

Desperation and conscription produced more Florida regiments. The 9th Florida Infantry Regiment was shipped to Lee in April 1864, and in early June a 10th Florida Infantry Regiment also went to Virginia. An 11th regiment was formed and traveled northward, but it represented the last of the Florida reserves. Merging units, forming a patchwork to meet needs, had allowed the creation of all three of the final regiments.

The Florida Brigade was further decimated by the butchery in the Wilderness and the other bloody battles of the 1864 campaign. Florida's final regiments joined their fellows in what was now called Finegan's Brigade, for its commander, former Florida resident Brigadier General Joseph J. Finegan. The brigade took massive losses in the battles, then held the front trenches of Petersburg as Lee's army dug in for a significant siege. During the next ten months, Finegan's men would be rallied to participate in a number of skirmishes around the city, but they never made significant strategic gains and constantly lost men they could not replace.[8]

The story of Florida's troops in the western theater began at the Chattahoochee Arsenal, with the organization of the 1st Florida Infantry Regiment under the command of Colonel James Patton Anderson. The regiment saw duty in Pensacola during the long stalemate, with some of its members taking part in the Battle of Santa Rosa Island. The regiment was sent to join the command of General Albert S. Johnston's Army of Tennessee in Mississippi though its enlistments ran out while the soldiers were on their way. Many men opted not to re-enlist, so only a battalion reached the Battle of Shiloh. Florida's soldiers benefitted from the excellent training and discipline of General Bragg, who had whipped them into shape in Pensacola. Now a brigade commander, Anderson liberally praised the Florida men for their courage under fire. In May 1862, the 1st Florida Regiment was reorganized.[9]

Bertram H. Groene, "Civil War Letters of Colonel David Lang," *Florida Historical Quarterly* 54 (January 1976): 356–57.

[8]Board of State Institutions, *Soldiers of Florida*, 206–207, 219; Wynne and Taylor, *Florida in the Civil War*, 50–56.

[9]Summerall, "Soldiers Connected with Florida History," 249; Larry Rayburn, "'Wherever the Fight is Thickest': General James Patton Anderson of Florida," *Florida Historical Quarterly* 60 (January 1982): 316–17; George C. Bit-

The 3rd Florida Infantry Regiment was mustered into Confederate service in August 1861 and reorganized in May 1862. Following initial service in Florida and Mobile, the regiment finally joined what was now Bragg's army. Both the 1st and 3rd Florida regiments were part of the invasion of Kentucky and took extreme losses at the Battle of Perryville, where the sharp black locust plants that covered the field lacerated the "virtually barefooted" Florida men. Decimated, the two regiments were combined to form the 1st and 3rd Consolidated Florida Regiment.[10]

The 4th Florida Regiment was formed in July 1861, reorganized in May 1862, and by December had joined its fellows in the Army of Tennessee. The Battle of Murfreesboro cost the Florida troops many men, but in May 1863 the Florida Brigade performed with distinction at the siege of Jackson. In late August, the Florida troops rejoined General Bragg and the Army of Tennessee, their ranks swelled by two more Florida regiments, the 6th and the 7th. All of these regiments saw action at the fierce Battle of Chickamauga, and all but the 7th suffered heavy casualties. The drain on manpower led to yet another reorganization of all the Florida infantry and the 1st Regiment, Florida Cavalry into a new brigade under the command of Brigadier General Jesse J. Finley.[11]

Bragg's failure to hold Chattanooga cost him the command of the Army of Tennessee. Under General Joseph E. Johnston, the battered Florida Brigade moved toward Atlanta. General John Bell Hood replaced Johnston in July 1864. Subjected by the blundering Hood to the battles of Franklin and Nashville, the Army of Tennessee was exhausted. Yet in early 1865 it was called to assist Lieutenant General William J.

tle, "Fighting Men View the Western War, 1862–1864," *Florida Historical Quarterly* 47 (July 1968): 25–26; Board of State Institutions, *Soldiers of Florida*, 38–39. The story of the Florida troops in the western theater can be found in Jonathan C. Sheppard, *By the Noble Daring of Her Sons: The Florida Brigade in the Army of Tennessee* (Tuscaloosa: University of Alabama Press, 2012).

[10]Dickison, "Military History of Florida," 43; Bittle, "Fighting Men View the Western War," 27; Board of State Institutions, *Soldiers of Florida*, 39–40, 100.

[11]Bittle, "Fighting Men View the Western War," 29; Summerall, "Soldiers Connected With Florida History," 252, Board of State Institutions, *Soldiers of Florida*, 118–19, 153–55.

Hardee, who was now squared off against Major General William T. Sherman in South Carolina. Hood resigned and Johnston, hoping to interpose the weary Army of Tennessee between Sherman and Grant, came out of retirement. A great final battle at Bentonville, North Carolina, proved the futility of the plan. The Confederate armies' days were numbered.[12]

Very few Floridians were Confederate sailors, an irony of the war in that the Confederate secretary of the navy was a Floridian. The Confederate navy was never larger than 4,450 enlisted men and 753 officers, with the Marine Corps at 749 individuals, including officers, noncommissioned officers, and rank and file. Almost every man qualified for naval service had already enlisted in the Confederate army before the navy was organized, and it was difficult to get them transferred. Only eighteen Floridians served in the Confederate navy, six of them on the crew of the steamer *Spray*, which had a career in the Gulf.[13] More numerous were the Floridians who took up the business of blockade running, an enterprise cloaked in patriotism but operated for profits. Some 160 blockade runners were eventually captured in Florida waters. The nature of their game makes it impossible to know how many more succeeded. While not all blockade runners were captained or crewed by Floridians, their exploits in and around Florida made them one of the most colorful aspects of Florida's Confederate endeavors.[14]

Florida's soldiers were initially overenthusiastic and undisciplined, as were all Civil War volunteers. Florida's adjutant general described the typical recruit's attitude toward war: "that it is all hunting, and in a fight each man on his own hook, our people are invincible." Like most Confederates, Floridians were inordinately proud of their home state. "Hurra for Florida," Washington Ives wrote in 1862, "I'd rather be a soldier from her than any other state of the Confederacy." Before battle, he assured

---

[12]Board of State Institutions, *Soldiers of Florida*, 102, 155; Wynne and Taylor, *Florida in the Civil War*, 69–73.

[13]Raimondo Luraghi, *A History of the Confederate Navy*, trans. Paolo E. Coletta (Annapolis: Naval Institute Press, 1996) 22, 26; Board of State Institutions, *Soldiers of Florida*, 317.

[14]Dodd, *Florida in the War*, 28–30.

his family of his comrades' courage. "There is no telling what moment we may be compelled to leave here to engage the enemy, but you may be assured that Florida will not be ashamed of her sons...."[15] Florida's soldiers expressed bravado. John Hosford of the 5th Florida Infantry bragged that he and his friends were ready "to hunt the yanks to see if we could get a fight." Captain Hugh Black of the 1st Florida Regiment entertained his family with stories of how he and his men had mocked the Yankees for being bad shots, encouraging them to aim higher or lower. "They would yell as though we were playing a game of town ball instead of fighting a battle," he wrote, perhaps in an effort to ease his wife's fear for his safety. If Yankees were such inept opponents, no more dangerous than a rival ball team, what was there to fear from them?[16]

War was not a game, however, and Florida's troops soon found that both physical and mental stamina were required. A soldier had to learn to be indifferent to horrific scenes and the suffering of others. Francis P. Fleming's musing, on a Virginia battlefield in 1862, echoed those of soldiers across the ages: "I thought, at one time, that such sights would be more than I could bear to look upon but seeing so many men shot and cut to pieces, one soon becomes accustomed to it, as it were, and such a sight as would in ordinary times be shocking in the extreme makes but a slight impression on a callous mind." Florida's soldiers were also faced with the grim fact that they were truly far from home. Inadequacies of transportation meant they had much less chance of returning to Florida on a furlough or of receiving visits from their kin. Even the mail from Florida was less reliable, especially as more areas of the state fell under Union control.[17]

[15]Ibid., 34; Jim R. Cabaniss, ed., *Civil War Journal and Letters of Serg. Washington Ives, 4th FLA C.S.A.* (Tallahassee: Jim R. Cabaniss, 1987) 20, 22.

[16]Dodd, *Florida in the War*, 34; Mellon, "A Florida Soldier in the Army of Northern Virginia," 245; Elizabeth Coldwell Franco, ed., *Letters of Captain Hugh Black to His Family in Florida during the War between the States, 1862–1864* (Evansville, IN: Evansville Bindery, Inc., 1998) 54–55.

[17]John P. Ingle, Jr., "Soldiering with the Second Florida Infantry Regiment," *Florida Historical Quarterly* 59 (January 1981): 337; Waters and Edmonds, *A Small but Spartan Band*, xi.

Throughout the war, Florida's soldiers were constantly in need of food and clothing. Pay was poor and erratic at best, and basic items such as blankets, knives, and socks could be difficult for an ordinary soldier to acquire. Troops relied upon the generosity of their families, friends, and communities. On September 6, 1863, Washington Ives wrote to his mother from a camp in Tennessee: "I wish the people of Florida would make up a collection of little things such as black pepper, salt, sugar, soap, ect. to send the boys out here, our regiment is nearly destitute of clothing, shoes, hats and pants...."[18]

Despite the hardships, war was a great social adventure, especially for young men who had never traveled far from their Florida homes. Many had not seen mountains or experienced a snowfall. John Hosford recorded his impression of a Virginia snowstorm, and the snowball battle that followed, admitting that his experience in such matters had been very limited. The ever-observant Hosford also noticed that his fellow Floridians missed the flowers of their homeland. Curiosity ran both ways, as boys left behind in Florida wrote to friends and brothers in service, eager for details about the places they visited and the people they encountered, especially those of the female persuasion. John Hanna passed along a friend's query in a wonderfully untutored letter to his son Calvin: "he sais have you seen aney girls in that place & wear they pretty." Perhaps to even the score, young men at home tended to brag that they were getting all the "widows and girls" while their elders were away.[19] Letters that carried gossipy tales of bad behavior in both camp and at home were always popular. Colonel David Lang freely admitted, "anything is eagerly sought for as recreation which withdraws the mind even for a few moments from the contemplation of the monstrous treadmill existence which we lead here." Colonel William Stockton was more direct while stationed near Chattanooga. "I hear horrible stories

---

[18]Cabaniss, ed., *Civil War Journal and Letters of Washington Ives*, 41.

[19]Mellon, "A Florida Soldier in the Army of Northern Virginia," 250, 268; John B. Hanna to Calvin Hanna, 4, 13 August 1863, Hanna Family Papers, State Archives of Florida.

about the Quincy women, as well as Tallahassee," he wrote to his wife. "Tell me about them."[20]

Temptations for soldiers to misbehave were plentiful when men were freed of community controls. George Washington Parkhill, a captain in the 2nd Florida Infantry, told his wife that the "soldiers fool the ladies sometimes and say they are single when they are married in order to have a little fun, so it is hard to know who to believe." Parkhill admitted that he had taken dinner with six buxom young ladies but "none of them had the finely chiseled features & bright, affectionate eye of my wife.—No, Lizzie, there is not another being on earth with the soul such as beats in the bosom of my angel & therefore their eyes cannot be as bright nor their features as pretty."[21] Lizzie Parkhill might have been reassured of her husband's devotion, but other wives worried about sexual infidelity, with very good reason, as sexually transmitted diseases were easily contracted but impossible to cure. Octavia Stephens took Winston to task for visiting a Jacksonville home she believed was a brothel, warning him that such allurements might turn him into a "bad boy."[22]

The image of nineteenth-century Southern men as taciturn, distant, and patriarchal fathers is a myth. Florida's soldier fathers were, like their comrades across the Confederacy, thoroughly absorbed in their children's lives and eager to participate in affectionate parenting, even from a distance. Soldiers remembered their youngsters' birthdays and filled every letter with kisses, often with the added instruction to the child to "kiss ma for pa." Fathers delivered lectures against disobedience, but they also promised rewards for good behavior and commended offspring for taking on extra duties. Soldiers frequently remembered their entire family, even the ones who might think themselves beyond such affection. "Give my love to the old men," Hugh Black told his wife, and others saluted cous-

---

[20]Groene, "Civil War Letters of Colonel David Lang," 359; Herman Ulmer, ed., *The Correspondence of Will and Ju Stockton 1845–1869*, bound manuscript (State Library of Florida, 1984) 220–21.

[21]George Washington Parkhill to Elizabeth Bellamy Parkhill, 24 March 1862, George Washington Parkhill Letters, Florida State University Special Collections.

[22]Blakey, et al., *Rose Cottage Chronicles*, 129, 131.

ins, friends, and even favored slaves in their missives.[23] On rare occasions soldiers could entertain their families in camp, but few were as privileged as General James Patton Anderson, whose wife and young sons lived in camp with him during the summers of 1862 and 1863.[24]

All too aware of how easily they could perish, many Florida soldiers turned to religion for comfort and strength, as well as to please agitated family members who feared for their souls. Revivals and camp meetings were popular, both in the state and near the great battlefields. John Hosford felt the sermons in the camps "do more for the salvation of our men than all the sermons they ever heard before." Isaac Auld expressed gratitude for his mother's interventions with the Almighty: "Dear Mother it is a great comfort to me to know that I have such a good mother at home praying for me while enduring the hardships of soldiering. I am sorry to inform you that I lost my little testament," he admitted, "but I got another out of a Yankee knapsack which I will try to keep." Sallie Raysor urged her husband to read his Bible and pray daily so that he would go to heaven if killed, and Michael no doubt eased her fears for his salvation when he wrote, "I have made up my mind to give my heart to God."[25] Dallas Wood linked the present with the future in a message to his sister: "we all have the cheering assurance of a blissful home in Heaven where there will be no war and no parting again." His words reflected the antebellum Christian concept of the afterlife as a vast family reunion, where the domestic hearth would be recreated for eternity.[26]

---

[23]Tracy J. Revels, *Grander in Her Daughters: Florida's Women during the Civil War* (Columbia: University of South Carolina Press, 2004) 45–49; Franco, ed., *Letters of Captain Hugh Black*, 46–47. For a larger consideration of the relationships between antebellum fathers and children, see James Marten, *The Children's Civil War* (Chapel Hill: University of North Carolina Press, 1998).

[24]Rayburn, "Wherever the Fight is Thickest,'" 321, 326.

[25]Mellon, "A Florida Soldier in the Army of Northern Virginia," 249–50; Isaac McQueen Auld to mother, 22 September 1862, Auld Family Letters, State Archives of Florida; Sallie Raysor to Michael Raysor, 12 October 1862; 17 May 1863, Raysor Family Papers, P. K. Yonge Library, University of Florida.

[26]Dallas Wood to sister, 25 December 1863, Dallas Wood Letter, Florida State University Special Collections.

As much as soldiers were eager, in the first months of the war, to get into action, once the conflict was advanced a running theme within their letters was a great desire to come home. Furloughs and passes became increasingly difficult to acquire, especially as the ranks thinned and commanders were desperate to hold onto their remaining men. Even generals were not immune. Following the squandered battle of Murfreesboro, James Patton Anderson wrote to his wife, "I don't know when I can get home...I do want to see you and the boys so badly." Home became an obsession for many. "How we pray for peace that we may go home and see all our friends and enjoy the comforts of home," John Hosford told his sweetheart.[27]

While most soldiers tried to keep their letters optimistic, by the later stages of the war complaints were frequent and disillusionment was obvious. Camp life wore them down and increasingly they referred to the struggle as a "most cruel" or "wicked" war. In January 1864, Roderick G. Shaw of the 4th Florida reported the lack of enthusiasm for re-enlistment. Hugh Black confessed, "I don't see the use in the Army trying to do anything more. I think that they have done their *best* and *lost*."[28] John Hosford admitted that he was a "weak creature" but could not resist scratching down the lines, "would that God would put a period in this cruel war that we could all go home in peace and see our loved ones."[29]

The adventures of army life were not limited to the eastern and western theaters. Initial postings at camps of instruction and in Florida provided plenty of time for socializing, swapping tales, and basking in feminine attention. Middle Florida's distance from hostilities and its relative prosperity made it a favored arena for memorable events. Writing from Lake City on June 8, 1863, Quartermaster's Clerk Davis Bryant recorded the "gay doings," which included a big dance and two picnic

---

[27]Rayburn, "'Wherever the Fight is Thickest," 325; Mellon, "A Florida Soldier in the Army of Northern Virginia," 256.

[28]Groene, "Civil War Letters of Colonel David Lang," 346; Bittle, "Fighting Men View the Western War," 31; Blakey, et al., *Rose Cottage Chronicles*, 195.

[29]Mellon, "A Florida Soldier in the Army of Northern Virginia," 264.

parties aboard the railroad to Jacksonville to watch the reviews at Camp Finegan. Bryant noted that he had glimpsed General P. G. T. Beauregard as well as "eight ladies here from Madison." He assured his brother "and a wild time I *could* have if I wished to give up to such...."[30]

Soldiers assigned to duty in Florida did not, of course, spend every day enjoying their station. For many, their tasks were monotonous and their living conditions were appalling. "Times with us are very dull," was a common complaint. Diseases were rampant in even the best-managed camps, where soldiers quickly came down with mumps, measles, pneumonia, and the ever unpopular "itch." Soldiers in Pensacola left memorable records of how unpleasant the area became in a very short time, and mortality rates spoke when soldiers' pens were abandoned.[31]

Most men who remained in Florida after 1862 fought in irregular and militia units. Men at home generally resisted the idea of being subjected to stringent military discipline. Winston Stephens of the St. Johns Rangers admitted he ignored all attempts to "make Regulars out of my men." Guerilla warfare, which some units adopted, was a natural fit for a frontier state, especially where knowledge of swamps and woodlands provided unique opportunities to Florida's defenders. Stephens felt certain that despite his unit's small size, "we can kill four to one in these woods."[32]

Guerilla warfare required a constant readiness to fight, hard riding across vast tracts of wilderness, and enervating exposure to the elements. Captain John W. Pearson, leader of the Oklawaha Rangers, felt that Florida's infestation with Unionism necessitated his tactics: "I am now a guerilla in every sense of the word; we neither tell where we stay nor where we are going, nor when we shall return; assemble the company at the sound of a cow's horn." Guerilla units could be desperate and extremely violent, often bushwhacking and sniping at Federal landing parties along the coast. They could also be cunning. Pearson had his men

---

[30]Blakey, et al., *Rose Cottage Chronicles*, 230, 237–38.

[31]Ibid., 87; Sterx and Thompson, "Letters of a Teenage Confederate," 341.

[32]Blakey, et al., *Rose Cottage Chronicles*, 195; Ellen E. Hodges and Stephen Kerber, "'Rogues and Black Hearted Scamps': Civil War Letters of Winston and Octavia Stephens, 1862–1863," *Florida Historical Quarterly* 57 (July 1978): 68.

don disguises, including dresses and blackface, to lure Union sailors ashore to be shot. Florida's guerillas were not above foraging and outright plundering of civilian stock, and they gave little thought to the misery they caused when they torched property to keep it out of enemy hands. The *New York Herald* reported that residents of St. Augustine "are not privileged to go out because of bands of guerillas who are everywhere organizing. This has produced a reign of terror in the neighborhood. Guerillas do not hesitate to kill those who differ from them." They were also not opposed to hunting for conscripts and settling old scores in the name of patriotism. Especially in South Florida, the deprivations caused by Confederate guerillas drove many otherwise neutral or apathetic citizens into the Union fold.[33]

While the number of Floridians who joined the Confederate forces was exceptional, Florida did not see a genius rise from the ranks. The state produced a number of able military leaders, but none of the caliber of Robert E. Lee or Stonewall Jackson. Just three individuals—two generals and a member of the Confederate cabinet—are usually recognized as Florida's most notable Confederates.[34]

Born on the island of Trinidad in 1811 or 1812, Stephen Russell Mallory arrived in Key West at age nine and later spent a brief educational interlude at a Moravian school in Pennsylvania. Upon his return he helped his mother run her boardinghouse, living amid the wreckers, sailors, fishermen, adventurers, and "wanderers from the far corners of the globe." Mallory studied law under Judge William Marvin and soon had a thriving practice.[35] Mallory was elected to the U.S. Senate in 1850, and while serving as chairman of the Naval Affairs Committee he championed efforts to improve naval efficiency. Though Mallory was a supporter of the Ostend Manifesto, which called for the acquisition of Cuba,

---

[33]Zack C. Waters, "Florida's Confederate Guerillas: John W. Pearson and the Oklawaha Rangers," *Florida Historical Quarterly* 70 (October 1991): 133–43; *New York Herald*, 12 September 1862.

[34]Tebeau, *A History of Florida*, 218.

[35]Occie Clubbs, "Stephen Russell Mallory: United States Senator from Florida and Confederate Secretary of the Navy," *Florida Historical Quarterly* 25 (January 1947): 222–35.

many Florida politicians viewed Mallory as lacking true ardor for secession and opposed his appointment to the Confederate cabinet.

President Davis, however, saw past the bickering and partisan prejudice to Mallory's unique qualifications. Mallory held that since the South could not match the Union ship for ship, she should concentrate on a policy of destroying Northern commerce via sea-going raiders. Mallory soundly weighed the economic, political, and psychological effect of such a campaign. Evolving technology also fascinated Mallory. He recognized that the future of naval warfare rested with innovations, including steam power, rifled guns, and armored vessels. His expertise was vastly richer than the Confederacy's treasury, however. Challenged by the lack of conventional ships and munitions, Mallory was willing to experiment with novel methods. His work led to the creation of the first ironclad vessel, the *Virginia*, which revolutionized naval warfare. He authorized the construction of a crude submarine, the *H. A. Hunley*, which became the first submersible to sink an enemy vessel when it sent the *Housatonic* to the ocean bottom just off Charleston Harbor (though the *Hunley* accompanied its victim to a watery grave). Mallory's vision of advanced naval warfare often paralleled that of United States Secretary of the Navy Gideon Welles, but Mallory was hampered by a lack of resources and the constant criticism from more conservative officials, who faulted his inability to break the blockade or provide adequate defenses for the South's important rivers.[36]

Throughout the war Mallory remained one of Davis's most trusted advisers. He fled with Davis and the other members of the Confederate cabinet following the fall of Richmond but was arrested soon after the party dispersed in Georgia. At the end of a ten-month stint in prison, Mallory returned to his home in Pensacola where he resumed his legal practice. He died in 1873.[37]

---

[36]Joseph T. Durkin, *Stephen R. Mallory: Confederate Navy Chief* (Chapel Hill: University of North Carolina Press, 1954) x–xi; Tebeau, *A History of Florida*, 218–19; Rembert W. Patrick, *Jefferson Davis and His Cabinet* (Baton Rouge: Louisiana State University Press, 1944) 245–47.

[37]Durkin, *Stephen R. Mallory*, 338–44, 414; Tebeau, *A History of Florida*, 219.

A native of Wilmington, North Carolina, William Wing Loring arrived in St. Augustine as a child. He grew into a military career that spanned the Second Seminole War and the Mexican War, losing his left arm during the battle for Mexico City. Like many other Southern professional soldiers, he resigned from the United States Army soon after secession. Accepting a new commission with the Confederacy, Loring rose from brigadier general in 1861 to major general in 1862. Loring won a small measure of fame when, during the defense of Vicksburg, he rallied his men by mounting a cotton bale parapet and shouting "Give them blizzards, boys! Give them blizzards!" He was the senior major general in active field duty when he surrendered with General Johnston in 1865. Loring soon found more exotic employment as the inspector general of the Khedive of Egypt. Returning to the United States in 1879, Loring died in New York City in 1886.[38]

Florida's best-known soldier was a native son. Born to Yankee parents in St. Augustine in 1824, Edmund Kirby Smith attended West Point, where his classmates dubbed him "Seminole." Following service in the Mexican War, Smith returned to the United States Military Academy as a mathematics instructor from 1849 to 1852, then did a tour of duty in the American West. Resigning his commission in 1861, he entered the Confederate service. He was wounded at First Bull Run, but he recovered and rapidly rose in rank. In 1863 he was given command of all Confederate forces west of the Mississippi River. Cut off from easy communication, he was granted wide latitude by President Davis to make decisions for the Trans-Mississippi forces. One of only six Confederates to hold the rank of full general and the last Rebel general in the field, he surrendered to Major General Edward R. S. Canby on May 26, 1865. His post-war career included heading insurance and telegraph companies, as well as the University of Nashville. From 1875 to his death in 1893, Smith returned to what was his true calling, teaching mathematics at the University of the South.[39]

---

[38]Board of State Institutions, *Soldiers of Florida*, 324–26.

[39]Tebeau, *A History of Florida*, 222; Board of State Institutions, *Soldiers of Florida*, 323–34. See also the biography by Joseph Howard Parks, *General Edmund Kirby Smith, CSA* (Baton Rouge: Louisiana State University Press, 1954).

Whether they were famous in history or unknown except to their friends, Florida's soldiers endured all aspects of the Civil War. Some served with courage and honor. Others deserted or acted in reprehensible ways. The extreme number of men who entered the ranks, from such an underpopulated state, guaranteed that no white family went untouched in some way by the demands of Confederate service. Even free blacks and Unionists often found themselves forced by strange circumstances to work for the Confederacy. Slaves likewise were commandeered as drivers, laborers, and cooks. For a state so far away from the major engagements, its people still experienced the Civil War as an intensely intimate conflict.

Chapter 5

They Are Just Glorious

Florida's Confederate and Unionist Women During the War

"No moment is idle," Ellen Call Long proclaimed. "In the cars traveling, visiting, in the dark and in the light, the knitting needle is going perpetually to clothe the feet of our soldiers, who thus heeled with tender devotion, ought to be more than common soldiery." The humble sewing basket, with its needles and thread, symbolized women's work across the Confederacy. Though forbidden to shoulder rifles, women wielded domestic tools as substitute weapons and saw themselves as full partners in the Confederate enterprise, equals in patriotism and perhaps superiors in sacrifice. "I don't know how the women would do if they had to go be shot themselves," Long conceded, "but as it is they are tremendous in the desire to fight, and certainly in those offices pertaining to them they are indefatigable. They are just glorious."[1]

To focus only on women's work in support of the Confederacy and their elevated sense of patriotism is, however, to miss the larger story of their lives during the war, especially the nuances of their opinions and experiences. Not all Florida women gave their allegiance to the Confederacy. While many undoubtedly supported their state at the beginning of the war, others actively opposed it or had little interest in its issues. Once the excitement and the community celebrations faded, women of the cracker class realized that they had little to gain and virtually everything to lose in a "rich man's war and a poor man's fight." Florida was home to many women of Northern birth, and these recent immigrants had few attachments to Southern ideals. Taken as a whole, Florida's free women

---

[1]Long, *Florida Breezes*, 324, 330.

were self-reliant and pragmatic in the face of what many of them must have understood to be a hopelessly lost cause.[2]

* * *

The months preceding secession and the first year of the war were the glory days for Florida's Confederate women, who were integral to the growing groundswell for disunion and the enthusiasm for independence. Debates raged around dinner tables and in community meetings, which women attended in significant numbers. While the nineteenth-century doctrine of "separate spheres" discouraged women from expressing political inclinations, Florida's women benefitted from both a frontier existence and unusually tumultuous issues, which freed them from the most rigorous restrictions. Once the war began, women stepped outside of their sphere in novel ways. Actions that would have garnered disapproval and even community shaming—such as public speaking, publishing, and aggressive fund raising—were now appropriate and encouraged, all in the name of Confederate patriotism. This was clear as early as November 6, 1860, when Helen, Margaret, Maria, and Florida Broward, a quartet of sisters living on the Broward's Neck plantation in Duval County, drafted a letter to the *Jacksonville Standard*. While acknowledging that "silence in the affairs of men and in particular that of politics, should be the place and province of females," they confessed their inability to remain "idle spectators of the passing scenes and excitement." Taking "Submissionists" to task, they urged ladies to "reserve their crinolines to present to our Southern Politicians who have compromised away the rights of the South" and promised that should war come "we will like our Revolutionary matrons forgo our amusements and apply ourselves to our cards, spinning wheels, and looms." While drafts of the letter were preserved,

---

[2]For a consideration of the vast diversity of Florida women and their wartime experiences, see Tracy J. Revels, *Grander in Her Daughters: Florida's Women during the Civil War*. To expand the study to Confederate women across the South, consult Drew Gilpin Faust, *Mothers of Invention: Women of the Slaveholding South and the American Civil War* (Chapel Hill: University of North Carolina Press, 1996).

the loss of all copies of the *Jacksonville Standard* makes it impossible to know if this fiery salvo was ever published. Considering the number of references to female involvement in the push for secession, it seems probable that it was.[3]

Women attended the secession convention, which was something of an embarrassment to Edmund Ruffin, who did not want to be called upon to speak in front of ladies. They were in the crowd at Tallahassee's celebration, and in Madison, Tampa, and other towns across the state. They unfurled "national flags" and wrote songs and poetry for the occasion.[4] Some gave inspirational speeches to local companies, or performed in symbolic plays before ushering their sons and brothers off to war. Confederate veteran H. W. Reddick claimed that sixty recruits were added to the company rolls after the women of Eucheeanna marched through town shouting "Go boys, to your country's call! I'd rather be a brave man's widow than a coward's wife!" An all-night dance then launched the volunteers into service. The ladies of St. Augustine caught the attention of a Philadelphia reporter in their city in February 1861. He wrote, "The citizens of the Flowery are determined to maintain their rights at all hazards; and the fair daughters of Florida are prompt to encourage and cheer their bold defenders."[5]

While war seemed to be either unlikely or short and glorious, Florida's Confederate women excelled in making uniforms and flags. Volunteers were often outfitted by their own families or through community efforts. The first trappings were splendid and colorful, if completely impractical and non-regulation.[6] C. Seaton Fleming was proud of the uni-

---

[3]Samuel Proctor, "The Call to Arms: Secession from a Feminine Point of View," *Florida Historical Quarterly* 35 (January 1957): 266–71.

[4]*Tallahassee Floridian and Journal*, 12 January 1861; Graham, "The Home Front," 21.

[5]William Warren Rogers, ed., "Florida on the Eve of the Civil War as Seen by a Southern Reporter," *Florida Historical Quarterly* 39 (October 1960): 155–56; H. W. Reddick, *Seventy-seven Years in Dixie: The Boys in Gray of 61–65* (H. W. Reddick: Washington County, FL, 1910) 9; *Philadelphia Inquirer*, 2 February 1861.

[6]In the memorable words of Bell Irvin Wiley, early Confederate uniforms "indicated considerably more zeal than skill" but "many of the companies were

forms of "hunting-shirt" pattern that the ladies of St. Augustine produced for the local companies, and throughout the war men would write
to their female relations asking for particular types of coats and shirts,
often with complaints that may have offended feminine sensibilities, such
as when Samuel Palmer noted that the "knit" shirts his spouse sent him
"proved too much hiding place for lice."[7]

Flags served symbolic purposes, so Florida's women filled them with
artistic reminders of the state's beauty and ties to its Southern sisters.
Classical and historical mottoes including *"Dieu et Mon Droit"* (God and
My Right), *"Semper Paratus"* (Always Ready) and *"Crescit Eundo"* (It
Grows as it Goes) swirled amid these emblems.[8] Women endowed flags
with physical reminders of themselves, so the silk, satin, and velvet ban-
ners reflected the wealth of the wardrobes pillaged to make them. The
flag of the Captain John J. Dickison's company was stitched in part from
his wife's shawl. The rings holding the flag to its lance were forged from
jewelry donated by the ladies of Orange Lake and the ferrule was made
from the silver comb Mrs. Dickison had worn on her wedding night.[9]
Everywhere in the state, Florida's Confederate women eagerly enforced
the notion that the defense of Southern rights was also a defense of female virtue.

---

resplendent," Wiley, *Life of Johnny Reb: The Common Soldier of the Confederacy*
(New York: Bobbs-Merrill, 1943) 108–109.

[7]Francis P. Fleming, *A Memoir of Capt. C. Seton Fleming of the Second Florida Infantry, C.S.A.* (Jacksonville: Times-Union Publishing House, 1884) 26–27;
Revels, *Grander in Her Daughters*, 22–23; Samuel Augustus Palmer to Mary
Rebecca Gassaway Palmer, 2 August 1863, Palmer Family Letters, State Archives of Florida.

[8]Reid Mitchell, *Civil War Soldiers* (New York: Viking Penguin, 1988) 19–
20; Mary Elizabeth Dickison, *Dickison and His Men*, 1890 facsimile ed. (Gainesville: University of Florida Press, 1962) 161; Steven M. Stowe, ed., *A Southern
Practice: The Diary and Autobiography of Charles A. Hentz, MD* (Charlottesville:
University Press of Virginia, 2000) 357; Graham, *The Awakening of St. Augustine*, 84; Daisy Parker, "Battle Flags of Florida Troops," *Apalachee* 1 (1948–
1950): 5–6. The mottoes on flags reflected the classical education that elite Floridians received.

[9]Dickison, *Dickison and His Men*, 19–22.

The illusion that the war would be brief and relatively bloodless was quickly shattered. For Floridians, the war came home with the fight at Santa Rosa Island on October 9, 1861. Susan Bradford, who only weeks before had enjoyed parties and target practice with local volunteers, now attended the grim funeral of her handsome cousin, Captain Richard H. Bradford, who was killed in Florida's first battle. A large crowd gathered for the burial at Pine Hill plantation, and Governor Milton gave the eulogy. War lost its nobility and romance as death became an ever-present companion to Florida's women.[10]

For all women left behind, the immediate task was to provide for their families while their principal breadwinners were away. Most Floridian women were far from the helpless belles of fiction. They were, to a large degree, frontier women who understood not only planting and cultivation but also trade and the operation of firearms. Cracker women were already famous for driving hard bargains with merchants and operating rustic inns. The lonesome women of South Florida were accustomed to long separations from spouses who were away chasing herds or sailing ships, and even elite Middle Florida women took charge of estates while their husbands rode law circuits or attended meetings of the General Assembly. One of Florida's wealthiest planters was female, and women excelled in a number of professions ranging from cooking and washing to operating the occasional "house of pleasure."

Women, however, were not abandoned to a single-gender world during the war. Many men remained at home for a wide variety of reasons, from age and disability to youth or disinclination to fight. For a time, overseers and cattle drivers were exempt from conscription. Almost every woman in Florida had some masculine resource to turn to for advice and aid, even if the male she preferred to rely on was on the battlefield.[11]

---

[10]Eppes, *Through Some Eventful Years*, 151, 159–60; Michael Gannon, *Florida: A Short History* (Gainesville: University Press of Florida, 1993) 43–46.

[11]James M. Denham, "Cracker Women and Their Families," in Mark I. Greenberg, William Warren Rogers, and Canter Brown, Jr., eds., *Florida's Heritage of Diversity: Essays in Honor of Samuel Proctor* (Tallahassee: Sentry Press, 1997) 18–23; Smith, *Slavery and Plantation Growth*, 215–22; Russell Garvin, "The Free Negro in Florida before the Civil War," *Florida Historical Quarterly*

How a Florida woman faced the challenge of the providing for her family depended on many variables, including her age, overall health, experience, level of self-confidence, and assistance from friends, family, and possibly slaves. While some women crumpled and suffered from physical ailments and deep depression, most found a way to endure. Many women tried to help each other. Tragically, relatively few letters from women to men survive, as men at the front were unable to store letters as cherished possessions. However, by reading backwards from the responses that men at war provided, as well as the post-war recollections and family traditions, one can gather a moving portrait of women's endurance on the Florida home front.[12]

Farmers and planters were as quick to issue orders to their wives as to their slaves. Soldiers on distant fields were enthusiastic about their own acres back in Florida, always wanting to know about harvests and yields, or to remind spouses about planting, hoeing, and spreading manure. They worried about their livestock as well. John S. Thomas told his wife to have their slave "feed the hogs well you have plenty of corn and now is the time to begin to push them and make them grow."[13] Soldiers advised their wives on storing and saving food; they occasionally even encouraged wartime profiteering. The Reverend Edmund E. Lee of Manatee County found time from his chaplain duties to urge his wife toward ever more elaborate easy-money schemes, from manufacturing lime juice to selling roof shingles. Michael Raysor assured his wife, Sallie, she had proven to be a better farmer than he was. Council A. Bryan worried that his wife, Cornelia, was exhausting herself with a combination of household chores and entrepreneurial efforts. He urged her to cut back, promising that after the war they would "commence to get rich" together.[14]

---

46 (July 1967): 12; Rogers, "A Great Stirring in the Land," 159; Revels, *Grander in Her Daughters*, 56–57.

[12]Revels, *Grander in Her Daughters*, 57, 65, 70.

[13]Elizabeth H. Sims, *A History of Madison County, Florida* (Madison: Jimbob Printing, 1986) 73.

[14]Sheehan-Dean, "'If It Was Not For You I Would Be Willing to Die,'" 400; Revels, *Grander in Her Daughters*, 65; *Civil War Letters of Edmund C. Lee* (Jacksonville: Historical Records Survey, 1937) 9, 19, 28–30; Council A. Bryan

Managing slaves was a wartime challenge. Most mistresses engaged in a complicated dance of rewards, threats, and punishments to keep their slaves obedient and productive. Before the war, plantation mistresses generally supervised their "house servants" and oversaw medical care and tended to the spiritual lives of those on their estates, but they were spared from physically punishing slaves. With husbands and later overseers gone, Florida's plantation mistresses gained many unwelcome responsibilities. Octavia Stephens found she had to administer beatings to her slave children, a task she had always had the luxury of avoiding. Other women fought a battle of wits and wills with their slaves, many of whom took advantage of every opportunity for disobedience. Being the mistress did not guarantee total victory over one's bondsmen. Though Sarah Jones admired Caroline Milton as the epitome of a Southern lady, she also conceded that the Milton household at Sylvania was in turmoil with the hen houses broken, the hogs loose in the gardens, and the slaves asking for and receiving inflated prices for the fish they caught and the eggs they found. While some women succeeded in becoming estate administrators, others began to wish their slaves on the Yankees or make the self-serving claim that mistresses were the biggest slaves on plantations.[15]

Along with keeping the family farm or business operational, women were eager to support their men at the front. They forwarded baskets and packages, filled with everything from cooked chickens and hams to gloves and socks, as well as precious mementoes like daguerreotypes. Soldiers weren't above asking for special items. Augustus H. Mathers wrote to his wife for "A few little dainties.... For instance a small box of sugar cakes and any other things of that Class You might be disposed to fix up." Requests and thanks sometimes came in the same letters. At times, soldiers tried to reciprocate by buying essentials such as coffee,

---

to Cornelia Archer Bryan, 2 October 1863, Council A. Bryan Papers, State Archives of Florida.

[15]Blakey, et al., *Rose Cottage Chronicles*, 128, 132; Jones, *Life in the South* 2:277; Eppes, *Through Some Eventful Years*, 87.

pins, needles, thread, and stamps for their families, or by sending money home.[16]

Though far removed from the largest battles of the Civil War, Florida's women were not spared a key obligation of women across the Confederacy: the care of the wounded. Florida's most famous nurse and Confederate heroine was Mary Martha Reid. A former territorial first lady and a widow, Reid decided to leave her Fernandina home and travel to Richmond in 1862, writing to her worried stepson that "others can and will fill my place here and there I feel something calling me." She assisted in setting up Florida's designated hospital in the Confederate capital, serving as the hospital's chief matron and publicity agent. Her work earned her the nickname "Mother of the Florida Boys."[17] But for most Florida women, nursing was a local calling. Towns had some form of hospital, often inside a church, hotel, or civic structure. "Wayside hospitals" near train depots might be little more than a local residence hastily converted for the reception of wounded. The knowledge that a nearby battle could turn a blissful home into an abattoir in hours was always present. Captain Hugh Black described a Richmond, Kentucky, house where "there were piles of arms and legs as high as table." Hopeful they would never be caught unprepared for such an event, hospital committees of women organized to procure sheets, bandages, and cooking utensils, and to take turns as nurses and assistants. These Floridian Florence Nightingales were often the bane of doctors, who posted "No Admittance" signs on their wards keep out women, especially the young and pretty ones.[18] Princess Murat often sent her carriage to collect convales-

---

[16]Revels, *Grander in Her Daughters*, 23–25; Franklin A. Doty, "The Civil War Letters of Augustus Henry Mathers, Assistant Surgeon, Fourth Florida Regiment, C.S.A," *Florida Historical Quarterly* 36 (October 1957): 111.

[17]Proctor, ed., *Florida a Hundred Years*, n.p.; Mary Martha Reid to Robert Raymond Reid, 14 July 1862, transcript, Reid Family Letters, P. K. Yonge Library, University of Florida; Edward C. Williamson, "Francis P. Fleming in the War for Southern Independence: Letters from the Front, Part I," *Florida Historical Quarterly* 28 (July 1949): 45; Mary Martha Reid, *What I Know of the Travers Family* (Jacksonville: Historical Records Survey, 1937) 14.

[18]Revels, *Grander in Her Daughters*, 26–28; "Notes on Secession in Tallahassee and Leon County," 67; Bittle, "Fighting Men View the Western War,"

cents in Tallahassee, treating them to hearty meals at her plantation; one can only imagine how their relatives must have reacted upon learning these men had dined with Napoleonic royalty in the Florida backwoods. While most women volunteered their services, others had nursing thrust upon them. Mattie English Bunch of Liberty County was often unsure whether the men who staggered to her door, desperate for nourishment, were Confederate soldiers, Yankee stragglers, or deserters of either camp. To be fair, she said, she "fed them out of the same spoon."[19]

Fundraising was another wartime expectation. Women were accustomed to soliciting donations for churches or genteel charities, but now they were encouraged to go public in ways that would have been nothing short of scandalous a few years before. "The ladies, whose recent efforts to raise a fund for the purchase of Mount Vernon were so signally successful, can, in these matters render efficient services," the *St. Johns Mirror* announced on May 7, 1861. "I presume no more is necessary than to call attention to the necessity of the movement."[20] In Middle Florida communities like Tallahassee, Quincy, and Madison, Confederate women planned a range of entertainments. Concerts, public lectures, and bazaars were held throughout the war; the public never seemed to tire of attending. Children were enlisted as performers. Tableaux, dramas involving static poses and stilted speeches, were popular in the state. Their common themes are suggested by the title of one organized by Julia Stockton in Quincy: *Cotton Ermine—Cotton is King.*[21] In 1863 the Ladies Dramatic Aid Society of Tallahassee commandeered the capitol building for a series of shows, which included scenes from Shakespeare

---

26–27; *Florida Sentinel* (Tallahassee), 26 August 1862; *Gainesville Cotton States*, 7 May 1864; David A. Avant, *J. Randall Stanley's History of Gadsden County, 1948* (Tallahassee: L'Avant Studios, 1985) 101–103; G. H. Dorman, *Fifty Years Ago: Reminiscences of 61–65* (Tallahassee: T. J. Appleyard, 1912) 4–5.

[19]Long, "Princesse Achille Murat," 35–36; Mattie English Bunch, "Story of Two Lovers," United Daughters of the Confederacy Scrapbooks, vol. 2, State Archives of Florida.

[20]*St. Johns Mirror* (Jacksonville), 7 May 1861.

[21]Mary Elizabeth Massey, *Bonnet Brigades* (New York: Alfred A. Knopf, 1966) 37; *Quincy Dispatch*, 21 April 1863; Ulmer, ed., *The Correspondence of Will and Ju Stockton*, 187–90.

and melodramas based on Florida history. The troupe charged a dollar per adult and fifty cents per child's admission and raised nearly a thousand dollars in three nights; the money went to impoverished wives and mothers of soldiers. Though never enough to counter inflation and destitution, this fundraising effort by amateur thespians was memorable for its uniqueness. It was a rare occasion of female initiative, leadership, performers, and beneficiaries.[22]

Florida's Confederate women had worked assiduously to support their men, but over time their enthusiasm for the war diminished. Some women supported the Confederate effort more out of community spirit than any personal zeal. Others had gone along because they feared social snubs if they seemed unpatriotic. "Women discipline each other," one observer concluded, "with intolerance towards any slacker...."[23] But when furloughs were denied and pleading for assistance went unanswered, Florida's female morale faded. Women turned from supporting the Confederacy to begging their husbands to come home. Even the stoic Confederate matron Julia Stockton wavered, earning a sharp rebuke from her husband, who felt honor-bound to remain in the service. From remarkably early in the war, many letters and diary entries reveal a despair that undermined patriotic efforts. "I think we can do no good worth counting," Octavia Stephens admitted to her husband in the privacy of their October 1862 correspondence, "as I believe there is no such thing as stirring up these country people, & without their help we could do nothing but knit a few pairs of socks."[24] Over time, many if not most of Florida's women were lost to the Confederacy, especially if decent rations and protection could be had for the cost of an oath of allegiance to the Union.

Florida's coastal women eventually faced a terrible decision: to remain in place and risk insults or atrocities of the enemy, or join the thousands of people across the South who had begun to flee. Leaving home

---

[22]*Tallahassee Floridian & Journal*, 26 May, 9 June 1863.

[23]Proctor, *Florida a Hundred Years Ago*, n.p.; *Gainesville Cotton States*, 7 May 1864.

[24]Ulmer, ed., *The Correspondence of Will and Ju Stockton*, 208–209; Blakey, et al., *Rose Cottage Chronicles*, 163.

meant losing all non-portable possessions. Women who chose flight often conducted an extreme yard sale. Abandoning Jacksonville, Maria Murphy packed up her husband's expensive medical library but sold off all her furniture, including "a side-saddle quite new, sold for $1.50, whatever offer was taken." While some families were given adequate notice, others had little warning. The *New York Herald* drew a memorable picture of Jacksonville families being evacuated by Union forces in April 1862:

> None of these had more than ten hours in which to make preparations…. It was sad to see them hurrying down to the wharf, each carrying some article too precious to forsake. Books, boxes, valises, portraits, pictures, packages of clothes, pet canaries and mocking-birds were most frequently seen. Stout-hearted and stylish officers, relieving Dinahs of their little charges and leading two-, three-, and four-year-olds added a humane and praiseworthy ludicrousness to the melancholy scene.[25]

While most women voluntarily chose to leave their homes, others were driven out, either expelled by Union occupiers or removed for their own safety in military evacuations. Some literally fled from exploding shells. Families in New Smyrna lost piano tops, and Newport residents counted dressers as casualties of gunboat projectiles. Tampa mothers took their children to the heights to watch their town being targeted. Some chose to stay for the war's duration, but many unnerved women and families left coastal cities for inland refuges.[26]

Refugee women faced constant challenges, from acquiring shelter to finding employment. Crowded into overpriced hotels and boarding houses, their money quickly ran out. Refugee women replenished purses by teaching, sewing, and doing laundry. Perhaps the greatest challenge they faced was learning to adapt and make friends in a strange community. St. Augustine resident Frances Kirby Smith clearly failed this test after being sent to Madison. She complained that the small town was provincial, its women "full of pretensions" and its men "engaged in

---

[25]Maria C. Murphy, "The 1st Evacuation of Jacksonville," United Daughters of the Confederacy Scrapbooks, vol. 1, State Archives of Florida; *New York Herald*, 22 April 1862. A "Dinah" was a female slave.

[26]Revels, *Grander in Her Daughters*, 115–17.

speculations great and small." Even bunking down with extended family could lead to unwanted drama. One Florida woman went home to her parents in North Carolina, only to find them so critical of her children that she fled back to Florida and life with her in-laws.[27] The experience of being homeless and unwelcome led many women to question their loyalty to the Confederate cause.

Unionism grew stronger as Confederate partisanship waned. Unionism among women was especially strong in East Florida and in Key West, but loyal women could be found across the state. Their hearts were often divided, especially if their sons chose to serve beneath the Stars and Bars. Though her son fought for the Confederacy, Ellen Call Long was as deep a Unionist as her famous father. Even as she participated in Confederate activities, she poured her skepticism and disgust with the Confederacy into her journal. In West Florida, an overseer's wife "would often fearlessly and with force and eloquence proclaim her love of the Union and her detestation of the Confederacy. After one of her sons was killed and one died in a hospital, woe be it to the Secessionist who dared to talk of war and politics in her presence."[28]

The most fortunate Unionist women were those who resided in areas that quickly fell under Federal control. In Fernandina, St. Augustine, and Key West, Unionist women welcomed the Yankee troops. Women like Clarissa Anderson, a wealthy, Northern-born widow, quickly became the peacemakers of the town, serving as advisers and liaisons between the Union officials and the simmering Confederate townspeople. Loyal female residents were soon enjoying the company of Yankee women, as many officers took the opportunity to invite their wives and daughters to Florida, often arranging for them to stay with Union sym-

---

[27]Mary Elizabeth Massey, *Refugee Life in the Confederacy* (Baton Rouge: Louisiana State University Press, 1964) 86, 118–19; Joseph Howard Parks, *General Edmund Kirby Smith*, C.S.A. (Baton Rouge: Louisiana State University Press, 1954) 346.

[28]Long, *Florida Breezes*, vii–xiv, 306–307; John Williamson Crary, Sr., *Reminiscences of the Old South from 1834 to 1866 and A Biographical Sketch of John Williamson Crary Sr. by May Crary Weller* (Pensacola: Perdido Bay Press, 1984) 85.

pathizers.[29] While most of these women came only for recreation or family reunions, a few, including Chloe Merrick and Esther Hill Hawks, came to Florida determined to inspire reform and provide educational opportunities for freedmen.[30] Women who were Federal partisans or simply had no great attachment to the Confederacy might enjoy romantic escapades with the Yankee invaders. Roscoe Charles Perry of Connecticut fell for Margarita Antonia Capo of St. Augustine, and the beauty of the town's "Spanish" women quickly became legendary among the occupying forces. Others, such as a "loyal woman" who arrived in Jacksonville during its third occupation, provided vital information to officers, making them aware of troop movements or runaway slaves in the area. In Key West, Union women participated in the same activities their Confederate counterparts did, presenting flags to troops, raising funds, and volunteering at the hospitals.[31]

Florida made war on women in an infamous 1864 incident. Sent to flush out a camp of bold Confederate deserters in the swamps of Taylor County, Lieutenant Colonel Henry D. Capers was unable to capture his prey, so he arrested their families instead. Two men, sixteen women, and a number of children were imprisoned in a specially-constructed stockade in Tallahassee, an action that infuriated Governor Milton, who poured his rage into a letter to General James Patton Anderson: "I am not convinced that any benefit has resulted from it, on the contrary it has made many women and children homeless and exposed them to disgrace and

---

[29]Graham, *The Awakening of St. Augustine*, 52–53; Jean Parker Waterbury, *The Treasurer's House* (St. Augustine: St. Augustine Historical Society, 1994) 118; James M. Nichols, *Perry's Saints: Or, the Fighting Parson's Regiment in the War of the Rebellion* (Boston: D. Lothop, 1886) 180.

[30]The life and work of these two remarkable Northern humanitarians can be found in Sarah Whitmer Foster and John T. Foster, Jr., "Chloe Merrick Reed: Freedom's First Lady," *Florida Historical Quarterly* 71 (January 1993): 279–99 and Gerald Schwartz, ed., *A Woman Doctor's Civil War: Esther Hill Hawks' Diary* (Columbia: University of South Carolina Press, 1984).

[31]William McGuire, "A Connecticut Yankee in St. Augustine, 1863," *El Escribano* 28 (1991): 62, 65; Capo Family Biographical File, St. Augustine Historical Society; Johns, *Florida during the Civil War*, 155; *Philadelphia Inquirer*, 2 November 1862; *Key West New Era*, 19 April, 20 September, 8 November 1862.

suffering. Some of these women and children *are the mothers and helpless brothers and sisters of patriotic and brave men who are soldiers in the armies of Virginia and the west.*" This mistreatment of poor families led to a malaise of morale that led to still more desertion and draft dodging, especially in Middle Florida.[32]

At war's end, it would be difficult to assess, with any hope of accuracy, the number of women who completely supported the Confederate cause, the true Unionists among them, or the ones who were primarily opportunists and had claimed loyalty based on the availability of food and protection. At the point of Confederate surrender, Ellen Call Long scoffed at the foolishness of Tallahassee's women, who were discussing cutting their hair to sell to raise funds for the troops.[33] A far more common reaction in the last year of the war was a desperate plea for the Divinity to intercede and bring the conflict to an end. Fatalistic feelings prevailed. "Sometimes I am led to think God has forsaken us, and intends to let us destroy each other," future Florida first lady Catherine Hart wrote to her family in New Jersey. Whatever their political inclination, and no matter their social class or place of birth, by 1864 the white women of Florida joined in the cry of Maria B. Taylor of Osceola: "When shall we again enjoy the blessings of peace?"[34]

[32]W. T. Cash, "Taylor County History and Civil War Deserters," *Florida Historical Quarterly* 27 (July 1948): 49–60; Ella Lonn, *Desertion during the Civil War* (New York: Century, 1928) 85; Eppes, *Through Some Eventful Years*, 223–24; John Milton to James Patton Anderson, 5 May 1864, *John Milton Letterbook, 1863–1865*, 60, State Archives of Florida.

[33]Ellen Call Long Diary, 16 April, 2, 10 May 1865, State Archives of Florida.

[34]Catherine Campbell Hart to Deborah Conger Campbell, Charlotte Campbell, Emma Campbell, and Charles G. Campbell, 5 January 1865, Dena E. Snodgrass Collection, P. K. Yonge Library, University of Florida; Maria B. Taylor to Mrs. Bonskett, 15 August 1864, Maria B. Taylor Letters, Lewis G. Schmidt Collection, State Archives of Florida.

Chapter 6

Make Ready to Go

Slavery in Florida

Slavery was deeply rooted in Florida. The Spanish conquistadors held African slaves in the 1500s, and slavery continued under the English occupation from 1763–1783. During the second Spanish period, slaves never formed a significant proportion of the Florida population. In the early 1800s some slaves escaped their masters and forged alliances with the Seminoles, but with the American purchase of the territory, the "peculiar institution" of African American slavery would quickly become a linchpin of the Florida economy.

Slaves migrated into Florida with their masters or were purchased from slave traders. The frontier nature of the state presented both challenges and opportunities for Florida's bondsmen and women. Natural increase and immigration soon led to a significant rise in the numbers of slaves in Florida. By 1860, approximately 44 percent of the state's population was enslaved.

During the Civil War, Union troops arrived in Florida as forces of liberation. But freedom did not come only through soldiers bearing the Emancipation Proclamation. By running away, by volunteering to fight for the Union, and by simple acts of resistance on farms and plantations, many of Florida's slaves demonstrated courage, sacrifice, and a determination to seize freedom for themselves.[1]

---

[1] Edwin L. Williams, Jr., "Negro Slavery in Florida, Part I," *Florida Historical Quarterly* (October 1949): 93–107; Rivers, "Dignity and Importance'," 406–407; Smith, *Slavery and Plantation Growth*, 27. For a consideration of the ways that slavery worked within the Seminole tribe, see Kevin Kokomoor, "A Reassessment of Seminoles, Africans, and Slavery on the Florida Frontier," *Florida Historical Quarterly* 88 (Fall 2009): 209–36. For information on how slaves were bought and sold, see Julia F. Smith, "Slavetrading in Antebellum Florida," *Florida Historical Quarterly* 50 (January 1972): 252–61.

* * *

Florida's bondsmen and women were subjected to the same hardships and traumas of slaves across the South. They were stripped of personhood and denied their most basic human rights. They owned neither their bodies nor their time and were deprived of education. Slaves were relegated to inferior houses and diets and frequently suffered brutal punishments for the least infraction of strict rules, which they had no voice in making.[2] Family life, though encouraged by masters as a source of pacification and moral improvement, had no legal foundation. Family members could be sold away at an owner's whim. By 1860, manumission was virtually impossible. Most slaves worked at agricultural tasks though some achieved favored domestic positions as valets, cooks, maids, and nannies. But even these elevated assignments carried high risks, as intimate "house servants" were the easiest targets of an owner's rage or lust.[3]

Florida's frontier environment sometimes altered the contours of slavery. Trust between master and bondsman was essential for survival. The vast distances between farms and towns often required owners to have confidence in their slaves' abilities and obedience to perform tasks miles from their residences. When Sarah Jones arrived in Tallahassee to tutor Governor Milton's children, she was shocked to find that the governor expected her to travel two days in a carriage with no companion other than William, the governor's body servant. She soon discovered that William was not only a competent carriage driver but also an honorable chaperone and a backwoods naturalist familiar with all species of Florida flora. Some small planters, such as Winston Stephens, were con-

---

[2] Gary M. Mormino, "Florida Slave Narratives," *Florida Historical Quarterly* 66 (April 1988): 409–11; Work Progress Administration, *Slave Narratives: A Folk History of Slavery in the United States from Interviews with Former Slaves*, vol. 17, *Florida Narratives* (St. Clair Shores, MI: Scholarly Press, 1976) 17: 35, 96.

[3] Rivers, "Dignity and Importance'," 414–15, 419. For a look at the legal codes governing slavery in Florida, see Joseph Conan Thompson, "Toward a More Humane Oppression: Florida's Slave Codes, 1821–1861," *Florida Historical Quarterly* 71 (January 1993): 324–38.

tent to do without overseers, allowing the slave "driver" or foreman to manage the fieldwork and supervise other slaves.[4] Sharing the rough frontier conditions with their masters, slaves at times appeared to develop a kind of camaraderie with their owners. Touring South Florida before the war, future Freedmen's Bureau Commissioner Oliver Otis Howard noted blacks and whites working together at many professions. He wrote, "Slavery here is a very mild form. You wouldn't know the negros were slaves unless you were told."[5] Masters who treated their slaves with basic human decency and some paternal indulgence would be rewarded during the war with behavior that they interpreted as great faithfulness, but which was more likely opportunism on the part of the black "family members."

Florida conditions could also, at times, work against a slave's welfare. Especially on small plantations or when a homestead was being initially developed, there was little division of labor by gender. In Florida, slave women engaged in heavy and dangerous tasks beside slave men; they not only picked cotton but also cut trees, dug ditches, and built fences.[6] Slaves forced to migrate with their owners from other Southern states left behind family members and friends whom they were unlikely to meet again. Marriages between slaves on distant plantations were difficult to maintain. And perhaps most tragically, residence on a frontier far from other whites who might disapprove of cruel or negligent behavior placed slaves even more at their owners' mercy. Masters were free to devise vicious punishments or to use chains, whips, and torturous devices without any rebuke from their peers. For slave women, the lack of com-

---

[4] Jones, "Governor Milton and His Family," 45; Christopher E. Linsin, "Skilled Slave Labor in Florida: 1850–1860," *Florida Historical Quarterly* (Fall 1996): 187; Granade, "Slave Unrest in Florida," 21.

[5] Irvin D. Solomon and Grace Erhart, "Race and Civil War in South Florida," *Florida Historical Quarterly* 77 (Winter 1999): 322.

[6] Rivers, "'Dignity and Importance'," 422–23; Blakey, et al., *Rose Cottage Chronicles*, 61, 94.

munity controls made them even more vulnerable to unwanted sexual attention.[7]

Despite what some masters may have believed, slaves were neither stupid nor passive. In Bartow, a slave woman spoke plainly to her mistress, announcing that she had been made to wash another woman's clothes "to help her husband fight to keep us slaves."[8] From the very beginning, slaves understood the fundamental cause of the war, perhaps better than some Southern whites did. When news of the war reached one Madison County plantation, an elderly slave gathered his fellows together for secret prayer, beseeching God to protect the Union soldiers. Most slave owners had female slaves in their home, doing domestic chores on at least a part-time basis, and eavesdropping has always been a servant's art form. Some slaves had secretly learned to read, despite laws forbidding their literacy, and they passed along information to their cohorts. Masters and mistresses attempted to keep slaves ignorant (a hopeless task) and resorted to scare tactics, warning bondsmen of the "devilish" Yankees and the agonies they inflicted on slaves they "captured." They also turned to religion, preaching private sermons on obedience and subjecting their slaves to endless Bible readings. None of these efforts were particularly successful at quenching slaves' desire for freedom.[9]

Florida's civic leaders feared that the war's disruptions and the lack of male supervision would enable slaves to plot murder and mayhem. Frontier-era trust evaporated for lawmakers, who in 1861 attempted to tighten patrol laws and better regulate slave movements. The lack of

---

[7] Joan E. Cashin, *A Family Venture: Men and Women on the Southern Frontier* (New York: Oxford University Press, 1991) 105; Smith, *Slavery and Plantation Growth in Florida*, 59–60, 93.

[8] "Memory Diary of Mrs. George Gibbs," 203, Gibbs Family Biographical File, St. Augustine Historical Society.

[9] Bell Irvin Wiley, *Southern Negroes, 1861–1865* (New York: Rinehart, 1938) 12–18; Schwartz, ed., *A Woman Doctor's Civil War*, 77; George P. Rawick, ed., *The American Slave: A Composite Autobiography*, vol. 17, *Florida Narratives* (Westport, CT: Greenwood Publishing, 1972) 17: 98, 214–15; Blakey, et al., *Rose Cottage Chronicles*, 90, 215.

manpower meant that these new regulations were rarely enforced.[10] Masters who retained confidence in their own bondsmen feared the slaves belonging to absent neighbors. Winston Stephens instructed his wife to get a relative "to shoot Gardners negroes if they come about the place and I will be responsible for the damage."[11]

Petty disobedience, rather than violent rebellion, became common on Florida's farms and plantations, especially in the female ranks. From Rose Cottage plantation on the St. Johns, Octavia Stephens reported a "great deal of grumbling about hard work" and repeated incidents of insolence from her bondswomen, much of it aimed at her visiting mother. Illness occurred at suspiciously regular intervals; Jane, a Stephens's slave, swore that a fever would "carry her off." It did not kill her, but it exempted her from ploughing chores.[12] On Sylvania plantation, a pair of slave maids antagonized the already overwhelmed English governess. One frustrated Sarah Jones's best efforts to keep the schoolroom clean, and the other poisoned the relationship between Jones and Mrs. Milton by altering the character of messages she carried between them.[13]

Acts of resistance such as feigning illness, breaking tools, or failing to work diligently were common in the entire era of slavery. What seems to have changed in Florida during the war was their frequency and the way they were directed at the mistresses, who were already in emotional distress. Some slaves cunningly waged a kind of psychological guerilla warfare on the home front. In Tampa, Sarah Brown found her mistresses weeping for her husband, who was on the battlefield. Sarah, who had been torn from her mother as a child and been beaten for her tears, coolly informed her mistress "not to cry, as it would not do her any good."[14]

For most slaves, the war increased their responsibilities and burdens. Planters expected more out of their slaves and regularly sent orders to them. Slaves might be reassigned to new jobs that would aid the Confed-

---

[10] Granade, "Slave Unrest in Florida," 27; Davis, *The Civil War and Reconstruction in Florida*, 220–21.

[11] Blakey, et al., *Rose Cottage Chronicles*, 69, 80.

[12] Blakey, et al., *Rose Cottage Chronicles*, 100, 198.

[13] Hopley, *Life in the South* 2:266–67, 283–85.

[14] Rivers, *Slavery in Florida*, 212–17; "One-Time Slave Sheds Light on Life in Tampa," *Tampa Tribune*, 5 June 1988.

eracy, such as salt making or cattle driving, or laboring to build fortifications. Some slave women were taken to hospitals to serve as cooks and maids for the Confederate wounded. Other slaves were forced to flee with their mistresses, packing up wagons and herding livestock to new residences. Refugee bondsmen sometimes faced the prospect of being assigned to temporary masters, to work in unfamiliar fields and live in cramped housing. Separation from family members was a constant hardship, especially when masters drafted men and boys to accompany them to war as teamsters and body servants.[15] Refugee whites might choose to leave trusted slaves behind to care for property. David Yulee's slaves, considered unusually faithful to their master, were unable to prevent the burning of his sugar plantation on the Homosassa River. George Washington Scott, fearful that his wife would need to abandon their plantation near Tallahassee, sent her an exhaustingly detailed letter on how to proceed, including instructions on what to pack, how to erect tents, and which slaves could be trusted with particular assignments. "Aunt Gina," an elderly slave, was to be left behind to watch the house and the other slaves' belongings. Scott presumably hoped that any invading Yankees would take pity on the old woman and not burn the house over her head. How Aunt Gina might have felt about the possibility of being left alone in the woods is a mystery.[16]

During the war, another very significant threat to Florida's slaves was the possibility of being sold or hired out. A slave was a readily liquefied asset, disposable as wartime inflation and deprivations took their toll, and slaves were especially vulnerable when creditors' claims had to be satisfied. Slave prices rose during the war. Gadsden County records show that the price of a prime field hand doubled from $1,000 in 1860 to $2,000 in 1863. While women and children brought less, they were also

[15] Rivers, *Slavery in Florida*, 237–39; Wiley, *Southern Negroes*, 4–6; Daniel L. Schafer, "Freedom Was As Close As the River: African Americans and the Civil War in Northeast Florida," in Daniel R. Colburn and Jane L. Landers, eds., *The African American Heritage of Florida* (Gainesville: University Press of Florida, 1995) 168, 172–73.
[16] Yulee, "Senator David L. Yulee," 5–7; Clifton Paisley, "How to Escape the Yankees: Major Scott's Letter to His Wife at Tallahassee, March 1864," *Florida Historical Quarterly* 50 (July 1971): 56–57.

seen as less essential in keeping a plantation operational and might be disposed of for needed funds. Newspaper ads for slave sales announced "chance for bargain" and "remarkably low price *for cash*."[17] Slaves who were not sold might risk being hired out to other families. Owners who were refugees and did not want to make arrangements to move their human property, or who possessed particularly troublesome slaves, were often tempted to hire their slaves to another plantation or as servants in town. Absent masters frequently urged mistresses to give control of slaves to someone else, often a neighbor more experienced in their management. While a skilled slave might benefit from this arrangement, especially if allowed to hire his own time, field hands had very little to gain by being marched to another plantation and turned over to a supervisor who had no emotional attachment to their welfare. Being hired out also divided slave families. Some owners even used this threat of sale or hiring out as a way to control slave behavior.[18]

Wartime material shortages took a greater toll on slaves than whites. Slave clothing had always been second rate, but during the war it became ragged and minimal. In the 1850s, planters had purchased cotton and linen fabrics in variations called osnaburg, domestic, shirting, sheeting, and stripes, along with kersey, a wool and cotton mixture, for less than twenty-five cents a yard. These fabrics skyrocketed in price, putting them beyond the reach of most mistresses, who turned to homespun fabrics. Slave women now had the added burden of weaving cloth for the entire plantation. Slaves had previously inherited clothing from their owners, but this supply ended as whites desperately patched, mended, and made do rather than passing along old clothing to their slaves. Shoes also vanished from the slave wardrobe. Winston Stephens urged his wife to keep the slave children near the fire rather than try to purchase footwear for them during the winter. He confessed his fear that extended depriva-

[17] Larry Rivers, "Slavery and the Political Economy of Gadsden County, Florida: 1823–1861," *Florida Historical Quarterly* 70 (July 1991): 17–18; *Pensacola Weekly Observer*, 4 June 1861; *Florida Sentinel* (Tallahassee), 9 December 1862.

[18] Linsin, "Skilled Slave Labor in Florida," 192; *Pensacola Weekly Observer*, 9 June 1861; Revels, *Grander in Her Daughters*, 97–98.

tions, especially in terms of clothing, might cause his generally obedient slaves to "go off on that account."[19]

Especially difficult for slaves and masters alike was the loss of the small luxuries that had served as incentives to good behavior. By the second Christmas of the war, slaves and children agreed that Santa Claus had been "shot by the Yankees." Owners, unable to dispense paternalistic tokens such as new clothes, tobacco, and trinkets, were painfully aware of the disgust such austerity caused. Slaves also shared with many owners the loss of religious comfort when churches that had both black and whites on their membership rolls closed.[20]

Florida's natural bounty made it unlikely that slaves on plantations would starve, but their diets became ever more monotonous as the war dragged on. Slaveholders had little choice but to allow slaves more opportunities for hunting and fishing, which in turn gave slaves additional chances to share information or perhaps escape. Increasingly, slaves in Florida faced the temptation to "go to the Yankees."[21]

Self-liberation was easier during the Civil War than it had ever been before. Initially, Union officers considered runaway slaves a species of wandering property that needed prompt return. In Pensacola, before hostilities erupted, slaves who reached Fort Pickens were escorted back to their owners.[22] Once the war began, however, officials in Florida readily followed the example of General Benjamin Butler at Fort Monroe, Virginia, and declared escaped slaves to be "contrabands" of war.

---

[19] Margaret T. Ordonez, "Plantation Self-Sufficiency in Leon County, Florida: 1824–1860," *Florida Historical Quarterly* 60 (April 1982): 434, 438; Wiley, *Southern Negroes*, 24–26, 28–30; Blakey, et al., *Rose Cottage Chronicles*, 279; Ellen E. Hodges and Stephen Kerber, "'Rogues and Black Hearted Scamps': Civil War Letters of Winston and Octavia Stephens, 1862–1863," *Florida Historical Quarterly* 57 (July 1978): 76.

[20] Eppes, *Through Some Eventful Years*, 253; Ellen Call Long Diary, 25 December 1864, State Archives of Florida; Robert L. Hall, "'Yonder Come Day': Religious Dimensions of the Transition from Slavery to Freedom in Florida," *Florida Historical Quarterly* 64 (April 1987): 413–16.

[21] Blakey, et al., *Rose Cottage Chronicles*, 71; Mormino, "Florida Slave Narratives," 412.

[22] Pearce, *Pensacola during the Civil War*, 50.

The name stuck, and when the Emancipation Proclamation went into effect on January 1, 1863, liberating slaves became one of the principal missions of Federal troops. Disrupting the institution meant depriving the South of vital labor, as well as extending the ideal of liberty to African Americans.[23]

In East Florida, Federals held Fernandina and St. Augustine from 1862 onward and frequently occupied Jacksonville. Slaves in this region soon realized that freedom was theirs if they could reach the St. Johns River. Hundreds fled into the area, turning up in pairs and in family groups, sometimes in canoes or on foot, always eager to reach Union lines. Union raiders brought them in as well, infuriating owners like Winston Stephens, who insisted that his slaves should take to the woods at the first sight of gunboats on the St. Johns.[24] Across the state, both escaped slaves and free blacks found their way into Pensacola as it was abandoned by the Confederacy in May 1862. Their stories of harsh treatment undoubtedly softened the hearts of Federal soldiers, who had considered the conflict a war for the Union but not for freedom. Robert, a former slave from a plantation on the Escambia River, told Major Willoughby Babcock that he had started for Pensacola with his wife but "de dogs ketched her, massa." Another escapee arrived with a "heavy iron bar on his leg," a manacle that he had dragged for "three weeks through woods and swamps."[25] In South Florida, some slaves fled to freedom in Key West, while raiding parties out of Tampa and Cedar Key scooped up others. These raiders had a tendency to take not only bondsmen, but horses, wagons, fodder, meat, and any firearms, leaving white Floridians without forced labor, food, or means of self-defense. Slaves were not always given a choice about staying with their masters. A Choctawhatchee resident noted that the Yankee soldiers "did not ask the negroes if they

---

[23] Masur, *The Civil War*, 28–29, 47–48.

[24] Schafer, "Freedom Was As Close As the River,"157; Blakey, et al., *Rose Cottage Chronicles*, 102–103, 215.

[25] Pearce, *Pensacola during the Civil War*, 169, 199.

wanted to go, they ordered them to hitch up the teams and make ready to go."[26]

Not all runaways were successful, and the major of Florida's slave population remained on their farms and plantations throughout the war. This should not be presumed as comfort in bondage or lack of initiative. Slaves longed for freedom, but they also sensibly weighed their chances of obtaining it. The vicissitudes of slavery had thoroughly ingrained caution into the black collective psyche. Areas endangered by the Federal presence nearby were the places most likely to have increased slave patrols. Shack Thomas, a slave in East Florida, recalled that during the war Confederate Regulators made extreme examples of the slaves they captured. Slaves caught without passes would be "gagged and tied in a squatting position and left in the sun for hours."[27] A sound whipping would be the least a recaptured runaway could expect during the war. Slaves also took into account they might be exchanging a known for an unknown master, and some were wary of being drafted into new forms of servitude. Religious convictions, community and family ties, age, physical disabilities, lack of knowledge, and a complicated affection for humane masters held others back. Slaves on well-established plantations may have assumed that at war's end they would be rewarded for years of faithful service, and that to run away was to risk this potential bounty. Whatever their reason, slaves hoped that, if they could not run to freedom, it would eventually march to them.[28]

Confederate Floridians could not defend against their slaves' almost intuitive knowledge of the landscape. Runaways carried maps in their minds, cartography etched by years of laboring in the fields and hunting in the woods. Appearing in Union camps, fugitive slaves frequently reported the details of community defenses (or lack thereof) and offered to guide their liberators through swamps and hammocks to places where

---

[26] Solomon and Erhart, "Race and Civil War in South Florida," 323; Rivers, *Slavery in Florida*, 231.

[27] Rivers, *Slavery in Florida*, 226–27.

[28] Ira Berlin, Barbara J. Fields, Thavolia Glymph, Joseph Reidy, and Leslie S. Rowland, *Freedom: A Documentary History of Emancipation*, 1861–1867, ser. 1, vol. 1, *The Destruction of Slavery* (Cambridge: University of Cambridge Press, 1985) 17: 111–12.

the enemy could be surprised. Though some officers were disinclined to accept the help or believe the stories, others were eager for assistance in strange territory. Israel, a fugitive from Jacksonville, guided Federal troops along Pablo Creek, and Isaac Tatwell, a former pilot on the steamer *St. Mary's*, provided valuable intelligence on the eastern coastal defenses. Colonel Thomas W. Higginson credited the success of the 1st South Carolina Volunteers' 1863 foray up the St. Marys River to Corporal Robert Sutton, who only a short time before had been enslaved on its shores.[29] Assisting the Federals was not without peril; the Oklawaha Rangers promptly hanged a slave suspected of providing intelligence to Yankees along the St. Johns River.[30]

Union commanders, like their fellow citizens in the North, held varying opinions on the nature of the war and the social position of the black race. While they ceased returning slaves to their masters, few officers viewed the contrabands as equals or even true men. Often Union commanders treated the escaped slaves shamefully. In some places, contrabands were shuffled into hastily erected camps without sanitation or health care. On Egmont Key, Unionist white refugees and runaway slaves found miserable sanctuary. Fear of Confederate attack, swarms of mosquitoes, and exposure to the baking heat left them sick and disheartened. Black men were often forced to work at sub-par wages and kept on the job during yellow fever epidemics due to the belief that they were immune to the disease.[31]

Despite such inequities, many of Florida's former slaves signed up to fight for the Union. Almost one thousand Florida freedmen wore blue before war's end, and some of them fought at Olustee and Natural Bridge. Many of these men became soldiers with great enthusiasm, eager to go to war for the freedom of their race. Dr. Seth Rogers heard a group of St. Augustine black recruits before he saw them, as they were singing the "John Brown hymn" while their boat came up the river. Other former

---

[29] Rivers, *Slavery in Florida*, 233; Richard A. Martin, "The '*New York Times*' Views Civil War Jacksonville," *Florida Historical Quarterly* 53 (April 1975): 416.

[30] Waters, "Florida's Confederate Guerillas," 138.

[31] Rivers, *Slavery in Florida*, 234–35.

slaves became sailors with the West Gulf Blockading Squadron, serving in integrated vessels and putting their knowledge of Florida's irregular coastline to good use.[32] Just as with their former owners, black families were often separated by their wartime service. In Pensacola in early1862, slave women and children who reached Fort Pickens were sent to New York while men were "enrolled as Uncle Sam's laborers, paid $15 a month and one ration per day." Other families were divided when one partner ran for freedom while a spouse was left behind. Jake, a bondsman from Duval County, escaped and enlisted in the Union army. During the war he returned to rescue his wife, only to learn that their master had sold her in his absence.[33]

Former slaves on the eastern coast were concentrated at Fernandina, Jacksonville, and St. Augustine. Many of them simply squatted in abandoned homes. Humane reformers, such as Esther Hill Hawks, a physician who arrived in Jacksonville during its fourth occupation, worked to bring cleanliness, order, and education to the newly freed people. She established the first integrated school in Jacksonville, drawing not only children but also soldiers from black regiments, all of whom expressed a great desire to learn to read. In Fernandina, Chloe Merrick founded an orphanage for black children in the former home of Confederate general Finegan. Black mothers were intensely interested in the Union forces' programs to assist their offspring.[34] In these Florida enclaves many formerly enslaved women were able to put their domestic skills to good use, earning money as cooks and laundresses. They soon formed the same types of social circles that white women did, organizing and catering special occasions. In St. Augustine and Key West, freed families marched in Emancipation Day parades, and in Fernandina two women's commit-

[32] Solomon and Erhart, "Race and Civil War in South Florida," 326–27, 337; Thomas Wentworth Higginson, ed., *Letters of Major Seth Rogers, M.D., Surgeon of the First South Carolina Volunteers* (Boston: John Wilson and Son, 1910) 344; Rivers, *Slavery in Florida*, 234.

[33] Pearce, *Pensacola during the Civil War*, 168–69; Schafer, "Freedom Was As Close As the River," 168–73.

[34] Gerald Schwartz, "An Integrated Free School in Civil War Florida," *Florida Historical Quarterly* 61 (October 1982): 155–58; Foster and Foster, "Chloe Merrick Reed," 286–93.

tees—all married ladies, known to be excellent cooks—organized an Independence Day celebration. "The affair," the Fernandina newspaper noted, "promises to be a complete success."[35]

By varying degrees, Florida's slaves were joining the ranks of its pre-war free black population. Free blacks, less than a thousand in number in 1860, had long resided in a strange limbo, not enslaved and yet far from truly free, relegated to an awkward position that acknowledged their right to earn money from their labors, but little else. Unable to vote or testify in most trials, free blacks were subjected to excessive fines for any indiscretion and exorbitant fees for all social activities. Worship was only permitted in white churches, where prayer could be supervised. Free blacks were required to have white guardians and to register with civic authorities. Any free black deemed "idle" could be arrest and enslaved. For free blacks, the war did not so much change their status as offer the hope that they would finally be openly respected as what they had quietly been for decades: model citizens of the country.[36]

In Confederate areas of Florida, free blacks remained under suspicion and often had to act as Confederate allies to protect themselves. In Jacksonville, before the outbreak of hostilities, a group of free black men volunteered to help build a gun battery as a way of deflecting possible abuse. But in Union-held communities, soldiers and other observers found free blacks a study in self-reliance, with Yankee values on display. Elias A. Bryant of the 4th New Hampshire Regiment visited the St. Augustine home of a man who had purchased his family's freedom before the war. "They are a very sharp, shrew, intelligent-looking people," he recorded, "not a little proud of having achieved their own liberty."[37] Many free blacks continued in their pre-war professions, and those in Union-occupied towns benefitted from heartier paychecks. Yankee soldiers had two constants: dirty laundry and a craving for home cooking. Free black women, many of whom already had community reputations

---

[35] *Fernandina Peninsula*, 2 July 1863.

[36] Rivers, "'Dignity and Importance'," 427.

[37] Garvin, "The Free Negro in Florida," 8; Schafer, *Thunder on the River*, 30; Elias A Bryant Diary, 66, Lewis G. Schmidt Collection, State Archives of Florida.

for these services, quickly found work. At Fort Jefferson a former slave named "Aunt Eliza" won fame for her recipes as well as her quirky behavior, which included threatening a younger lover with an ax.[38]

In their journey to freedom, black Floridians frequently faced white prejudice, which came in many forms. Just as former masters could be cruel, liberators could be patronizing and inconsiderate. In St. Augustine, a woman identified as "Aunt Rhoda," who claimed a mixed heritage of African, Seminole, and Spanish blood, became the victim of a series of soldiers' pranks, including having cows tethered in her house and pigs stuffed down her chimney. Black women remained vulnerable to sexual abuse, even by those men charged with protecting them. After witnessing the hanging of three black soldiers of the 55th Massachusetts Regiment for an "outrage" against a white woman, Dr. Hawks confided to her diary that many white officers were guilty of the same crime against defenseless black women.[39]

Though most slaves remained with their owners (and many demonstrated a remarkably forgiving attitude at the war's conclusion), those who did make their way to freedom often relished the way that fate had turned the tables. In Jacksonville a contraband girl wanted to learn to read and write so that she could send a sarcastic letter to her old mistress. In Key West a former maid could not resist leaning on a fence, watching her former owner sweat while working in a garden, and then asking her "how she liked it."[40]

Decades after the war, Susan Bradford Eppes proudly claimed, "We felt every confidence in our dear black folks; every faith in the affection for us; and never a doubt of the loyalty." Elizabeth Coffee Sheldon, in a United Daughters of the Confederacy article titled "My Old Black Mammy," described a sentimental farewell scene on a Madison County

[38] Rogers, "A Great Stirring in the Land," 156–59; "At the Dry Tortugas during the War: A Lady's Journal," *Californian Illustrated* (June 1892): 87–93; Revels, *Grander in Her Daughters*, 106.

[39] Henry F. W. Little, *The Seventh Regiment New Hampshire Volunteers in the War of the Rebellion* (Concord, NH: Ira C. Evans, 1896) 86; Schwartz, ed., *A Woman Doctor's Civil War*, 61.

[40] Schwartz, ed., *A Woman Doctor's Civil War*, 69–70; "At the Dry Tortugas during the War," 103.

plantation with her father entrusting "his home, his wife, his two little girls, his all" to his slaves.[41] The idea that slaves had been good and faithful servants became a cornerstone of the Lost Cause, a historical interpretation sympathetic to the antebellum South. But a careful examination of primary documentation produced during the Civil War—in contrast to memoirs written years after the conflict—reveals plentiful examples of Florida slaves who wanted to be free and acted resolutely on this desire. Whether they ran away, bore arms for the Union, or antagonized for their owners via small but unceasing acts of resistance, slaves demonstrated agency. "I have often heard you tell the Negros that you wished the Yankees had them," Samuel Palmer wrote to his wife, Mary, "and I am afraid that it will not be very long before your wish will be consummated."[42] Florida's slaves were unable to record their thoughts, but their actions spoke clearly to their desire to be free.

---

[41] Susan Bradford Eppes, *The Negro of the Old South: A Bit of Period History* (Chicago: Joseph G. Branch Publishing, 1925) 106–107; Elizabeth Coffee Sheldon, "My Old Black Mammy," United Daughters of the Confederacy Scrapbooks, vol. 3, State Archives of Florida.

[42] Samuel Augustus Palmer to Mary Rebecca Gassaway Palmer, 4 September 1863, Palmer Family Letters, State Archives of Florida.

Chapter 7

Dire Necessities

Florida's Provisions for the Confederacy

Even though Florida appeared abandoned by the Confederacy, the new nation still required Florida's resources in the struggle to achieve independence. A number of Florida-produced commodities were essential to the war effort, but Richmond both failed to recognize the importance of Florida's commodities and to protect their production until it was too late. Floridians on the home front generally entered the war with a patriotic determination to provide provisions, but soon opportunism, self-interest, and a simple struggle against destitution changed the nature and amount of goods that Florida could offer to the Confederate cause.

* * *

During the antebellum period, the South had experimented with bringing the cotton mill to the cotton field. Three factories for the manufacture of cotton cloth and yarn were built in Florida before the Civil War, but 1861 found only the Bailey Cotton Mill (known officially as the Jefferson Manufacturing Company) still operational. Located just east of Monticello, the brick mill had been completed in 1853 and was equipped with 1,500 spindles and 50 looms. Though it averaged 600,000 yards of cloth and 100,000 pounds of yarn annually, and it employed 40 men and 25 women, the business was unprofitable because superior Yankee cloth could be purchased more cheaply. When the blockade created a sudden demand for Confederate production, the mill gained new life. General William Bailey, the mill's owner, was a dedicated Confederate who kept prices low and donated bales of yarn and cloth to be distributed to needy families; this generosity earned Bailey accolades from the legislature and Governor Milton. When male mill workers were conscripted, disabled soldiers took their place. The Confederate government threatened to seize the factory in 1864, and in a rare moment of intransience, the governor fought for the mill to remain in local hands. Milton won his argument with the War Department, but one mill could never hope to meet the needs of the state, much less make a significant contribution to the Confederacy. Though it remained operational throughout the war, the mill (with the motto "Southern Rights") disappeared soon afterward. Other manufacturing businesses that survived for some or all of the war (but made negligible contributions) were the Madison Shoe Factory, an iron foundry in Newport, and the Florida Card Company, which produced cotton and wool cards that one housewife deemed "not worth buying."[1]

One commodity that the Confederacy hoped to acquire in Florida was saltpeter or niter (potassium nitrate), the main ingredient of gunpowder. Nathaniel A. Pratt, a professor from Oglethorpe University, was sent to inspect a number of caves in Middle Florida in hopes of finding niter-rich soil. Though his report does not survive, another message to the Confederate War Department indicated that Florida's caves were too small and wet to be of use, but "plantation earth" should prove more viable. Tallahassee resident Charles H. Latrobe was in charge of this project. Producing niter artificially was a thoroughly disgusting process. Rotting vegetable matter, solid animal matter (including manure, offal, and carcasses), liquid wastes (urine), and crude earth materials such as lime, marl, and dirt dug from beneath buildings were placed in pits (called beds) under protective sheds. The beds were stirred weekly, with new material added when necessary. They were considered mature when a white mold appeared on the surface. The earth would then be scooped out and leached in a barrel. Three niter sheds were constructed in Tallahassee, where a crew of truly unlucky slaves was hired to work them. The exact amount of niter produced in Tallahassee is unknown. It is possible

---

[1]Dorothy Dodd, "The Manufacture of Cotton in Florida before and during the Civil War," *Florida Historical Quarterly* 13 (July 1934): 3–15; Johns, *Florida during the Civil War*, 124–27. Cards were wooden boards with iron teeth. Cotton and wool were pulled through these cards as the first step in transforming these resources into finished materials. Cards wore out very quickly. For a detailed discussion of Southern home textile production and an illustration of cotton cards, see Faust, *Mothers of Invention*, 48–49.

that none of the beds actually matured before the war ended. What is certain is that Florida's niter operations were the least productive of any state east of the Mississippi.[2]

While niter was scarce, corn was presumed plentiful. Thanks to its balmy climate, exaggerated pre-war assessments cast Florida as a magical cornucopia of cereals and vegetables. Planters willingly cut back on cotton to plant corn in the first year of the war, but in 1863 rumors of an early peace and hopes for a boom market changed production schedules in favor of traditional and inedible cash crops such as tobacco and cotton. Soldiers despised this about-face. Colonel David Lang of White Springs spoke for many of his comrades:

> Nothing is so disheartening to the soldier, for the poor man who has left a large and almost helpless family to risk life and limb in the cause of independence, to see those who are permitted to remain out of the army for the purpose of raising provisions embark in the thoughtless, heartless, and most unpatriotic enterprise of planting large cotton and tobacco crops when the country is almost on the verge of famine.[3]

The demand was not just for soldiers' rations. The horses and mules of the armies consumed vast amounts of fodder, and feeding them elevated the price of corn. In response to the need for more food, in 1863 the Florida legislature passed an act allowing planters just an acre of cotton for each slave between the ages of fifteen and sixty. The remainder of their land was to be committed to food production. Tobacco acreage was also limited.[4]

Though Florida succeeded in helping meet the demands of the Lower South in 1862, the harvests of 1863 and 1864 were inadequate to

---

[2]Marion O. Smith, "Confederate Nitre Bureau Operations in Florida," *Florida Historical Quarterly* 74 (Summer 1995) 40–46. Charles H. Latrobe probably would have based his methods on those described by Joseph LeConte in *Instructions for the Manufacture of Saltpetre*, published in Columbia, South Carolina, in 1862.

[3]Robert A. Taylor, *Rebel Storehouse: Florida in the Confederate Economy* (Tuscaloosa: University of Alabama Press, 1995) 66–67; Groene, "Civil War Letters of Colonel David Lang," 349.

[4]Taylor, *Rebel Storehouse*, 70; Johns, *Florida during the Civil War*, 144–45.

meet more than domestic needs. There was no Florida corn to send to the besieged Confederates at Charleston in 1864. Floridians refused to sell their private stock at any price, and many of them had discovered clever methods of hiding their family's supply from impressment agents. No doubt this sharp drop in Florida's corn supply caused resentment across the South toward a state that the *Southern Cultivator* had hailed as "a great country."[5]

The war led to renewed industries and creative adaptations. Distilling was a popular backwoods pursuit, and occasionally it was even legal. Florida moonshiners made personal contracts with Richmond to supply medicinal alcohol. Strong liquor was often the only painkiller available for horrific surgeries. Florida's ladies were encouraged to grow garden poppies for the production of narcotics. Barrels of oranges, limes, and lemons were sent northward in the first two years of the war, but the harsh winter of 1863–1864 turned citrus fruit into a rare treat. The small Florida sugar industry was revitalized, but much of its product was seized by impressment. A small number of fisheries opened on the Gulf Coast. By 1864, with the use of slave labor, fishermen packed 100,000 barrels of mullet. All of these operations—some patriotic, others more profit-oriented—failed to make any significant contribution to the Confederacy's vast need for food and drugs.[6]

Salt, by contrast, was one of Florida's most important exports. In an age before refrigeration, salting meat, fish, butter, and other perishables was the only reliable method of preservation. Salt was also necessary for making leather and as a supplement to the diet of draft animals on farms and plantations. Southerners could not imagine eating their meals without it. With millions of people to be fed and various purposes to be supplied, the traditional sources of salt (among them Great Britain and the West Indies) were eliminated by the blockade. Fortunately for the Confederacy, Florida's coastline was a natural production ground for this

[5]Taylor, *Rebel Storehouse*, 71–73.
[6]Ibid., 73–77, 82–83.

mineral. Many Floridians saw the advantage in turning to salt production, which was fast, uncomplicated, and lucrative.[7]

By 1862 the Florida Gulf Coast was dotted with small saltworks.
No specialized machinery or technical knowledge was required. One
simply boiled seawater and collected the salt upon the water's evapora-
tion. Floridians showed great ingenuity in creating vessels for salt boiling,
using old iron sugar kettles and halves of steamboat boilers, as well as
metal harbor buoys converted into vats. Saltworks were "unique affairs"
to a visitor's eyes. They may also have been an affront to the visitor's
nose, as the furnaces usually produced an unpleasant aroma from the
boiling brine and smoke.[8] Plantation owners were familiar with the salt-
making process because they had used it in the past, usually producing
enough salt in one session to last their households for an entire year.
They knew the bays and inlets and were well acquainted with vast
stretches of pine that could be felled for fuel. The main obstacle to selling
the salt was the lack of transportation. Getting the salt back to inland
civilization was torturous, but the potential payoff encouraged their efforts. At first, salt-making was seen as patriotic. Tallahassee's *Florida
Sentinel* put out calls for more workers and lobbied for their protection by
the government. Mindful of the need and the profits, Floridians eagerly
responded to the paper's charge to *"save your bacon!"* by making salt for
food preservation and other uses.[9]

Atlantic saltworks were minimal. The favored location for the activity was on the Gulf, particularly between Tampa Bay and Choctawhatchee Bay. The largest collections of saltworks were located on St.
Andrew Bay because it featured a number of secluded small inlets. Industry could be established along these watery tendrils, out of sight and
hopefully out of reach of any enemy vessels that entered the deep-water
bay. A lengthy drought in this region had increased the water's salinity,
so the salt produced was high quality. Soon not only Floridians but also

---

[7]Ella Lonn, *Salt as a Factor in the Confederacy* (Tuscaloosa: University of
Alabama Press, 1965) 13–18.

[8]Taylor, *Rebel Storehouse*, 46–47.

[9]Lonn, *Salt as a Factor*, 19; Johns, *Florida during the Civil War*, 128; *Florida
Sentinel* (Tallahassee), July 15, 1862.

residents of Georgia and Alabama were arriving to establish salt production along the coast. The Florida legislature legalized their activity and extended an invitation for all citizens to come and make salt. The first year and a half of the enterprise was a boom time. In the phrase of historian Ella Lonn, "the salt-workers throve and grew great, both in the amount of the commodity produced and in the boldness with which the industry was pursued."[10]

The industry was not entirely a blessing for the state. The blockade made it unsafe to transport salt via steamer, which meant that hundreds of wagon teams were required to move workers and their product. These animals consumed fodder. This was at first a boon for farmers with hay, oats, and corn to sell, but the vast needs of the animals soon outstripped supplies in West and Central Florida. By 1862, many Florida farmers were forced to buy feed for their own livestock at inflated prices. Speculation soon raised its viperous head. Governor Milton worried that speculators would buy prime real estate for saltworks and then charge exorbitant fees for its repurchase or use. Some operators refused to accept Florida treasury notes in payment, all while upping the price of Florida salt from $3 per bushel in 1862 to $16 to $20 a bushel less than a year later. Milton railed against these speculators, calling them cowards and traitors, but there was little he could do to stop them except withdraw from sale all public lands suitable for saltworks. Approved individuals could use these public spaces for a more patriotic form of enterprise.[11]

With the rise in speculation, the public perception of salt makers began to change. Though initially hailed as heroes for the cause, salt workers came under suspicion when they were able to evade the Confederate Conscription Act. Soldiers like Michael Raysor resented ablebodied men who avoided the draft and made money at the same time, especially when these men were his relatives.[12] Though salt makers were

---

[10]Johns, *Florida during the Civil War*, 128–29; Ella Lonn, "The Extent and Importance of Federal Naval Raids on Salt-Making in Florida, 1862–1865," *Florida Historical Quarterly* 10 (April 1932): 167–68, 175.

[11]Johns, *Florida during the Civil War*, 129–30.

[12]John F. Reiger, "Deprivation, Disaffection, and Desertion in Confederate Florida," *Florida Historical Quarterly* 48 (January 1970): 287.

not officially exempted from the draft, agents recognized the need for salt and generally left the workers alone. With the extreme profits many were making, the public and even the *Florida Sentinel*, formerly a cheerleader for salt production, soured on the workers, protesting any special treatment and the assignment of three companies of troops to St. Andrew Bay as a protective force. "How, then," the paper asked, "can such men ask or hope for protection at the hands of the very poor people upon whose dire necessities they are speculating?"[13] Militia protection was withdrawn, and in fall 1862 the General Assembly put protecting the saltworks into the hands of the salt makers. All workers were required to organize into military companies, with first lieutenants appointed by the governor. The state promised to provide arms and ammunition. This solution was pathetic at best. On January 9, 1863, the governor's agent reported that only 498 men had been enrolled on the coast between the St. Marks and the Suwannee rivers and that they had only forty-three workable guns between them. Three hundred of these men were under forty years of age, and the vast majority of them were deserters from the Confederate army. The best the governor could hope for was that the Yankees would be blind to the smoke rising from the coastline.[14]

Yankees, however, had excellent vision. They were also aided by the keen eyes and quick wits of Unionists and escaped slaves. Beginning in 1862, raiding saltworks became a sport for bored blockaders.[15] The first significant attacks came along the St. Joseph Bay and the St. Andrew Bay in September 1862. The commander of the *Kingfisher* was gentlemanly enough to signal his intent under a flag of truce and give the workers two hours to depart. But things became less genteel after a Union crew under a flag of truce was ambushed on October 4 while destroying a presumably abandoned saltworks at Cedar Key.[16]

Upon discovering a saltworks, Union commanders would shell the area, directing fire at any structures and hiding places, putting its workers

---

[13]Johns, *Florida during the Civil War*, 129–30; *Florida Sentinel* (Tallahassee), 14 October 1862.
[14]Johns, *Florida during the Civil War*, 131.
[15]Rivers, *Slavery in Florida*, 234; Johns, *Florida during the Civil War*, 131.
[16]Lonn, "The Extent and Importance," 168.

to flight. Raiding parties supplied with small arms would come ashore. Half the men would fan out as skirmishers while the other half did the heavy work of breaking up boilers, kettles, and other equipment. Any slaves found would be liberated and taken aboard. If a site appeared too well defended or presented the appearance of a long day's work to destroy, howitzers were brought in and fired point-blank into the works. Union soldiers slaughtered any mules and cattle, and they ruined the remaining salt by mixing it with sand. Occasionally, humor accompanied the work, as when a noncombatant informed a Union captain, who was struggling to smash a thick kettle, that the Yankees had gotten "hold of Vicksburg this time." But for the most part, the union raids and destruction were time consuming and risky. Floridians and their Southern companions had amazing resilience and ingenuity. Whenever one saltworks was destroyed, another would appear within days. One frustrated Union officer reported that saltworks were repaired "as fast as he demolished them."[17]

The most intensive series of raids on the Gulf Coast came in December 1863, when St. Andrew Bay was attacked and some five hundred saltworks were torched, most by Federals but many by Confederates who did not want their supplies to fall into enemy hands. The devastated area had produced an estimated 15,595 bushels of salt a day until flatboats, sloops, and oxcarts, as well as hundreds of buildings and thousands of kettles and iron boilers were destroyed. Approximately $6,000,000 in government and private property was lost. Yet less than two months later, most of the works had been rebuilt, leading to another orgy of destruction in February 1864. This was accompanied by a similar fury at St. Marks and Goose Creek, where $4,000,000 in property was reduced to ashes and broken metal, depriving the Confederacy of 2,500 bushels per day. Continued harassment in 1864 went as far as Tampa Bay, with the final great raid occurring in St. Andrew Bay in February 1865.[18]

---

[17]Johns, *Florida during the Civil War*, 131–33; Lonn, "The Extent and Importance," 172, 179.

[18]Johns, *Florida during the Civil War*, 133–34; Lonn, "The Extent and Importance," 176–177.

Salt-making was simply too essential to abandon. Despite the ever-present threat of death or capture and the recurrent destruction, salt makers always returned to their boilers, kettles, and profits. Even respectable planters and military leaders, such as Colonel George Washington Scott, maintained investments in the enterprise.[19] The lure of manufacturing a patriotic necessity while growing rich in the process helps explain why the Federals were unable to shut down all of Florida's saltworks. Raids were intense but isolated, and victory was never completely achieved. Perhaps the profits—more than any sense of Confederate patriotism—prevented the Federals from shutting down all of Florida's saltworks.

Florida's other great material contribution to the Confederacy was beef. The crack of the cattle driver's whip was a familiar sound in the state, especially in its central and southern regions. The 1860 census estimate put Florida herds at 388,060 head. State law required fencing only for cultivated fields, so all unfenced land remained common range. In the last great frontier east of the Mississippi, thousands of branded and unmarked herds wandered freely. Florida's "scrub cows" were a genetic mix of the *criollo* herds imported by the conquistadors and the Anglo cattle brought south by American pioneers. Scrubs were hardy creatures, accustomed to foraging. Though small, they had developed an impressive immunity to common diseases, such as tick-borne fevers. Weighing about 600 pounds at prime market size, a scrub would yield about 300 pounds of beef. Modern diners would find Florida's 1860 brand of beef tough and unappealing, but cooks of the era claimed it possessed a flavor like venison, and it was highly prized for spicy Cuban dishes.[20]

Before the war, Florida cowmen (a more common term than ranchers) followed a seasonal routine. In the winter they devoted very little attention to their herds, allowing the cattle to graze freely on hammocks

[19]Ellis and Rogers, *Tallahassee and Leon County*, 13; Lucas, "Civil War Career of Colonel George Washington Scott," 132.

[20]Joe A. Akerman, Jr., *Florida Cowman: A History of Florida Cattle Raising* (Kissimmee: Florida Cattleman's Association, 1976) 83; Dillon, Jr., "South Florida in 1860," 440; John S. Otto, "Open-Range Cattle Herding in Southern Florida," *Florida Historical Quarterly* 65 (January 1987): 317, 320.

and prairies, where moss, wiregrass, and maidencane provided ample fodder. Supplements such as mineral licks were unknown, as was veterinary care. In the spring, cowmen burned over forests to promote spring grasses and palmetto to sprout. Newborn calves were penned with their mothers to protect them from wolves and other predators, which the cowmen delighted in hunting and killing. Once the summer "cow-hunt" began, a cowman depended on the help of his kinsmen, neighbors, and a few good "cur-dogs" to get the job done since very few of the cowmen owned slaves to assist in their efforts. Cattle were branded, sorted, and then driven to market.[21] A drive of forty days could shave 150 pounds off an already lean animal. These annual cattle drives were made to coastal cities, sometimes as far north as Savannah, or to the railhead at Baldwin, where the animals could be transported to Jacksonville and beyond. Tampa became a more important destination in the late 1850s when James McKay, a Scottish-born merchant, opened a bi-monthly trade to Cuba. McKay was popular for his contacts with important cowmen in the Hillsborough region and for the fact that he paid in cash, usually in Spanish gold. By early 1860 he was sending 400 cattle per month to Havana.[22]

Though Florida was one vast cow pen, the Confederacy did not significantly look to Florida until 1863. By that spring, Tennessee had been scoured of herds and the depot in Atlanta had a mere 4,000 head, all of them earmarked for consumption by the Army of Northern Virginia. Patchwork supplies saved the Army of Tennessee for a time, but on July 4, 1863, the fall of Vicksburg to the Federals meant that cattle could no longer be imported from the Trans-Mississippi region. Florida now became essential to Confederate supply efforts. To provide foodstuffs more

---

[21]Otto, "Open Range Cattle Herding," 321–23; John S. Otto, "Florida's Cattle-Ranching Frontier: Manatee and Brevard Counties (1860)," *Florida Historical Quarterly* 64 (July 1985): 53, 54–55, 60.

[22]John S. Otto, "Florida's Cattle-Ranching Frontier: Hillsborough County (1860)," *Florida Historical Quarterly* 63 (July 1984): 78; Akerman, *Florida Cowman*, 85, 88.

effectively, the state was divided into five commissary districts under the control of Major Pleasant W. White of Quincy.[23]

Richmond wanted 3,000 head of cattle a week from Florida, though even this number would represent a substantial reduction in rations for the men. Confederate leadership understood numbers, but not the realities of Florida cattle-driving. As historian Robert Taylor writes, "Collecting and driving semi-wild bovines was an assignment that only experienced wranglers could handle effectively." Pushing their herds ten to twelve miles a day, instead of the usual eight, cowmen were lucky to find pens at night where cattle could be protected. Stampedes could be caused by lightning strikes or panther screams; "such was the perversity of the beast," according to one cowman. Florida's scrubs were ornery and even scrawnier than usual by the time they had been herded at break-neck speed from South Florida ranges to depots in North Florida.[24]

August was traditionally the final month of the cattle-driving season, but 1863 was an extraordinary year of need. On August 25, White received a request from General Bragg begging for more cattle. White promised to try to continue to supply at least 1,000 head a week. This was simply impossible due to the difficulty of herding them that far and finding fodder for them along the way, and while hundreds of cattle did continue the exceptional migration north, they were far too few to meet the needs of Bragg's men in Chattanooga and Beauregard's men in Charleston, who were also pleading for food. White's unenviable task was made even more frustrating by the large number of speculators operating in Florida and by the purchasing power of agents from other states and railroad companies. By December there was simply not enough fodder along the trails for cattle to arrive in decent condition. Still the requests came and White attempted to answer them, even if the livestock he was sending northward would arrive as little more than bags of bones.

---

[23]Robert A. Taylor, "Cow Cavalry: Munnerlyn's Battalion in Florida, 1864–1865," *Florida Historical Quarterly* 65 (October 1986): 196.

[24]Robert A. Taylor, "Rebel Beef: Florida Cattle and the Confederate Army, 1862–1864," *Florida Historical Quarterly* 67 (July 1988): 19; Joe A. Akerman, Jr., and J. Mark Akerman, *Jacob Summerlin: King of the Crackers* (Cocoa: Florida Historical Society Press, 2004) 54–55, Akerman, *Florida Cowman*, 90.

White also worked to have cattle that could not move forward be butchered in-state, though the lack of barrels and boxes hampered the processing task. By February 1864 he ordered all of Florida's available pork and bacon sent to the front lines as well.

The February 1864 Federal incursion that climaxed with the Battle of Olustee was, in part, an acknowledgement of Florida's role in Confederate food production. Cutting off the supply line from Florida would have doomed the troops in Charleston. Olustee was something of a wake-up call to Floridians, but no amount of renewed patriotism could counter the laws of nature or the actions of those opposed to the Confederate cause. Herds had been depleted by the past year's efforts, and in South Florida cattle were prey for Federals, Confederate deserters and draft-dodgers, and even Seminoles. Rising dissatisfaction with the war seemed to cause falling numbers of available cows. White was tugged viciously by demands from both Atlanta and Charleston, with nothing close to the numbers that either force required. Adding to the demand and confusion was the desperate need for Florida beef to be sent to Andersonville, where 26,000 Union prisoners languished by late summer 1864. During the summer and into the winter, cows continued to straggle northward in lean and hungry ranks. Richmond hoped for 100,000, a ridiculously optimistic figure. In 1864, Florida could offer fewer than 20,000.[25]

Sherman's march to the sea and the problems of winter foraging ended the movement of cattle for a short period after January 9, 1865. Drives resumed in the spring and continued until the war's end in May 1865. The Confederate government had collected approximately 75,000 cattle from Florida over the course of the war. Private sales, poaching, and the senseless slaughter that took place in South Florida during the fighting between Federals and the Cow Cavalry in early 1865 had further thinned Florida's bounty of beef. Many cowmen who did have cattle to sell undoubtedly preferred dealing with any agency but the Confederate government, which would pay in worthless currency if it paid at all. Jacob Summerlin, the "King of the Crackers" and one of the largest cattle own-

---

[25]Johns, *Florida during the Civil War*, 163; Taylor, "Cow Cavalry," 208.

ers in the state, said he "was not given a copper" for his substantial contributions to the Confederate commissary.[26]

Other, perhaps more insidious, forces had worked against Florida's role as a stockyard for the Confederacy. Historian Canter Brown, Jr. argues that James McKay, the pioneer of the Cuban trade who had been hired by White as a collection agent, was possibly a covert agent for the Union. McKay had lost significant property to the Confederacy in 1861 and been branded a traitor in his hometown of Tampa. Following his arrest and a "long and acrimonious" trial, McKay slipped out on bond and visited Federal-controlled Key West, where a witness recalled that McKay "expressed disgust at the Confederate rule in Florida."[27] Following a brief arrest and detention in Fort Taylor, McKay was summoned to Washington where he conferred with Secretary of State Seward and signed an oath of alliance to the United States. Allowed to return to Tampa through the blockade, McKay proved his Confederate loyalty and regained his popularity via successful blockade running. He also accepted a position as an agent with White, a natural offer considering his knowledge of the area and his contacts with local cowmen.

Once in authority, McKay did everything to slow the process of collection. The knowledgeable agent with plenty of contacts suddenly could not find cows. McKay complained about everything from the weather to his health, and he schemed to get relatives (including his son) released from the Confederate army to be cattle drivers. Even with his favorite cowmen at his service, he somehow only managed to round up poor quality cattle, claiming that the best ranges were out of his reach. To make matters worse, in early 1864 local cowmen were said to be supplying the Yankee outposts at Useppa Island and Fort Myers. McKay quickly latched onto this as a reason to suspend operations.[28]

---

[26]Akerman and Akerman, *Jacob Summerlin*, 51; Akerman, *Florida Cowman*, 85, 91.

[27]Canter Brown, Jr., "Tampa's James McKay and the Frustration of Confederate Cattle-Supply Operations in South Florida," *Florida Historical Quarterly* 70 (April 1992): 418–19.

[28]Ibid., 409–28.

When the Confederate draft exemption for cattlemen was repealed in February 1864, McKay proposed a special military unit to protect the herds and assist in collection, insisting "no Cattle may be expected from this District until the enemy is got Rid off." President Davis appointed Charles J. Munnerlyn, a Georgia lawyer and planter, to recruit and command a "battalion of cow drivers." Munnerlyn eventually formed nine companies of the 1st Battalion, Florida Special Cavalry, better known across the state as the Cow Cavalry. These men who joined had exemption from regular army service but also full combatant-status, which would be a benefit to them if they were captured. They were a colorful and diverse lot; some were under-aged, and many were much more interested in defending their communities and incomes than any notion of Confederate patriotism. Their task, to guard a line over 300 miles long, in a state "infested with traitors and deserters," was daunting.[29]

Union forces seemed to mock their efforts. The 2nd Florida Cavalry (a Unionist force made up largely of men from the Fort Myers area) made a jaunt to Tampa on May 6, 1864, then plundered and burned Fort Meade on May 19, all without significant challenge. The Cow Cavalry unit was unable to establish control over the southern ranges until fall 1864. By then it was too late to be of much good to the beef supply operation.[30]

Whether McKay was truly a double agent or merely a skillful opportunist, he succeeded in assisting his friends and partners in the cattle business. Despite McKay's reports of depleted herds, when his post-war trade with Cuba resumed there were plenty of cattle available to be shipped out at $17 to $27 a head. Hillsborough, Manatee, and Polk county cowmen had reported 106,130 head of cattle for tax purposes in 1861 and 115,653 in 1866, figures that clearly demonstrate the improbability of extreme sacrifice on their parts.[31]

---

[29]Brown, "Tampa's James McKay," 428; Taylor, "Cow Cavalry," 198–209; Akerman, *Florida Cowman*, 93.

[30]Brown, "Tampa's James McKay," 428–29.

[31]Ibid., 429–33.

Considering the circumstances, Florida had provided diligently for the Confederacy, but officials were delusional when it came to estimates of Florida's available herds and appallingly ignorant of conditions within the state. One doubts that the leadership of the Confederacy, including most of its generals, had ever roped a recalcitrant steer or slogged through a snake-infested marsh to rescue a wayward calf. The Confederacy's reluctance to provide adequate defenses for the men who herded its cattle demonstrated typical shortsightedness. Inefficiency in collection, along with the usual selfishness and chicanery of speculators plus the possibility of subtle sabotage by leading citizens, left Confederate soldiers with empty plates that Florida perhaps could have filled.

Chapter 8

Anxiety and Suffering

Unionism in Florida

In May 1862, the *St. Augustine Examiner* applauded the efforts of "twenty-five ladies in town, who have openly espoused the Union cause throughout the troubles, and they deserve great credit for their courage and fidelity, sustained under the most perilous and trying circumstances."[1] It was an open recognition of a fact that Confederate Floridians found disturbing: there were "traitors" in their midst, friends and neighbors who gave aid and comfort to the enemy. Many of these Unionists had been faithful from the start, while others had switched their allegiance from the CSA to the USA at a precipitous moment. Unionism in Florida, its numerical strength and intensity of passion, has been a subject of debate from the opening days of the war to present times. Whether a silent majority or only a few thousand true believers, pro-Union sympathizers caused trouble for Florida's participation in the war efforts and raised the specter of a state divided. Their swelling ranks also reflected the Confederacy's failed promises.

* * *

Floridians had never been united on secession. Pro-Union sentiment was strong on Florida's East Coast, especially in Jacksonville, which depended on trade and shipping ties to the North for its livelihood and was home to many recent Yankee immigrants. St. Augustine's nascent tourism industry relied on invalid visitors from colder climates, and small towns along the St. Johns knew development would cease with secession. Complete Confederate loyalty in Key West was an illusion. Pensacola had its share of divided families, and Unionism had been a vital force in

---

[1] *St. Augustine Examiner*, 1 May 1862.

West Florida's old Whig counties. Impoverished Floridians who were apathetic at the war's outset could easily be swayed to the Union cause if the Confederate one demanded excessive sacrifice. The Confederacy's pointed abandonment of the state turned some Floridians into Unionists, whether out of disgust or opportunism. Governor Milton was keenly aware of Unionism's potential as a disruptive force. In September 1862 he warned President Davis:

> You are apprised that in Florida a very large minority were opposed to secession, and in many parts of the State combinations existed to adhere to and maintain the United States Government, and even now in some portions of the State there are men who would eagerly seize any opportunity that promised success to the United States.[2]

Exactly how many Floridians were or became Unionists will never be known. Florida's first Civil War historians dismissed the Unionist numbers as miniscule—no more than 4,000 individuals—though they agreed Unionist ranks swelled during the war. More recent historians have questioned the assertion that Unionists were a tiny fraction of Florida's population at secession. An examination of the 1860 presidential vote, in which Breckinridge had only a 1,369-vote majority over Douglas and Bell combined, "may be interpreted as a manifestation of continuing, strong pro-Union sentiment." Some people of the era believed Florida's love for the Union ran deep though it was not stated boldly. John Francis Tenney, a Northerner who left Florida before the war, later claimed that "an undoubted majority of the people" of the state wanted to remain in the Union, but had been deprived of a fair vote. Historian Jerrell Shofner holds that a "significant minority" of Floridians were Unionists. The intimidation Unionists faced from their virulent Confederate neighbors

---

[2]Kathryn Trimmer Abbey, *Florida: Land of Change* (Chapel Hill: University of North Carolina Press, 1941) 289–90; Brian R. Rucker, "West Florida's Unionists" *Pensacola History Illustrated* 2 (Winter 2012): 21–22; Paul D. Escott, *After Secession: Jefferson Davis and the Failure of Confederate Nationalism* (Baton Rouge: Louisiana State University Press, 1978) 97; Reiger, "Florida after Secession," 134.

forced them to maintain a veil of secrecy that, a century and a half later, remains almost impossible to pierce.[3]

Unionists sought ways to survive. Social standing could afford some protection. Richard Keith Call's pre-eminent status as a former territorial governor protected him from violence though his family clearly believed his "illness and suffering" were caused by the issues that "weighed heavily upon his mind" before his death on September 14, 1862. Marianna physician Ethelred Philips denounced secession as "the greatest act of folly and crime that ever disgraced the earth," but his advanced age and his sons' Confederate service prevented harassment. Many Unionists chose to abandon the state and did not return until the war was over. But most Florida Unionists decided, at the start of the war, that professing loyalty to their state was the more logical choice, a way to protect themselves and their property. Some Unionists even wore Confederate gray. George T. Ward, a delegate to the secession convention who had urged delay and who stated, as he signed the ordinance, that he wished to be known as "the last man to give up the ship," died in battle for a cause he did not wholeheartedly support. Others embraced passivity as a viable (if not commendable) option. Their divided hearts and contradictory actions reveal the complexity of the Civil War in Florida, where choosing sides was often a matter of pragmatism and opportunism, rather than deeply held ideology. Undoubtedly all Unionists shared the sentiment of future Florida governor William Marvin, who later recalled the "great mental anxiety and suffering" he had experienced as a Unionist in Key West during the secession furor.[4]

Partisanship divided families. James W. Bryant, a Jacksonville businessman known for his public support of the Union, spent the war years

---

[3]Davis, *Civil War and Reconstruction in Florida*, 246–47; Johns, *Florida during the Civil War*, 154; Reiger, "Secession of Florida from the Union," 361–63; Jerrell H. Shofner, *Nor Is It Over Yet: Florida in the Era of Reconstruction* (Gainesville: University Press of Florida, 1974) 1.

[4]Shofner, *Nor Is It Over Yet*, 1; Caroline Mays Brevard, "Richard Keith Call," *Florida Historical Quarterly* 1 (October 1908): 20; Shofner, *Nor Is It Over Yet*, 2; Herbert J. Doherty, Jr., "Union Nationalism in Florida," *Florida Historical Quarterly* 29 (October 1950): 95; Kevin E. Kearney, "Autobiography of William Marvin," *Florida Historical Quarterly* 36 (January 1958): 213.

outside of the state, leaving behind his wife and daughter, as well as sons and a son-in-law who served in the Confederate army. He had only one visit with his family under a flag of truce, and would lose both his wife and son-in-law before war's end. St. Augustine siblings Isabel Benet and Colonel Stephen Vincent Benet took opposing sides: she was Secessionist, he, as a West Point graduate, chose the Union.[5] Northerner Alvan Wentworth Chapman and his Southern spouse reached an unusual truce. He later told an interviewer that his wife "was a Secessionist, and when she would not change nor see my point of view, we agreed to part. She went to her home in Marianna. I stayed here [Apalachicola]. I never saw her those four years." He added that they had only a single moment of correspondence, when she sent him four shirts and he thanked her for them. He confessed to having missed her "some," but "those were very stirring years." The couple was fortunate; they reunited after the war.[6]

Divided cities posed more threats to Unionists. Jacksonville had been a center for vigorous debate before the war, but following secession the town became ever more anxious. Vigilance committees were organized, supposedly to keep watch over slaves, but also to spy on and terrorize Unionists. Calvin Robinson, a Northern merchant, thought he could endure the insults on the street, but he worried for his family's safety. He rigged a primitive alarm system in his home, and both he and his wife took to sleeping in their clothes, ready to bolt at a moment's notice. While they chose to believe the vigilantes represented only a vicious minority and not the opinions of most fellow citizens, Jacksonville Unionists turned their homes into virtual fortresses and met in strictest secrecy.[7]

---

[5]Blakey, et al., *Rose Cottage Chronicles*, 59; Jean Parker Waterbury, ed., *The Oldest City: St. Augustine, Saga of Survival* (St. Augustine: St. Augustine Historical Society, 1983) 175.

[6]Rogers, *Outposts on the Gulf*, 7; Winifred Kimball, "Reminiscences of Alvan Wentworth Chapman," *New York Botanical Garden Journal* 22 (January 1921): 4.

[7]Richard A. Martin, *The City Makers* (Jacksonville: Convention Press, 1972) 29, 33; Richard A. Martin and Daniel L. Schafer, *Jacksonville's Ordeal by Fire: A Civil War History* (Jacksonville: Florida Publishing, 1984) 52–53.

The small-town milieu of even Florida's largest cities meant that gossip could quickly become denunciation. Unionists had to hide their true feelings or act a false role. They were keenly aware of being watched. In St. Augustine, where the town's obvious vulnerability to Federal attack made passions run high before the inevitable occupation, Dr. John Peck encouraged his wife and daughters to maintain social ties with Frances Kirby Smith, the city's most aggressive Confederate, in order to protect his position as the city's physician. It was perhaps a wise move, as Mrs. Smith was one of the most suspicious women in the town, always eager to root out the Northerners she suspected of being in league with abolitionists.[8]

Unionists often found themselves in the crossfire. In Pensacola, in January 1861, the families of Union soldiers stationed at Fort Barrancas were hurriedly rushed to Fort Pickens under a flag of truce to bid farewell to their husbands and fathers before being shipped off to New York. The loss of property and homes was devastating, leading one furious matron to volunteer to man the guns herself.[9] The first invasion of Jacksonville in March 1862 sent Calvin Robinson and his family on a desperate dash to escape the Regulators who were torching the town prior to the Union landing. Even during the Federal occupation, Robinson and others felt unsafe, and entire families carried guns at all times.[10] In South Florida, Unionists faced repeated harassment from Confederate neighbors and guerilla units. In 1864, Unionist families in the vicinity of Fort Meade were rounded up and incarcerated, only to be rescued by Federal troops from Fort Myers.[11] Fearful of persecution and conscription into Confederate forces, Floridians often fled to Union lines, or tried to flag down blockading vessels. In January 1863, the crew of the *Sagamore* found a woman and her children living in a tent on an inlet of the Indian River, and later that year another miserably tattered and hungry family was

---

[8]Waterbury, *The Treasurer's House*, 120; Revels, *Grander in Her Daughters*, 11.

[9]Parks and Johnson, eds., *Civil War Views of Pensacola*, 26–28; Mary Reed Bobbit, *With Dearest Love to All: The Life and Letters of Lady Jeb* (Chicago: Henry Regnery, 1960) 36–38.

[10]Martin, *The City Makers*, 39–41; Martin, "Defeat in Victory," 25–30.

[11]Brown, *Florida's Peace River Frontier*, 169–76.

picked up by the *Pursuit*. The fighting and guerilla action in East Florida in 1864 rousted hundreds of families from the swamps. Gaunt, ravenous, and ragged, the men would often take the oath of allegiance and enlist, especially if such actions would ensure food and refuge for their families.[12] With ever tightening enforcement of taxes and conscription, Floridian morale plummeted and people fled to the arms of the enemy. Even if they were Unionists only because their bellies were empty, in a state as underpopulated as Florida, the loss of every family mattered.

Union sympathizers—male and female, black and white—provided valuable information to the enemy. In 1864, a *New York Times* correspondent with the byline "WHIT" described a local man who led scouts from Jacksonville to Lake City as "the most valuable auxiliaries we have in our command." "WHIT" credited the man with knowing "every road and bypath," plus having "better military judgment than half of the Generals in the field." Though unnamed by the reporter, it is likely this essential resource was John Alsop, a Jacksonville lumberman who also led Federals on a mission up the St. Marys River, where a vast amount of war material was seized. A Unionist identified as J. E. Whithurst "expressed his intention of fighting for no flag but the one he was brought up and had always lived under" and proved his loyalty by providing extensive information on Tampa prior to a 1862 shelling of the city.[13] But not every informant was so lucky. Captain John J. Dickison tricked a "loyal Union woman" into giving him the location of her Confederate deserter sons by pretending to be a Union officer, a charade his men found hilarious.[14]

The most serious efforts to restore Florida to the Union came from a combination of civilian urgency and political machinations. Though these attempts failed, they highlighted the dangers of Unionism and the

---

[12]William J. Schellings, ed., "On Blockade Duty in Florida Waters," *Tequesta: The Journal of the Historical Association of Southern Florida* 15 (1955): 67–70; *New York Tribune*, 20 February 1864.

[13]Martin, "The '*New York Times*' Views Civil War Jacksonville," 416–17; Frank Falero, Jr., "Naval Engagements in Tampa Bay, 1862," *Florida Historical Quarterly* 46 (October 1967): 135.

[14]Dickison, *Dickison and His Men*, 117–19.

impact of Confederate abandonment of Florida's most urbanized areas so early in the war.

Jacksonville, in the words of historian Richard A. Martin, was "a focal point for politicians, adventurers, and visionaries who regarded northeast Florida as the ideal place for launching their various schemes."[15] Union forces first occupied Jacksonville in March 1862. The majority of citizens who remained in the town following a "reign of terror" by Confederate Regulators professed intense loyalty to the American flag. They sought to repudiate secession and organize a loyal state government for Florida. Though the original incursion into Jacksonville was supposed to be very brief, General Thomas W. Sherman, commander of all the troops in action in Florida, met with citizens and decided to enlarge the occupation force and extend its time in the city.[16]

On March 20, 1862, about a hundred Union men assembled at the courthouse. Placing their names on Union rolls was tantamount to signing their death warrants, should Jacksonville fall back into Confederate hands. The Jacksonville Unionists adopted resolutions that declared secession invalid and pronounced Florida "an integral part of the United States." They called upon loyal citizens to "raise up a State government," a resolution that met with Sherman's approval. General Sherman in turn issued a proclamation to the "People of East Florida" assuring them of protection and urging them to "throw off that sham government which has been forced upon you." Jacksonville Unionists immediately took the lead, holding a second "Union meeting" on March 24, which was attended by delegates from throughout Northeast Florida. This gathering called for a convention to assemble on April 20 for the purpose of "reorganizing the civil authority" in Florida. The arrival of another Federal regiment in Jacksonville was taken as a sign of permanent occupation, and more Unionists came forward. Calvin Robinson, a leader in the movement, rejoiced, feeling "that nearly the whole country was in sympathy with us," as elections were expected to take place in St. Johns, Nas-

---

[15]Martin, "The '*New York Times*' Views Civil War Jacksonville," 410.
[16]Martin, "Defeat in Victory," 18–21.

sau, Putnam, Clay, Volusia, Orange, and Brevard counties.[17] Sherman was optimistic, but on March 31, Brigadier General Horatio G. Wright, the Union commander at Jacksonville, reported a rumor that Confederate forces were assembling to retake the town, which he could not hold without reinforcement. His superior, General David Hunter, was not willing to gamble on thin promises of Florida Unionism, and on April 6 Wright received orders to withdraw. Jacksonville Unionists were both outraged and terrified, knowing that if they were left behind they would probably be murdered. Approximately one hundred Union families were taken on board Union transport vessels, many of them eventually making their way to New York, where their plight inspired collections for their welfare. The Jacksonville adventure also met with condemnation and a congressional investigation that fueled criticism of Lincoln's war policies.[18]

In 1862 the *New York Times* argued the merits of colonizing Florida with freedmen. The New England Emigrant Aid Company explored the possibility of planting a colony as well though the plan did not materialize during the war. In 1863 Northern enthusiasts such as Eli Thayer gave speeches encouraging white colonization of the area between the St. Johns River and the Atlantic Ocean, with the twist that the 20,000 volunteers for the occupation would be rewarded with Florida land once the region was secure. The national government would benefit both from the occupation of enemy territory and the nucleus of a free state government, which could be rapidly organized and allowed to re-enter the Union. A delegation of German-Americans met with Lincoln and expressed that they were "ready and anxious" to participate in this proposed colonization of Florida. Despite Lincoln's kind words to the delegates, their proposals went nowhere.[19]

---

[17]Schafer, *Thunder on the River*, 68–60, Martin, "Defeat in Victory," 19–23.

[18]Martin, "Defeat in Victory," 24–28; Shofner, *Nor Is It Over Yet*, 4; Martin, "The '*New York Times*' Views Civil War Jacksonville," 412.

[19]Robert L. Clarke, "Northern Plans for the Economic Invasion of Florida, 1862–1865," *Florida Historical Quarterly* 28 (April 1950): 262–64; Martin, "The '*New York Times*' Views Civil War Jacksonville," 410–12.

The approaching 1864 election found the Republican party divided. Conservative and Radical divisions as well as personal ambitions made for an intricate dance among Lincoln's famous team of rivals. Salmon P. Chase, Lincoln's secretary of the treasury, hoped to win support from the Radicals, and receiving credit for bringing Florida back into the Union would make him more attractive. To achieve the goal of rescuing Florida, Chase relied upon the services of a political opportunist and adventurer named Lyman D. Stickney, a man who had once partnered with a slave smuggler but who now professed to be a dedicated Unionist. Along with Harrison Reed, a Wisconsin editor, and John S. Sammis, a resident of Jacksonville (though of Northern birth), Stickney had been appointed a Federal tax commissioner for Florida in October 1862. Stickney was full of ideas for ways to return Florida to the fold (and perhaps line his own pockets in the process).[20]

In 1863, Stickney joined with Colonel Thomas W. Higgison to promote a third expedition to Jacksonville. A noted abolitionist, Higgison was eager for his black troops to see more action and prove their merit to a skeptical Northern public. General David Hunter approved the plan, and on March 10, 1863, Higgison and his men arrived in Jacksonville with Stickney in tow. The presence of black troops infuriated Confederates stationed some ten miles west of town, leading to vicious attacks on pickets and lone soldiers. Things grew so unsettled in the city that the Federals agreed to evacuate all women and children, sending them to safety in Lake City. Following more skirmishes, a bid for reinforcements for a permanent occupation failed, and on March 28 Jacksonville was ordered evacuated once again. Higginson was bitterly disappointed. As the troops were preparing to board their transports, fires broke out in the town. A *New York Daily Tribune* correspondent described the scene:

> On every side, from every quarter of the city, dense clouds of black smoke and flame are bursting through the mansions and the warehouses. A fine south wind is blowing immense blazing cinders right into the heart of the city.... The whole city, mansions, warehouses, trees,

[20]Johns, *Florida during the Civil War*, 192–93; Shofner, *Nor Is It Over Yet*, 4–5.

shrubbery, and orange groves; all that refined taste and art through many years have made beautiful and attractive, are being lapped up and devoured by this howling fiery blast.... Is not this war—vindictive, un-relenting war?[21]

As the Federals sailed away, they left nearly a third of the main business area in ashes.[22]

Stickney now realized that Unionism in Florida—and support for Chase's presidential ambitions—would not flourish without a serious military operation, hopefully one that brought the entire area of East Florida under Union control. To this end, he advised Major General Quincy A. Gillmore to come up with a plan for such action and present it to United States General-in-Chief Henry W. Halleck. Gillmore obliged on December 15, 1863, arguing that an invasion of East Florida could accomplish a number of objectives, including gaining Federal control over the most valuable part of the state, cutting off enemy supplies, and adding freedmen to the ranks of Union soldiers. Halleck approved, giving Gillmore permission to use his own discretion, provided the Charleston campaign was not weakened by the Florida invasion.[23]

On December 8, Lincoln had issued his Proclamation of Amnesty and Reconstruction, forever known as the Ten Percent Plan. Amnesty would be extended to all Southerners willing to take an oath of future loyalty to the Union. In any Confederate state, once a number of persons equal to 10 percent of the state's 1860 voters had sworn the oath, Lincoln would recognize the government they formed. This raised the stakes considerably; now both Lincoln and Chase would want the loyalty of Florida Unionists. Lincoln dispatched his secretary, John Hay, to Beaufort with instructions to accompany Gillmore into Florida. Hay carried with him a major's commission and the paperwork for administering the

---

[21]*New York Daily Tribune*, 8 April 1863.

[22]Proctor, "Jacksonville during the Civil War," 352–53; Shofner, *Nor Is It Over Yet*, 4–6; Schafer, *Thunder on the River*, 158–59. Who was responsible for burning Jacksonville has long been a subject of debate. Higginson proclaimed his men "guiltless" of the arson but admitted they "were excited by the occasion" and "recalled their favorite imagery of Judgment Day, and sang and shouted without ceasing" as they departed. See Schafer, *Thunder on the River*, 160–61.

[23]Shofner, *Nor Is It Over Yet*, 8–9.

oath of allegiance and enrolling loyal voters. Sent ahead to Fernandina before the expedition launched, Hay's work ran counter to the efforts of Stickney, who claimed to be organizing a "Free State League" and a "Chase League." Both agents reported success in finding loyal Union men who, of course, would support each man's master.[24] The invasion became a reality, with Union troops arriving in Jacksonville on February 7, 1864. Skepticism of the chances of turning Florida blue perhaps ran higher among the soldiers than the schemers. Lieutenant C. M. Duren of the 54th Massachusetts wrote home that captured Florida combatants "are glad to take the oath—and go to their homes, but I would not trust them as good Union Men out of my sight, that's as much confidence as I have in them."[25]

This occupation was Jacksonville's final one and led to the Federal defeat at the Battle of Olustee. Union optimism crumbled with the loss. Hay had reported securing many names, but by March 1 he was forced to admit that he would never be able to acquire the 10 percent of Florida voters needed to establish a loyal government under Lincoln's plan. Ever the manipulator, Stickney wrote to Chase that he had molded Hay's opinion "in harmony with my own. He now works with me, and for the measure I wish to prevail."[26]

Chase withdrew from the presidential nomination race in March 1864 and Stickney found his leadership of Florida Unionists eroding as business partners and fellow tax commissioners accused him of corruption. A convention of Unionists was held in Jacksonville on May 17, 1864, with the purpose of electing delegates to the Republican convention, which was meeting in Baltimore on June 7. The convention was filled with Stickney's enemies, and it selected a slate of Lincoln men led by Calvin Robinson. Though Stickney also sent a delegation to Baltimore, the convention only seated the Robinson delegation. They were denied voting rights, but Robinson, who had once slept in his clothes

---

[24]Johns, *Florida during the Civil War*, 194; Shofner, *Nor Is It Over Yet*, 8–9.

[25]C. M. Duren, "The Occupation of Jacksonville, February 1864 and the Battle of Olustee: Letters of Lt. C. M. Duren, 54th Massachusetts Regiment, U.S.A," *Florida Historical Quarterly* 32 (April 1954): 266.

[26]Johns, *Florida during the Civil War*, 199–200.

and turned his house into a fortress against Confederate vigilantes, was named to the Republican Union National Committee. Stickney's attempts at being a master manipulator ended in humiliating defeat. Florida did not raise a loyal government, but foundations for Reconstruction had been laid among the East Florida Unionists. In May 1864 a Federal officer could state, with confidence, that "the people on the east side of the St. Johns are called Florida Yankees and the majority of them are Union men."[27]

Unionism in Jacksonville was, to a large degree, dependent on Union troops to protect it until the final year of the war. In contrast, Key West never truly left Union control, and St. Augustine was surrendered without a shot in early 1862. Both of these towns quickly became strongholds of Unionism in the state and were never seriously threatened with recapture.

Key West was initially divided in sentiment, though Confederates on the island were more vocal than determined, all bark and very little bite. Promptly reinforced, the Federal forces were sufficient to make sure Union authority was never questioned though all but two United States officials at Key West resigned their posts at secession. One of these stalwarts was District Judge William Marvin, who squared off in May 1861 with McQueen McIntosh, a secession leader who had been sent to replace him. Marvin refused the demand to surrender his office and all records, and he arranged for McIntosh to be escorted off the island rather than arrested. This was the sole Confederate attempt to hold onto Key West, and it failed with embarrassing swiftness for the Florida government. Union military authorities promptly solved the problem of Confederate sympathizers in town by declaring martial law on May 10, 1861. All persons were required to take the oath of allegiance or leave the island. Confederates either muffled their complaints or fled, and by June 6, the *New York Herald* would report that Key West "has a thoroughly Union-loving population." Though probably only a small minority of Confederates abandoned their homes, there were enough outraged men to

---

[27]Ibid., 200; Shofner, *Nor Is It Over Yet*, 12–15; Reiger, "Florida after Secession," 139.

organize a company colorfully named the "Key West Avengers" and enter Confederate service.[28]

Key West became an important station for the blockading fleet, and for many of the men on duty there, it was a colorful and romantic world where foreign accents and customs merged with both Yankee and Southern folkways. The stores were well stocked and holidays vividly celebrated. Dances, concerts, and serenades broke up the otherwise monotonous service on blockading vessels. "After more than three months' cruising on the blockade it is very pleasant indeed to come once more within the pale of civilization, for here we find the greatest of all civilizers, the society of refined, cultured ladies," a correspondent for the *Philadelphia Inquirer* reported.[29] Love affairs between sailors and local women, whether "secesh" or Unionist, appeared to flourish, leading one wit to claim that whenever a naval officer died, at least one woman went into overly dramatic mourning for him, asserting that she had been his "affianced Bride, and that Death alone has separated them." Yellow fever posed the greatest threat to Union control of the town and the strength of the blockade. Captain John Augustus Wilson of the 2nd Regiment, United States Colored Troops, admitted that despite the beauty of the surroundings, the deaths of so many of his friends from the mysterious disease had caused him to ponder, "Is this indeed Paradise or is it Hell?"[30]

Perhaps its great distance from the fray explains Key West's unique position during the war. Though firmly in Union hands and unquestionably loyal, there was little sense of political excitement on the island. Homer G. Plantz, Chase's private secretary, was sent to Key West as a Federal district attorney in 1863. After less than two weeks at his post, Plantz reported an "absence of all manifestations of National or even

---

[28]Johns, *Florida during the Civil War*, 155–56; *New York Herald*, 6 June 1861. For the experiences of one of the "Avengers," see R. Thomas Campbell, ed., *Southern Service on Land and Sea: The Wartime Journal of Robert Watson, CSA/CSN* (Knoxville: University of Tennessee Press, 2002).

[29]*Key West New Era*, 20 September 1862; *Sunbury (Pennsylvania) American*, 9 January 1864; *Philadelphia Inquirer*, 22 January 1862.

[30]Robert B. Ely, "This Filthy Ironpot," *American Heritage* 19 (February 1968): 49–50; Millicent Todd Bingham, "Key West in the Summer of 1864," *Florida Historical Quarterly* 43 (January 1965): 265.

State feeling. Political apathy prevails." He quickly determined that "what everybody wants is to be let alone; not to be required to take sides on any questions; and, better and chiefly, not to have any questions to take sides about."[31]

St. Augustine initially presented more problems for the Union officers and the Union sympathizers within it borders. While the surrender was without bloodshed, enough residents remained vocal in their partisan sentiments to threaten Union safety. Guerilla snipers were a constant danger to Union pickets. Few men were willing to sign up for city defense, and the Confederate women of the town were particularly offensive to Federal soldiers, which finally led to an ultimatum condemning their "grossly insulting" actions and warning them of "strict arrest" if these displays did not cease. The attempt to muffle St. Augustine's Confederate dames paralleled, in many ways, General Benjamin F. Butler's infamous "Woman Order" in New Orleans.[32]

Following an abortive 1862 attempt to cleanse the city of Confederate sympathizers, in January 1863 all citizens having a male relative in Confederate service were expelled. The Reverend L. R. Staudenmeyer of Trinity Church noted that remaining residents were adjusting more gracefully to Yankee rule: "At the beginning the families kept their houses closed against Yankee visitors, but in the process of time many welcomed them, and you would see some women walk arm in arm with the Yankee officers on the seawall and on the streets!"[33] Half a dozen regiments were rotated through St. Augustine before war's end for rest and relaxation. "These soldiers live in clover," the *Sacramento Daily Union* reported in summer 1863, "having a delightful climate, a fine old town, plenty of fresh meat, fish, vegetables, fruit and milk, and being in good quarters at the old fort built by the Spanish." John Hay toured the town during his search for loyal voters in 1864 and claimed that he found "a

---

[31]Reiger, "Florida after Secession," 140.

[32]East and Jenckes, "St. Augustine during the Civil War," 84–87. The "Woman Order" announced that any female who insulted Union soldiers would be treated "as a woman of the town plying her avocation" (Jefferson Davis Bragg, *Louisiana in the Confederacy* [Baton Rouge: Louisiana State University Press, 1941] 108–109).

[33]Graham, "Homefront," 34; Graham, *The Awakening of St. Augustine*, 103.

quiet and almost unconscious admission of superiority of the North" among its residents.[34] But St. Augustine and Key West were the exceptions, not the rule, in Florida.

Ironically and tragically, some Florida Unionists were abandoned and betrayed by their presumed comrades. The Jacksonville loyalists of 1862 were encouraged to go public with their sentiments, which exposed them so clearly to Confederate wrath that most chose to sacrifice their homes and businesses rather than remain behind when the Federals abruptly departed. In St. Augustine, loyalists who had sons in the Confederate army were unceremoniously ejected from the town and the same fate was barely avoided by Unionists in Key West. Commanders of Union vessels became increasingly suspicious of refugees, and in 1864 an admiral's order denying transport to peddlers and foreign nationals put even more pressure on Florida Unionists to prove their sincerity or stay behind and face community retribution.[35]

Though Unionism held strength and sway in a few Florida communities, for Floridians to profess dedication to the United States was to risk everything: friends, community respect, property, and even life itself. Unless exercised in the shadow of Union guns, American patriotism could prove fatal. "Union men they threaten to hang, and do shoot, as we have lamentable proof," one Union agent wrote from South Florida.[36] The Unionist Mitchel family of Apalachicola remained in town, protecting their property, until a son was conscripted into the Confederate army. On his furlough, the family arranged a desperate dash to a Federal blockade vessel for father and son, with the mother and other children to follow them to sanctuary in Rhode Island. Before she could take her children to safety, Mrs. Mitchel learned that local men suspected of aid-

[34]East and Jenckes, "St. Augustine during the Civil War," 83; Staudenraus, ed., "A War Correspondent's View," 61; Tyler Dennett, ed., *Lincoln and the Civil War in the Diaries and Letters of John Hay* (New York: Dodd, Mead, 1939) 162–63.

[35]Staudenraus, ed., "A War Correspondent's View," 62; Browne, *Key West: The Old and the New*, 96; David J. Coles, "Unpretending Service: The *James L. Davis*, the *Tahoma*, and the East Gulf Blockading Squadron," *Florida Historical Quarterly* 71 (July 1992): 51–52.

[36]Waters, "Florida's Confederate Guerillas," 142–43.

ing Unionists had been "tied to trees and shot at" by an entire company of Regulators.[37] And in April 1864, Brigadier General Alexander Asboth, commander of the Union forces in West Florida, filed one of the most chilling reports of the war: "In Walton County 7 citizens were hung last week for entertaining Union sentiments, and a woman, refusing to give information about her husband's whereabouts, was killed in a shocking manner, and two of her children caught and torn to pieces by bloodhounds."[38]

---

[37]Mitchel, *Reminiscences of the Civil War*, 8–14, 29.
[38]This gruesome report can be read in United States War Department, *The War of the Rebellion: A Compilation of the Official Records of the Union and Confederate Armies* (Washington, 1880–1901) Ser. 1, vol. 35, pt. 2, 64.

Chapter 9

This Unequal Struggle

Deprivation, Desertion, and Death

"Tivie has learned to card and spin—I can knit though very slow at it—All our soap and candles are made at home too," Rebecca Bryant reported to her son in 1863, updating him on the family's progress in domestic skills. "Don't you think we will do to live in the Confederacy?"[1] Her playful pride in the art of making-do mocked a harsh reality. By 1863 many Floridians had passed beyond the point of finding sacrifice and salvage patriotic, much less amusing. The war was testing not only their skills, but also their resolve.

To some degree, Florida's frontier status made wartime shortages easier to endure. People in rough, unsettled areas were accustomed to living without the niceties and small luxuries that were common to urban life. Florida's crackers were unlikely to miss ink, perfume, or fancy soap. Their women had always worn homespun, not silk or satin. Even wealthy Floridians repaired objects rather than replacing them, as the culture of built-in obsolescence was unknown in the mid-nineteenth century. Many Floridians had never been to school, and many rarely attended church and thus would not mourn the loss of intellectual and spiritual routines. A number of regions avoided attacks or even much threat of violence, and as long as a Floridian possessed a gun, a fishing pole, and a small plot of land, Florida's natural bounty assured a subsistence level of nourishment. Certainly Floridians fared better as a whole than did the residents of the Shenandoah Valley or the citizens who stood between Sherman and the sea.[2]

---

[1] Blakey, et al., *Rose Cottage Chronicles*, 208.

[2] Brown, *Florida's Peace River Frontier*, 287; Clifton Paisley, "Tallahassee through the Storebooks: War Clouds and War, 1860–1863," *Florida Historical Quarterly* (July 1972): 44; Abbey, *Florida*, 287.

But deprivations did come, and many Floridians suffered and were driven to desperate measures. Some turned against the Confederate government or on their neighbors. By 1863, Florida's loyalty was no longer a strong cornerstone of the proud Confederacy, but instead a crumbling pillar propping up an ever more dilapidated home.

* * *

At the beginning, Floridians seemed energized and responsive to calls to mobilize in support of the Confederacy. Farmers pledged to obey General Beauregard's request to plant vegetables rather than cotton. This promise was quickly forgotten as the profits from running cotton through the blockade were recognized. Governor Milton sternly disapproved of cotton profiteering, as well as bringing anything besides arms and munitions through the blockade, but his admonishments were dismissed at all levels. Visiting Tallahassee in March 1862, Major General John C. Pemberton found that many planters "had a disposition to plant cotton the coming season" rather than the corn and wheat the Confederacy desperately needed.[3] Those who did have surplus corn were also quick to perceive its potential as a necessary commodity and to hoard bushels while waiting for higher prices. An April 12, 1863, letter to Tallahassee's *Florida Sentinel* accused a "blood-drinker" planter of Jefferson County of refusing the cash offerings of poor widows. "Surely, if God does not visit such with a just retribution in due time, the people will," the writer warned. Exposure of profiteering remained a newspaper crusade. The *Floridian and Journal* demanded publication of the names of those who grew cotton rather than corn, including the "rich widows" who were "by no means helpless" and just as unpatriotic as their male colleagues.[4]

The blockade was the cause of much of Florida's suffering, but citizens bore some responsibility as well. As one Southerner noted, "Every man in the community is swindling everybody else." By encouraging

---

[3]Dodd, *Florida in the War*, 30; Reiger, "Deprivation, Disaffection and Desertion," 279.

[4]Proctor, ed., *Florida a Hundred Years Ago*, n.p.; *Florida Sentinel* (Tallahassee), 12 April 1863.

loved ones to hoard and gouge commodities, even dedicated Confederate soldiers contributed to the spiral of inflation. Michael Raysor urged his wife at home in Jefferson County to ask top prices for their excess bacon: "for when we buy we have to pay high & when we sell we ought to sell high that's my motto."[5] As historian John F. Reiger explains, "Speculation in necessities of life was a major problem in Florida throughout the war. Like all manifestations of indifference toward Confederate war aims, this evil increased and spread as it became more and more obvious that the South was headed for defeat." Matters were hardly improved when blockade runners stuffed their cargo bays with luxury items like gold pens, violin strings, shaving cream, morocco gaiters, parasols, dolls, picture books, and toupees, rather than essential commodities such as food and medicine.[6]

Things Floridians had become accustomed to purchasing or perhaps bartering for were no long available or were exorbitantly priced. Grotesque inflation was the bane of the southern Civil War home front. Prices varied greatly, but always seemed outrageous. The price of kerosene, a common lighting fluid, tripled from 1861 to 1862. Kitchen staples such as flour, sugar, salt, and spices were especially dear. Governor Milton informed the legislature that rum worth fifteen to twenty cents a gallon was selling for forty to eighty dollars. Meanwhile, First Lady Caroline Milton saw mustard, black pepper, rice, molasses, and baking soda vanish from her pantry. To add insult to injury, many shopkeepers who had graciously extended credit in antebellum days now demanded cash. In January 1863, Tallahassee merchant Philip T. Pearce informed his customers that, "after the 20th of this month, I will expect them to pay cash for all articles of marketing purchased of me. I find myself alone in the credit business, and, as the ladies say, one had better be out of the world than out of fashion, I prefer adopting fashion at this time." By

---

[5]John Christopher Schwab, *The Confederate States of America 1861–1865: A Financial and Industrial History of the South during the Civil War* (New York: Yale University Press, 1904) 230; Sheehan-Dean, "'If It Was Not For You I Would Be Willing to Die,'" 391, 400.

[6]Reiger, "Deprivation, Disaffection and Desertion," 280–81; Helen R. Sharp, "Samuel A. Swann and the Development of Florida, 1855–1900," *Florida Historical Quarterly* 20 (October 1941): 174–75, Dodd, *Florida in the War*, 30.

war's end, very few Floridians could have enjoyed purchasing consumer goods or even savored a meal cooked with antebellum flair.[7]

Families substituted things that were plentiful for things that were not. With less beef, pork, and poultry on the table, more fish, opossum, squirrel, and fox appeared. Alligator was not unknown. Octavia Stephens found black bear especially pleasing: "I had a fine baked piece of it and it was as tender and nice as any beef I ever tasted, and came just in the nick of time as we were out of meat."[8] With creative adjustments to the recipe, plain corn bread was modified into Rebel bread, Jeff Davis muffins, Jackson batter cakes, and Stonewall hoe cakes. Sarah Palmer Williams confessed that despite her best efforts in enriching her Confederate cake, its "cornmeal foundation was against its popularity." To try to improve flavoring, Floridians turned to "long sweetening," a dark mush made from cane, as well as dried fruits, berries, figs, peaches, and watermelon rind.[9] Perhaps most unappetizing to imagine are the many substitutes Floridians concocted for coffee and tea. Almost any vile brew would be consumed, including drinks made from parched corn, corn shucks, grits, peanuts, and okra.[10]

Unable to obtain cloth from English or Yankee mills easily, Floridians quickly became preoccupied with their wardrobes. Acquiring, patching, and altering garments had never been more essential. Even the most inferior calico cloth, which had sold for ten to thirty cents before the war, was priced at four to eight dollars a yard in 1863. In that same year, the *Philadelphia Inquirer* noted, "Articles as calico, muslin, and dry goods are entirely out of date, and the female portion of the community are wear-

---

[7]Dodd, *Florida in the War*, 49–50; *Philadelphia Inquirer*, 21 May 1863; Hopley, *Life in the South*, 2:276–77; Paisley, "Tallahassee through the Storebooks: War Clouds," 49–50; Proctor, *Florida a Hundred Years Ago*, n.p.

[8]Blakey, et al., *Rose Cottage Chronicles*, 71, 137.

[9]Untitled article, United Daughters of the Confederacy Scrapbook, vol. 6, State Archives of Florida; Mrs. M. M. Scarborough, "Suffering of Southern Women," United Daughters of the Confederacy Scrapbooks, vol. 1, State Archives of Florida; James M. Denham and Canter Brown, Jr., *Cracker Times and Pioneer Lives: The Florida Reminiscences of George Gillett Keen and Sarah Pamela Williams* (Columbia: University of South Carolina Press, 2003) 122.

[10]Revels, *Grander in Her Daughters*, 59–60.

ing out their old rags—the relics of better days."[11] Men were not spared the cost of store-bought articles or the humiliation of homemade attire. In 1862, William D. Slasser purchased a pair of trousers, a coat, and a handkerchief, shelling out twice what he had paid for these masculine essentials before secession. Other men wore pants and shirts made from curtains, drapes, and the skirts of their wives' old dresses. Any opportunity to purchase thread or other dry goods brought in through the blockade would spark a near riot.[12]

Middle class and elite Floridians sought instruction in the art of spinning and weaving from those who had never enjoyed the privilege of buying finished goods. Slaves and cracker women taught other women the domestic arts that had been lost as economic status rose. Slave women were especially well versed in plant lore and could demonstrate which combinations of berries, bark, and roots would achieve the desired color of dye. Newspapers conveniently carried dye recipes for determined Confederate fashionistas.[13] Perhaps the most necessary color was black, the hue of mourning. Nineteenth-century etiquette prescribed somber attire for those who had lost close relatives, though the *Florida Sentinel* condemned this as a wasteful practice, arguing "mourning clothes adds great to our expenditure and detracts to that extent from our ability to maintain this unequal struggle."[14]

Home production was suddenly extensive across the social classes. Thimble brigades continued their work, providing not only replacement uniforms and blankets to the troops, but community and comfort to the

[11]Hopley, *Life in the South*, 2:276–77; Dodd, *Florida in the War*, 49–50; *Philadelphia Inquirer*, 21 May 1863.

[12]Paisley, "Tallahassee through the Storebooks: War Clouds and War," 49; Scarborough, "Suffering of Southern Women"; Mrs. T. R. Leigh, "The Burdens Women Bore," United Daughters of the Confederacy Scrapbooks, vol. 5, State Archives of Florida.

[13]Lillie B. McDuffee, *The Lures of Manatee: A True Story of South Florida's Glamorous Past*, 2nd ed. (Atlanta: Foote & Davies, 1961) 149; *Tallahassee Floridian and Journal*, 11 March 1865.

[14]Lou Taylor, *Mourning Dress: A Costume and Social History* (London: George Allen and Unwin, 1983) 123–24, 132; *Florida Sentinel* (Tallahassee), 19 August 1862.

people left behind. Floridians wove hats from sawgrass and palmetto plants, and cut blankets from carpets and piano covers. Shoes were repaired with bed ticking and velvet scraps. While families tried to respond promptly to battlefield requests for clothes and food, they could not ignore their own needs. Confederate patriotism would not fill stomachs or cover nakedness.[15]

Medicine and medical care were casualties of war. "Medicines there were none, of any consequence," Sarah Jones recalled, of her days on the Milton plantation. "Stimulants there were none." Castor oil went for twenty dollars a gallon. Quinine sold for twenty dollars an ounce.[16] Caregivers turned to home remedies, many of them (including one that involved blackberry roots, buttermilk, and rusty nails) of dubious efficiency. Slave women, particularly the aged "grannies" and "doctor women," earned new respect from their owners, now that so many trained physicians had abandoned their practices for the army.[17]

Another painful shortage for many Floridians was reliable information. The delivery of newspapers, magazines, and letters had never been exactly timely on the frontier, and the disruptions of the war, including attacks on mailmen by deserter gangs, only made things worse. Even the governor's family often went weeks without a newspaper, and then was vexed when the postmaster threw away the backdated papers, apparently "thinking stale news unprofitable." Families ran out of paper, ink, and stamps. Keeping up a steady correspondence was a Herculean task, yet it was an essential one. Soldiers begged for letters more than they begged for clothes or food. Fighting with Lee's army, Francis P. Fleming requested more mail from his family. "Please bear in mind that the principal, and I might almost say the only enjoyment that a soldier up here has is the reception of letters from 'The loved ones at home,' deprived as we are of all society, it is about the only link that connects us

---

[15]Revels, *Grander in Her Daughters*, 61–63.

[16]Reiger, "Deprivation, Disaffection, and Desertion," 280; Hopley, *Life in the South*, 2:255, 276–77.

[17]Susan Bradford Eppes, *The Negro of the Old South: A Bit of Period History* (Chicago: Joseph G. Branch Publishing, 1925) 109–11; Deborah Gray White, *Ar'n't I a Woman?: Female Slaves in the Plantation South* (New York: W. W. Norton, 1985) 124–25.

with its enjoyments and keeps us alive within us an appreciation of home associations." Fleming would have agreed with Colonel David Lang of White Springs, who considered letters from family and friends "sacred."[18]

Not knowing the progress of the war and the fate of loved ones was among the greatest hardships. Worry, loneliness, and despair broke the spirits of all but the strongest of those left behind. No war is easy to bear, but the knowledge that Americans were slaughtering Americans gives a pointed pathos to the messages and thoughts of Floridians who endured the Civil War.

Departure was difficult, especially for couples that held contrasting views on duty and honor. "I am sorry that you is greaving so much," Michael Raysor wrote to his wife, Sallie, after his departure from Monticello. "You know you is all & all to me & if it was not for you I would be willing to die" but "you know the situation of our country and some body will have to do the fighting & it is as much my duty to defend my state as any body else."[19] Families did their best to stay connected during the conflict, as their letters testify. Soldiers wrote of battles and adventures and the foibles of their comrades in camp. Wives composed "domestic pictures" for their husbands of their children at play. Christian mothers proselytized to errant sons. Parents cooperated, even at great distances, in the discipline of naughty youngsters. Husbands tried to mend family feuds via the mail. Kisses for ma, pa, and all the children were never in short supply, at least on paper.[20] Florida's Civil War letters resonate not

---

[18]Jones, "Governor Milton and His Family," 49; Johns, *Florida during the Civil War*, 164; Williamson, ed., "Francis P. Fleming in the War for Southern Independence: Part II," 143; Groene, "Civil War Letters of Colonel David Lang," 340, 350.

[19]Sheehan-Dean, "'If It Was Not For You I Would Be Willing To Die,'" 392.

[20]Ulmer, ed., *The Correspondence of Will and Ju Stockton*, 88–90, 93, 278; Sarah Ann Fletcher to sons, 6 May 1861, Zabud Fletcher family papers, State Archives of Florida; J. Russell Reaver, "Letters of Joel C. Blake," *Apalachee* 5 (1962): 8–9, 16; Michael O. Raysor to Sallie Raysor, 5 February 1863, Raysor Family Papers, P. K. Yonge Library, University of Florida; George Washington Parkhill to Elizabeth Bellamy Parkhill, 1, 3 October 1861, George Washington Parkhill Papers, Florida State University Special Collections; Marten, *The Children's Civil War*, 21–22.

so much with the political issues of the day, or with assessment of battles and campaigns (those these are often discussed), but with the simple joys of human existence: family, romantic love, the affectionate regard of friends, and the hopes for a happier eternity.

Floridians of all stripes tried to be strong, to bear the struggle with Christian fortitude. Many survivors remembered parents who sacrificed without complaint. Others recalled their own willingness to contribute to the community, echoing the words of Mattie English Bunch of Liberty County: "I was young, healthy, and strong and felt that I must do something for the general good."[21] But often the most traditional sources of comfort were denied to Floridians, especially those in small communities and the backwoods. Schools were disrupted, breaking childhood routines. Across the state, churches lost pastors and lay leaders. Episcopal houses of worship were especially unlucky. St. John's in Warrington, St. John's in Jacksonville, and St. Luke's in Marianna were burned during military engagements. The rotting belfry of St. Mark's in Palatka made the sanctuary unsafe, and St. Paul's in Quincy was sold to pay the parish debts. Animals wandered through the neglected aisles of Trinity in St. Augustine. Wherever churches still operated, they were crowded on special days of prayer and fasting, as Floridians beseeched God to end "this wicked war."[22]

If God would not provide, perhaps the government would. Impoverished Floridians looked to their communities and to their state government to assist them. Governor Milton was sensitive to their plight and pressured the legislature to act. In 1862 the General Assembly appropriated $200,000 for the relief of 3,341 families (11,744 people), and further legislation in 1863 and 1864 increased this amount to $500,000 yearly. By 1864, Florida was attempting to assist at least one noncombatant for every soldier in the field. The state also invested in purchasing

<hr>

[21]Maria Louisa Daegenhardt Memoir, transcript, 5–7, Dena E. Snodgrass Collection, P. K. Yonge Library, University of Florida; Mattie English Bunch, "Story of Two Lovers," United Daughters of the Confederacy Scrapbooks, vol. 2, State Archives of Florida.

[22]Joseph D. Cushman, Jr., "The Episcopal Church in Florida during the Civil War," *Florida Historical Quarterly* 38 (April 1960): 298–300; Johns, *Florida during the Civil War*, 183–84.

wool and cotton cards for distribution to needy families, though the cards acquired were generally inferior and unlikely to be a source of self-sufficiency. County governments likewise attempted to aid their citizens, first with funds and then with cotton cards and food rations. Women's charities made contributions as well. But these efforts were more symbolic than successful, and they were unable to counteract the impact of inflation or come anywhere close to meeting the needs of Florida's poorest families.[23]

Atop the hardships of scarcity, inflation, and emotional deprivation were the twin demons of the Confederacy: taxation and conscription. Together, these factors destroyed Floridian's morale faster than any battlefield defeat. Both ran sharply counter to the foundational doctrine of states' rights. Politicians debated their nuances, but it was the poor people of the state who suffered the most and understood the least. The desperate measures the Confederacy took to ensure its survival in the field killed most of the loyalty to "the cause" in Florida.

The War Tax Act of August 19, 1861, imposed taxes on property, occupations, incomes, and sale of provisions. The Impressment Act of March 26, 1863, and the General Tax Act of April 24, 1863 (also known as the Confederate tithe), gave state tax collectors and Confederate commissary agents wide latitude to seize food, livestock, and basic supplies from citizens, who would receive only worthless Confederate notes in exchange. By the last years of the war these agents—whom Floridians regarded as rascals and thieves—took corn, beef, rice, peas, molasses, and sugar, regardless of a family's obvious destitution.[24] Complicating matters were the multiple currencies then circulating in Florida. Four types of legal tender were common during the war: Confederate treasury notes, state treasury notes, corporation notes, and paper notes of various municipalities. Bank notes and specie still occasionally passed from hand to

---

[23]Cash, "Taylor County History and Civil War Deserters," 47; Dodd, *Florida in the War*, 48; Jerrell H. Shofner, *History of Jefferson County* (Tallahassee: Sentry Press, 1976) 258–59. For a detailed accounting of how funds and items were allocated, see William Frank Zornow, "State Aid for Indigent Soldiers and Their Families in Florida, 1861–65," *Florida Historical Quarterly* 34 (January 1956): 259–65.

[24]Reiger, "Deprivation, Disaffection, and Desertion," 283–85.

hand, and foreign coinage was not unknown. Railroad notes for small amounts were known as "change bills" and circulated as currency at a discount. Towns also produced fractional paper currency nicknamed "shin plasters." While most of the town and railroad bills fell out of circulation by the end of the war, Confederate and state notes circulated at enormous discounts under gold.[25] Floridians in underpopulated areas conducted much of their ordinary business via barter. This wide variety of exchange mediums made even the simplest transactions confusing and the calculation of taxes excruciating. For women especially (as even those with farm management skills often had little experience in complex financial matters), the burden of paying taxes was crushing. Thoughtful husbands did their best to prepare their wives for the inevitable visit from the taxman, calculating on drumheads in distant army camps what was owed to the government on their Florida farms and plantations.[26]

The impressment acts stated that property necessary for the support of the owner and his or her family was not to be taken. Agents recklessly ignored this important clause. Governor Milton's desk was cluttered with letters of outrage from local leaders and private citizens. In 1863 the Reverend John R. Richards complained that

> there are soldiers' families in my neighborhood that the last head of cattle have been taken from them & drove off, and unless this pressing of cows is stopped there won't be a cow left in Calhoun County. I know of several soldier's families in this county that have not had one grain of corn in the last three weeks, nor any likelihood of their getting any in the next three months; their husbands slain at the battlefield in Chattanooga.[27]

Impressment went beyond the violation of political ideals or even the poverty it caused; it was a gut-wrenching betrayal of those who had already given their most cherished asset—the lives of their loved ones—

---

[25]Davis, *Civil War and Reconstruction*, 182–83.

[26]Ianthe Bond Hebel, ed., *Centennial History of Volusia County, Florida, 1854–1954* (Daytona Beach: College Publishing, 1955) 22; Revels, *Grander in Her Daughters*, 68–69.

[27]Dodd, *Florida in the War*, 53–54.

to the Confederate cause. It seemed insulting, ungracious, and even treasonous to deprive these families of what little remained.

The Confederate Congress approved America's first conscription act on April 16, 1862. It ordered all nonexempt white males aged eighteen to thirty-five into military service for three years or the war's duration. The act was modified throughout the war, with the age limit expanding to forty-five and, by early 1864, stretching to encompass men from seventeen to fifty. Early exemptions favored large slaveholders, but over the course of the war these dwindled. In 1864 the Florida cowmen, so essential to production of the state's greatest Confederate resource, were liable for service beyond its borders. Some Floridians were forced to join the 1st Georgia Regulars, which the *Florida Sentinel* called "an outrage upon the rights of Floridians, not to be submitted to quietly." Even sick and disabled men were dragged into camps, in hopes that they could be found fit for some type of military duty. Governor Milton wrote yet another incensed letter to President Davis, arguing that these men "would be of some service in taking care of and comforting women and children" rather than giving a military camp the appearance of an institution "for those afflicted with lameness and disease."[28]

A conscription agent was the nemesis of any man who was a Unionist, a neutral or apathetic observer, or simply an individual who put his family's welfare above the call to arms. Agents cared little for excuses. Formerly law-abiding men were their criminal prey. An observer in South Florida painted a vivid picture of conscription at work: "every man between the ages of 18 and 45 in that section of rebeldom [was] being remorselessly pressed into the rebel army, and if any objections are made they are handcuffed and tied, and marched off, no matter what the condition of their families."[29] Florida's white men were now, in essence, the Confederacy's slaves.

Many Floridians were unwilling to accept such a fate. George Carter of Alachua County held that his duty was to his wife and children. Like numerous others, he took to "laying-out" whenever officers were in his area. Carter nursed a fierce resentment toward those who

---

[28]Reiger, "Deprivation, Disaffection and Desertion," 286–88.
[29]Brown, *Florida's Peace River Frontier*, 152.

drove him from his home and forced him "to hide in the woods at night without fire, despite the inclemency of the weather." Military deserters often joined these draft dodgers in their swampland exile; both types of rebels were prominent in Florida by 1863. They were generally tolerated, despite calls from newspapers like the *Quincy Semi-Weekly Dispatch*, which alerted its readers to "some 50 or 60 men who need their necks stretched with stout ropes." Too many Floridians were sympathetic to the suffering of the "lay-outs" (even if they disapproved of them) to ever mount a hardy cry for their prosecution. Later, as these men organized into vicious guerilla forces, Floridians would be too intimidated to offer much resistance.[30]

More than two thousand Floridians deserted from military service over the course of the war. Their reasons varied from personal cowardice, disgust with the tediousness and hardships of army life, and disgruntlement with the lack of significant victories. Even the most dedicated soldiers could find themselves tempted to abandon the ranks. Captain Hugh Black wondered if it would "stand Me in hand to go and make peace with the Yankees," and urged his wife not to worry if he was reported missing. Many deserters had been opposed to the war from the start and embraced no cause but their own. The factor most readily associated with desertion was news of deprivation in Florida. Unfamiliar with or uninhibited by army discipline, men simply walked away to try to aid their families, with intention of returning to the ranks once the problems at home were resolved. Farmers who felt the need to return for planting or harvesting duties deserted at four times the rate of common laborers in the ranks. Washington Waters, a Madison County farmer, freely admitted that he "started for home to provide something for my family to eat." He was fortunate merely to be demoted from corporal to private for his misdeed. Floridians, like their brothers in arms, had great difficulty accepting the fact that military service, whether voluntary or conscripted, deprived them of their right to care for their families.[31]

---

[30]Reiger, "Deprivation, Disaffection, and Desertion," 288.

[31]Shofner, *Nor Is It Over Yet*, 2; Mark A. Weitz, *More Damning Than Slaughter: Desertion in the Confederate Army* (Lincoln: University of Nebraska Press, 2005) 221; Bittle, "Fight Men View the Western War," 32; Washington

Some Confederate officers felt that examples had to be made. Private William Keen of Company K, 3rd Florida Regiment, was shot for desertion at Dalton, Georgia. The *Gainesville Cotton States* blamed his wife for exaggerating her home front suffering. "Soldiers' wives cannot be too cautious in their letters to their husbands," the editor moralized. "Such letters cause more than half the desertions in the army." This was not necessarily editorial hyperbole. From Fredericksburg in 1863, David Lang reported a soldier executed for desertion "caused by an unfortunate letter full of complaints received from his wife." The ever-philosophical Lang mused over the impact of letters: "And may not the result of battles and the fate of the country rest upon these little messengers of weal or woe?" Whatever their cause, soldiers often found executions difficult to watch. John Hosford wrote that he had seen men cut down beside him in battle and been trampled by soldiers in their death throes, "but of all to see men shot tied to the stake for deserting" was far worse.[32]

Other soldiers paid for their acts of desertion with hard labor, forfeiture of pay, head shaving, whippings, and brandings. Such cruel treatment did little to change the attitudes of the offenders or raise the morale of the witnesses. Abusive punishments were more likely to backfire and cause further intransience. Washington Ives wrote to his family about deserters who were shamed by being forced to wear barrels around their bodies. In Ives's view, a man subjected to such treatment "cannot be persuaded to be of any benefit to any government which will allow him to undergo such treatment, every man in the 4th Fla. Reg't except one who has been bucked or had to wear a barrel or do anything else dis-

Waters to wife, 17 April 1864, Washington Waters Papers, State Archives of Florida; Yael A. Sternhell, *Routes of War: The World of Movement in the Confederate South* (Cambridge: Harvard University Press, 2012) 111. According to Weitz, 2,219 Florida deserters were listed on the official records and only 220 of them were returned to the ranks.

[32]*Gainesville Cotton States*, 14 April 1864; Groene, "Civil War Letters of Colonel David Lang," 351; Mellon, "A Florida Soldier in the Army of Northern Virginia," 259.

graceful have deserted and are all now enemies instead of soldiers of the Confederate gov...."[33]

In the swamps of Taylor County, a band of deserters and conscription dodgers organized themselves into a dangerous guerilla force under the leadership of William Strickland. Calling themselves the "Independent Union Rangers" or the "Florida Royals" of the "United States of Taylor," they were a significant threat to Middle Florida, providing information to Union raiding parties, engaging in sabotage, and even plotting to kidnap Governor Milton. They so terrorized Taylor County that one sheriff defected and another refused to collect taxes, noting that he had received a note from the Rangers and "thought it best to desist." The Confederacy's attempt to capture the partisans met with embarrassing defeat when only the Rangers' women and children were taken prisoner. Though Strickland was killed during the Battle of Natural Bridge, the presence of the Rangers illustrated the greatest danger home front Floridians faced: the war was degenerating into a conflict of neighbor versus neighbor, with old scores to be settled.[34]

The ultimate deprivation of the Civil War was the death of a loved one. Fortunes could be restored, but the loss of a relative in the conflict was so devastating that many of the bereaved never recovered. The home front of Florida took its greedy toll. Soldiers died in camps of instruction, often from typhoid, measles, and dysentery. A Pensacola boy was killed by the accidental discharge of a musket during a militia drill. Florida yellow fever carved a hideous path, especially among the Yankee invaders. One Key West officer feared that there would not be enough men in his unit to carry the coffins to the graves.[35] The crudity of preservation combined with the Florida heat made it unlikely that out-of-state relatives

---

[33]Jessica Slavin, "'Everyone is Tired of This War': An Examination of Desertion and Confederate Florida," *Apalachee* 11 (1991–1996): 18–22; Cabaniss, ed., *Civil War Journal and Letters of Washington Ives*, 56–57.

[34]Lucas, "Civil War Career of Colonel George Washington Scott," 138; Reiger, "Deprivation, Disaffection, and Desertion," 296–98; Johns, *Florida during the Civil War*, 164. For a detailed description of the wartime woes of Taylor County, see Cash, "Taylor County History and Civil War Deserters," 48–58.

[35]*Pensacola Weekly Observer*, 9 June 1861; Bingham, ed., "Key West in the Summer of 1864," 264.

could view the remains of sons who died in Florida. One Alabama officer left a stomach-turning description of the rapid decomposition of a teen-aged soldier who perished in Pensacola. It was not an advertisement for the effectiveness of zinc coffins. Despite the claims of their manufacturers, zinc coffins were not air-tight, and the officer wisely judged that "it would be no gratification" for friends and family to see the boy's body in such an "offensive" condition. [36]

Occasionally, a soldier was able to return home to die. Michael Raysor, who had been so diligent in his correspondence with his beloved Sallie, died of wounds and exhaustion after his return to Monticello in 1863. A condolence letter reminded Sallie how fortunate she had been, in having "had the satisfaction of nursing him and doing all you could to smooth his dying pillow."[37] Families longed to have the bodies of those who died in distant fields returned to them, but this was often impossible. Legends and relics took the place of corpses. Joel Blake's death at Gettysburg was so violent the pieces of his body could not be collected. Family tradition holds his mother screamed, "Oh my God, my Joel is dead!" at precisely the instant her son was lost, startling everyone around the dinner table. Helen Moore's brother was struck and killed by shrapnel in an Atlanta trench as he was writing a letter to her. She kept the missive as a treasure. [38]

When bodies were returned home, families took comfort in highly ritualized and sentimentalized burials. Women made these ever more elaborate affairs, covering the caskets with flowers and acting out the roles of the missing, standing as substitutes for absent family. Sergeant Charlie Dickison, the son of Captain John J. Dickison, was killed in a skirmish in August 1864. His body was sent home to Orange Springs, but neither of his parents could attend the funeral. Sarah E. Freyer described the event in a letter to Captain Dickison: "We accepted the remains of the young hero-martyr as a sacred trust.... Gentle maidens

---

[36]Sterkx and Thompson, "Letters of a Teenage Confederate," 344–45.

[37]Letter to Sallie Raysor, 23 February 1863, Raysor Family Papers, P. K. Yonge Library, University of Florida.

[38]Reaver, "Letters of Joel C. Blake," 5; Helen M. Edwards, "Memoirs," *Keystone Kin* 11 (December 1997): 3.

kissed his calm, pale brow with sisterly affection, and twined a laurel-wreath (around it). Kind matrons kissed him for his absent mother."[39]

Floridians made many sacrifices of food, goods, and time. They paid exorbitant taxes and met cruel conscription demands. But as early as 1862, a dark malaise had begun settling over many citizens, a kind of apathy that undermined Confederate patriotism. Now with every coffin or condolence letter, Floridians had to ask themselves a simple question: was the war worth the cost?

---

[39]Dickison, *Dickison and his Men*, 77–78, 82. For a thorough understanding of how Americans dealt with death and grief during the Civil War, see Drew Gilpin Faust, *This Republic of Suffering: Death and the American Civil War* (New York: Alfred A. Knopf, 2008).

Chapter 10

The Whole Affair Was Bungled

Olustee and the South Florida Campaign, 1864

The year 1863 had passed with little Federal attention directed at Florida, except in the continued tightening of the blockade, the largely ineffective raids upon saltworks, and a brief, insignificant incursion into Jacksonville. Floridians had begun to suffer from war, however, even if the only military incidents in the state were skirmishes. The blockade was an economic garrote, and conscription was depriving Florida of what few healthy men remained to support and protect its dependent population. Impressment of food and livestock left already impoverished people with nothing but worthless Confederate bills to show for months of labor. Families were becoming disenchanted with the government. Many Floridians thoroughly resented how little the Confederacy seemed to value their state or appreciate their sacrifices. But at least 1863 had been relatively uneventful in terms of bloodshed on home soil.

The fourth year of the war ushered in a major campaign in East Florida and brought savage conflict to South Florida as well. The Union was finally recognizing Florida's importance to the Confederacy, seeing it as a storehouse of foodstuffs, particularly beef. Determined to cut off this supply, to starve the Confederacy into submission, Union attacks would once again commence and the war would come home.

* * *

The 1864 campaigns were rooted in a new appreciation of Florida's role as a Confederate supply center and from Republican political machinations. Reports (if erroneous) of thousands of cattle being driven from Florida ranges each week gave new impetus to plans for an invasion. The advent of an election year also made it imperative to win military victories if the Republicans were to retain control of the White House. Lincoln knew that both Democrats and fellow Republicans were scheming against him. As 1863 ended, rumors that Florida could easily be returned to the Union prompted Federal Tax Collector Lyman Stickley, an agent of potential presidential candidate Salmon Chase, to engage in the conspiratorial dealings that eventually led to General Gillmore proposing an expedition to Florida. Gillmore sold it as a mission that would capitalize on the ease with which Jacksonville could be claimed and the Confederate supply of beef interrupted. General-in-Chief Henry Halleck, the "Old Brains" of the Union command, gave Gillmore discretion to act, but in January 1864, Secretary of War Edwin M. Stanton questioned the value of the planned campaign.

In response to the secretary's comments, Gillmore sent a more thorough statement of his objectives: first, to procure an outlet for Florida products, such as cotton, lumber, and turpentine; second, to cut off the flow of cattle from South Florida and to prevent the iron from the Fernandina and St. Marks Railroad from being taken up to aid the Confederacy; third, to gain recruits for black regiments; and fourth, to "inaugurate measures for the speedy restoration of Florida to her allegiance" to the Union. It was an ambitious but sensible plan. Florida was generally presumed to be helpless, with few domestic troops to defend her. Confederate reinforcements would have to be drawn from the Georgia coast, and, without a railroad linking Georgia to Florida, their progress would be slow and painful. Properly handled, the campaign should succeed. Gillmore received approval.[1]

On February 4, 1864, Gillmore ordered Brigadier General Truman Seymour to begin embarking his troops from Hilton Head Island. Forty years old and a West Point graduate, Seymour had some experience in Florida, having served in the Third Seminole War. He was also notorious for having led the bloody frontal assault on Battery Wagner in 1863. This new mission was somewhat of a mystery to the roughly 7,000 men involved.[2] They included units from across the northeast, as well as the 54th and 55th Massachusetts regiments, the black soldiers who were al-

---

[1]George F. Baltzell, "The Battle of Olustee (Ocean Pond), Florida," *Florida Historical Quarterly* 9 (April 1931): 201–202.

[2]Baltzell, "The Battle of Olustee," 203; Schafer, *Thunder on the River*, 178.

ready on their way to immortality for their courage under fire. They set sail on February 6 and arrived in Jacksonville the next day. By noon on February 8, the entire force was ashore. One officer of the 54th Massachusetts described Jacksonville as having once been "a very pretty place—but War has *ravished* it. It is made desolate and lonely."[3] The troops moved rapidly through the devastated city, reaching Camp Finegan that night. This Confederate outpost had been so hastily abandoned that Union men found steaming kettles of beef, as well as assorted papers and books, and even coats and swords left behind. Penned poultry was plentiful; therefore "the order to charge hencoops was given...the feathers flew in all directions." The soldiers relished eating their enemy's dinner, viewing it as a proper reward for a long day of marching through woods and swamps.[4]

Baldwin, a hamlet nineteen miles west of Jacksonville, was captured early in the morning of February 9. This was a prize despite its tiny size, for it was the junction of two railroads and contained some half-million dollars worth of turpentine, resin, pitch, cotton, rice, and tobacco, as well as a three-inch gun and a caisson. Hungry troopers paid for their hotel breakfast with Confederate bills found in the depot's garbage. Moving on, the Federals reached Sanderson, a village thirty-three miles west of Jacksonville, and occupied it on February 11. Though the retreating Confederates had burned some supplies, the Federals collected oats, salt, and other commissary stores.[5] Victory seemed assured. "We have evidence here continually that the Confederacy is crumbling to pieces," one journalist wrote, noting the steady influx of enemy deserters. The Feder-

---

[3]Duren, "The Occupation of Jacksonville, February 1864," 263. For a insightful consideration of the use of black troops in Florida, especially in the Olustee campaign, see David J. Coles, "'They Fought Like Devils': Black Troops in Florida during the Civil War" in Mark I. Greenberg, William Warren Rogers, and Canter Brown, Jr., eds., *Florida Heritage of Diversity: Essays in Honor of Samuel Proctor* (Tallahassee: Sentry Press, 1997).

[4]Nulty, *Confederate Florida*, 90.

[5]William H. Nulty, "The Seymour Decision: An Appraisal of the Olustee Campaign," *Florida Historical Quarterly* 65 (January 1987): 300–303; Nutley, *Confederate Florida*, 91.

als felt certain Florida's northeastern corner had been "virtually abandoned" by the Confederacy.[6]

Some resistance was encountered as the Federals crept westward, but it was more token than deadly. General Joseph Finegan, commanding the District of East Florida, knew that the only hope of defending Florida rested in delaying a battle long enough to collect reinforcements from outside the state. His appeal to General Beauregard led to the release of Confederate troops from James Island and Savannah; these troops began to move south on February 11. Meanwhile, Floridians responded to the Yankee incursion with surprising calmness. A Tallahassee newspaper urged people to be of "good cheer" and not to "lend a credulous ear to false or exaggerated rumors." The area around Jacksonville was underpopulated and much of the land was covered with longleaf pines, scrubs, and grass. One Union soldier noted "for *my* part I can't see what there is in here worth sending an *army* after; but I suppose Gen. Seymour or some other general does."[7] If the Union forces settled around Sanderson they would be of little threat, but if they moved further west, as they were certain to do, they would threaten the plantation counties of Middle Florida and eventually the capital.

Governor Milton lacked faith in Finegan's abilities. Arguing that neither the soldiers nor the citizens of Florida trusted Finegan's leadership, Milton wired Secretary of War James A. Seddon to demand a change of commander. "All will be lost," Milton predicted, but the battle at Olustee (also known as the Battle of Ocean Pond) occurred before Richmond took action.

Finegan summoned his reinforcements to Lake City, the most significant town between Jacksonville and the Suwannee River. Units from South Carolina and Georgia were hastily organized into three brigades and one reserve artillery. Collectively, Finegan had 4,000 infantry, fewer than 600 cavalry, and a mere twelve guns. Facing him were five brigades

---

[6]Foster and Foster, "Historic Notes and Documents," 462.

[7]Robert P. Broadwater, *The Battle of Olustee: The Final Union Attempt to Seize Florida* (Jefferson, NC: McFarland & Company, 2006) 65; Vaughn D. Bornet and Milton M. Woodford, "A Connecticut Yankee Fights at Olustee: Letter from the Front," *Florida Historical Quarterly* 27 (January 1949): 255.

of Federals, which included men from New York, Connecticut, New Hampshire, Massachusetts, and Rhode Island, with black soldiers recruited from both the North and South. Approximately 5,500 men faced west beneath the Union flag.

Finegan also had an unknown advantage as he gathered his men: a case of Union cold feet. Writing from Baldwin on February 11, Seymour held that a further advance was impractical. He argued that he was outmanned and outgunned by the enemy. Nor was he hopeful of any sudden surge of Unionism; it would take more victories than his men could provide to bring Florida back into the Union. Political opportunism, not sound strategy, was putting his men at risk. Seymour recommended staying put, holding only Jacksonville and Palatka, which would allow the St. Johns River to serve as a base for future cavalry assaults. It was an opinion Gillmore may have helped shape and definitely shared, as the commanders had talked late into the night the evening before Seymour wrote his letter. In response to it, Gillmore instructed Seymour not to risk an advance on Lake City. In reports to Halleck, Gillmore appeared satisfied that a permanent occupation of East Florida and the St. Johns would work toward obtaining the goals of encouraging Unionism and diverting resources from the Confederacy. On February 14, Gillmore left Florida for his headquarters at Hilton Head.[8]

Meanwhile, Seymour sent out raiding parties. Successful expeditions to Gainesville and along the St. Marys River collected contrabands, refugees, and supplies. Emboldened, Seymour changed his mind about his chances of success. He now believed the "people of this state kindly treated by us, will soon be ready to return to the Union." He also believed that he could destroy the Suwannee River bridge, effectively slicing the state in half. A number of his officers pointed out the danger of advancing so far west with only one railroad to support them, a line that could be easily cut, leaving them trapped in enemy territory. But Seymour ignored their advice, and on February 16, he sent a message to Gillmore that he was ready to move westward across the state. In fact, "probably by the time you read this I shall be in motion."[9]

---

[8]Schafer, *Thunder on the River*, 183.
[9]Ibid., 184.

Gillmore was shocked and confused by Seymour's sudden announcement. He wrote a note immediately, ordering Seymour not to advance. Fate and bad weather intervened. The bearer of the message, Brigadier General J. W. Turner, was delayed in reaching Florida. By the time the note reached Seymour, the Battle of Olustee was over. Seymour's decision to advance remains mysterious, controversial, and tragic.[10]

On the morning of February 20, both sides began to move. Seymour's force pulled out of Barber's Ford, with the ultimate goal of destroying the railroad bridge across the Suwannee River, an action that would effectively sever travel and communication between East and West Florida. Finegan chose to make his stand at Olustee, thirteen miles east of Lake City, the only area that offered even a modicum of natural defenses. The Confederates were arrayed in a north-south line, solidly blocking the Union army's progress. To their north was Ocean Pond, a large lake, and to their south was a big swamp. The Florida, Atlantic, and Gulf railroad and the Jacksonville to Lake City road both bisected this line. If the Federals made it to the bridge, they would have to come directly through Florida's defenders.

Upon learning of the enemy's approach, Finegan sent out cavalry to skirmish and draw the Federals into his defensive works. The main force of Rebels and Yankees engaged at approximately 2 p.m. on a beautiful, clear winter day. The Union troops had been marching for seven hours without a break for a meal, covering sixteen miles of often mucky, exhausting road. As the struggle had begun with no prior planning, the best the Federals could do "was attack whatever was offering resistance in front of them."[11] By mid-afternoon the battle reached its climax. Patrick Egan, a Rhode Island veteran, recalled that the fighting "on both sides was something terrible. It seemed as if no one could possibly escape, the bullets appeared as thick as mosquitoes in a marshy land." The Confederates held a slight advantage in position though neither side had the

---

[10]Johns, *Florida during the Civil War*, 198–99; Nulty, "The Seymour Decision," 304–309.

[11]Nulty, *Confederate Florida*, 131–33, 136; Schafer, *Thunder on the River*, 186; Coles, "They Fought Like Devils," 35–36.

benefit of careful preparation or the ability to duck behind well-engineered defenses. Both sides fought bravely through virgin pine forest and across a cleared field, hemmed in by the lake, numerous bays, and the swamp. But the Federals were "outgeneraled," and Seymour foolishly sent his troops into battle piecemeal, which allowed them to be "defeated in detail" by the Confederates, who were obviously enthusiastic for the fight. Invigorated by action after seeing so little of it in Florida, Winston Stephens reported feeling "like I could wade through my weight in wild cats" during the battle.[12]

At just past six the Confederates ran short of ammunition, leading to a lull in the action that gave the Federals a chance to begin withdrawing. The black soldiers were brought into position to cover the retreat, preventing it from becoming a rout. Men from the 7th Connecticut, Henry's Cavalry, and Elder's Battery, along with the survivors of Company C, 3rd Rhode Island Heavy Artillery, also screened the departing troops. Despite their twelve ambulances, many of the Federal wounded fell by the wayside. As darkness conquered daylight, the only major battle fought on Florida soil came to a close. In the words of Seymour's telegram to Jacksonville, it had been "A devilish hard rub."[13]

The Union retreat was painful and exhausting. "By this time most of the army was in disorder," Patrick Egan remembered, "every one apparently looking out for himself." Stops were made to destroy materiel at Sanderson and Baldwin. A train filled with wounded broke down, and the soldiers of the 54th Massachusetts were sent back to attach ropes to the engine and lug the cars forward from Ten Mile Station to Camp Finegan, risking capture and certain death if the Confederates pursued them. "Does history record a nobler deed?" a sanitary commission agent

---

[12]Baltzell, "The Battle of Olustee," 211–21; Patrick Egan, *The Florida Campaign with Light Battery C, Third Rhode Island Heavy Artillery* (Providence: Soldiers and Sailors Historical Society of Rhode Island, 1905) 15; David J. Coles, "Southern Hospitality: A Yankee Prisoner at Olustee, Tallahassee, and Andersonville," *Apalachee* 10 (1984–1990) 16; Blakey, et al., *Rose Cottage Chronicles*, 319.

[13]Nulty, *Confederate Florida*, 168–69; Baltzell, "The Battle of Olustee," 222; Schafer, *Thunder on the River*, 187.

asked. Fortunately for the Union troops, the Confederates did not give chase after "probably one of the hardest fought battles of the war."[14]

The Confederates had won an indisputable victory. Along with forcing the Federals to retreat to Jacksonville and thwarting the Union incursion into Florida, the Confederates also claimed 5 cannon, 1,600 small arms, 400 accouterment sets, and 130,000 rounds of small arms ammunition as booty from the Federal flight. Casualties were significant on both sides, however. The Confederates tallied 93 killed, 847 wounded, and 6 missing. The Union lost 203 killed, 1,152 wounded, and 506 missing. For the Union, Olustee was proportionally the third bloodiest battle of the Civil War.[15]

Controversy haunts the field at Olustee. The exact number of Union soldiers taken prisoner and the treatment of their black comrades has long been a subject of debate. General James Patton Anderson assumed command of the Confederate forces shortly after the battle, and reported to his Union counterpart in Jacksonville that 349 Federals had been wounded and captured, with 7 dying while in Confederate care. Most of the prisoners were taken first to Lake City, then to Tallahassee, and finally to the hellhole that was the Andersonville stockade. While Anderson claimed that the black soldiers received equitable and honorable treatment, Union survivors swore they had seen Confederates murder wounded black troops on the battlefield. An unnamed Union soldier who endured imprisonment at Andersonville wrote of seeing wounded blacks "bayoneted without mercy" while their captive white officers were tortured and threatened with being buried alive amidst the black corpses. Just before the battle, Colonel Abner McCormick of the 2nd Florida Cavalry told his men that black troops would "run over the state and murder, kill, and rape our wives, daughters, and sweethearts. Let's teach them a lesson. I shall not take any negro prisoners in this fight." Multiple Confederate letters and memoirs mention the butchering of blacks; one

---

[14]Egan, *The Florida Campaign*, 16–19; Nulty, *Confederate Florida*, 176–79; Coles, "They Fought Like Devils," 38.

[15]Nulty, "The Seymour Decision," 298; Nulty, *Confederate Florida*, 203.

even suggests they were the victims of unnecessary amputations. Southern racism undoubtedly cost many wounded Union soldiers their lives.[16]

The victory at Olustee unleashed immediate relief and rejoicing across Florida. The state legislature joined with the Confederate Congress in voting a resolution of thanks to the previously maligned Finegan. In the days after the confrontation, families wandered that rarest of sights, a Florida battlefield, where they marveled over dead horses, tin cans, canteens, and broken weapons, then sneered that the Union prisoners held in town were "foreigners—substitutes—men hired to fight in the place of Federal soldiers." Despite their prejudice, and to their credit, they pitied the captives and brought food to them.[17] Some Floridians had found themselves caught up in the crisis, including a woman in a house near the Confederate field hospital. A survivor recalled her with simple eloquence: "She reddily gave every scrap of cloth but what she wore 7 of her bed ticks & a glorious & a grevious thing that from a humble & quiet life that within five hours after the Battle began six hundred wounded soldiers was laid down at this little woman's door. But she murmured not but was reddy to assist all night."[18]

For others, the victory was tempered, as Olustee brought war's impact home with shocking intensity. Riding across the battlefield the next day, Winston Stephens found his bravado stripped away:

> I went over the battle ground this morning...never in my life have I seen such a destressing sight, some men with their legs carried off, others with their brains out and mangled in every conceivable way and then our men commenced stripping them of their clothing and left

---

[16]Nulty, *Confederate Florida*, 128, 210–13; Coles, "Southern Hospitality," 17–18; Broadwater, *The Battle of Olustee*, 142; Coles, "They Fought Like Devils,"39.

[17]Maria C. Murphy, "Olustee," United Daughters of the Confederacy Scrapbooks, vol. 4, State Archives of Florida.

[18]Unsigned letter, United Daughters of the Confederacy Scrapbooks, vol. 3, State Archives of Florida. The survivor's quotation most likely refers to bed ticking, a cotton or linen fabric used to cover or hold together mattresses. By giving up all seven of her "bed ticks," which would have certainly been ruined by the blood of wounded men, the woman was making a sacrifice of her family's comfort.

their bodies naked. I never want to see an other battle or go on the field after it is over.[19]

In Madison, Margaret Vann joined with other women in bringing food and comfort to the Confederate soldiers returning via train from the battlefield. She was shocked to see a young soldier in a coffin, partially covered by flowers. "An old lady came forward, saying 'My son gave his life to Virginia and this son has given his life to Florida: let me kiss him for his mother.'" She then covered his face with her handkerchief. In Vann's memories, "It was all so sad, so pathetically sad...."[20]

On the Union side, General Seymour was thoroughly and publically castigated for his ineptitude. Northern press poured a withering fire on the general, accusing him of disobeying orders. Confidentially, in letters to family and friends, many soldiers had the same evaluation of their leader. Even before the battle, some had hated him for what they saw as harsh discipline. Missives from white and black soldiers expressed disgust with the way the battle had been mismanaged. "The whole affair was bungled," one Connecticut private wrote. He added, "Our men for the most part fought *well*, and the *darkies just as well as any.*"[21]

The great potential for stealing Florida away from the Confederacy had been lost. Federal forces were withdrawn to Jacksonville, which remained under Union occupation. Many veterans of Olustee would see action in other battles. The experience of fighting in Florida left a vivid impression in the minds of observant Yankees. One noted that Florida was "a rich country" and that "when the war is over, very many Northern men will move South...."[22] Serving in Florida stirred mixed emotions in the black troops who had once been enslaved. While not viewed as a significant battle in comparison to other clashes, Olustee had, in the end,

---

[19] Blakey, et al., *Rose Cottage Chronicles*, 320.

[20] Blakey, et al., *Rose Cottage Chronicles*, 320; Unsigned letter, United Daughters of the Confederacy Scrapbooks, vol. 3, State Archives of Florida; Mrs. Enoch Vann (Margaret Vann), "Reminiscences of the Battle of Olustee," United Daughters of the Confederacy Scrapbooks, vol. 1, State Archives of Florida.

[21] Bornet and Woodford, "A Connecticut Yankee Fights at Olustee," 247, 252, 255.

[22] Proctor, "Jacksonville during the Civil War," 355.

achieved certain objectives. For some time, it disrupted and diminished the flow of supplies from Florida. The fight drew Confederate troops away from other areas that could not afford to lose them, and it demonstrated the courage and skill of black soldiers.[23] On the fourth anniversary of the battle, Harriet Ward Foote Hawley, the wife of Connecticut governor Joseph Russell Hawley (who had been a lieutenant colonel of the 7th Connecticut) memorialized the struggle: "The battle with its terrible sacrifices was useless, save that the rebel losses of a few hundred counted a little toward that costly wearing away that finally brought the rebellion to its knees."[24]

Following the Union debacle at Olustee, another series of campaigns was waged in South Florida. Their objectives were similar to those of the Olustee expedition, if in a different location and on a much smaller scale. Disruption of cattle drives might be easier closer to the source of the herds, the vast plains and prairies of the Peace River valley. It was an area where Confederate loyalty was dubious at best. Waging war on Florida's southern frontier was unlikely to be glorious, but it might be crucial.

South Florida had not been greatly affected by the Civil War in the conflict's initial stages. In June 1862 a Tampa minister noted "very little excitement or apprehension of danger" in a country blessed "with abundance of the necessaries of life." In Brooksville, another reverend stated, "We are less affected here except taking almost all our men away, than any other portion of the Southern Confederacy." Blockade running was common along the coast and especially on the Peace River, but the tightening of surveillance was making the practice more difficult. Local legend Robert Johnson, a "daredevil of a fellow who feared neither God or man," so ruthless that even his allies considered him a pirate, was captured and imprisoned in 1863. For most South Florida families, however, the greatest threat was the presence of conscription agents dragging away

---

[23]Nulty, "The Seymour Decision," 297, 316. Surprisingly, Seymour's career survived his ignominious defeat, and he would eventually command a division in the Army of the Potomac. He remained in the U.S. Army until his retirement in 1876, and died in Florence, Italy, in 1891.

[24]Foster and Foster, "Historic Notes and Documents," 464.

reluctant draftees and the mistreatment of any individual who expressed Unionist sentiments.[25]

On December 2, 1863, Enoch Daniels, a Unionist refugee from the Charlotte Harbor area, arrived in Key West with a plan for military action in his home territory. Meeting with Union officers, he urged them to support the raising of a volunteer refugee force to "occupy and conquer the country between Charlotte Harbor and Tampa Bay." He was confident that Key West was home to enough loyal Union men, especially those who had fled South Florida, and that if they were mustered into service, armed, and accompanied by about 100 regular troops, they could set up a military post near the coast. This would encourage Unionism in their native territory and serve as a base for disrupting cattle collection in South Florida. Confederate deserters and draft dodgers would also be welcomed, and hopefully would choose to join the Union ranks. The Federal commanders were impressed with the scheme, and soon twenty-nine Key West refugees signed up, calling themselves the Florida Rangers and electing Daniels as captain. Brigadier General Daniel P. Woodbury, commander of the Federal District of Key West and the Tortugas, established three distinct goals for the expedition: first, encourage Union men in South Florida to enlist; second, recruit escaped slaves for service; and, third, supply Federal troops and ships with Florida cattle.[26]

As the Florida Rangers and their supporters embarked from Key West on December 17, South Florida was essentially defenseless, with nothing but roaming guerilla bands and a hundred-man garrison at Tampa to protect vast tracts of wilderness and the region's approximately 7,000 residents from Yankees and bandits. The blockade, labor shortages, and taxation had caused massive dissatisfaction with the Confederacy, but in some places Southern partisanship and tempers still ran hot. South Florida was an ideal environment to test a theory, that a small group of

---

[25]Brown, *Florida's Peace River Frontier*, 142, 150–53.
[26]Rodney E. Dillon, Jr., "'The Little Affair': The Southwest Florida Campaign, 1863–1864," *Florida Historical Quarterly* 62 (January 1984): 316–18.

Union men could win a significant block of territory from an otherwise Confederate state.[27]

The first incursion was unsuccessful. A skirmish with Confederate guerillas on the Myakka River prevented the accomplishment of Federal objectives. But Woodbury refused to abandon the plan of establishing a permanent garrison. Enoch Daniels's men and a small force under Lieutenant James Meyers remained on Useppa Island, and the *Gem of the Sea* continued its patrol of Charlotte Harbor. On January 5, 1864, Woodbury and a full company of the 47th Pennsylvania Volunteer Infantry sailed for the mainland, landing at the mouth of the Caloosahatchee near Punta Rassa on January 7. This detachment soon took control of an old Seminole War stockade called Fort Myers. Inside they found three men, two of them known Confederate blockade runners and possible Indian agents. The Federals imprisoned the Confederates and wisely sent a delegation to reassure the Seminoles that they would remain undisturbed in this war between whites.[28]

The Florida Rangers joined their colleagues and made necessary repairs to the fort. Soon refugees and Unionists began trickling into Fort Myers, and with these new recruits the Florida Rangers were reorganized as the 2nd Florida (Union) Cavalry, under the command of Captain Henry Crane, a man "well known and popular among the people of Lower Florida" and considered by Union officials as "a far superior stamp to the greater part of those who have come over to us." In February, the 2nd Florida Cavalry engaged in several skirmishes with Confederate guerillas. Their success in defeating guerillas gave Federal officers confidence in the Florida men, who were briefly responsible for the entire Union presence in South Florida while regular troops were being transferred.[29]

In spring 1864 an ever-increasing number of cattle were being driven down the Caloosahatchee valley to Fort Myers and to Punta Rassa,

---

[27]Dillon, "'The Little Affair,'" 315–16; Irvin D. Solomon, "Southern Extremities: The Significance of Fort Myers in the Civil War," *Florida Historical Quarterly* 72 (October 1993); 133. For a discussion of Floridian's anxieties about the Seminoles, see Robert A. Taylor, "Unforgotten Threat: Florida Seminoles in the Civil War," *Florida Historical Quarterly* 69 (January 1991): 300–24.

[28]Dillon, "The Little Affair," 318–26.

[29]Ibid., 327–28.

where the numbers necessitated the building of a wharf to handle the traffic. More volunteers arrived to fight for the Union. A survivor later explained the appeal of service at Fort Myers: "The people were poor, they were not able to move and maintain their families. If they joined the Confederate army they would have to move their families. They could go to Fort Myers and join the Federal army and be with their families." By May 1864 approximately 140 refugees had reached Fort Myers, and most of them joined a second company of the 2nd Florida Cavalry.[30]

Woodbury hoped for even greater things but met constant frustration from the Union War Department, which denied his grandiose plans for using South Florida as a launching pad to invade the Gulf Coast of the state. However, the garrison at Fort Myers continued to prove its usefulness and even its bravado. On May 6, 1864, two companies of the 2nd Florida Cavalry and a detachment of three companies of the 2nd Regiment, United States Colored Troops, along with naval support, seized Tampa. Though the town was abandoned in just a few days, Union forces had sent a clear message.[31]

The invasion of Tampa infuriated the Confederate forces in the region. The use of black troops was especially maddening to slaveholders, who considered armed freedmen the "ultimate insult." One South Florida historian holds that Woodbury purposefully used black troops as an irritant to racist Southerners, sending them on raids in the countryside as a way to "demonstrate the futility of the Confederate cause." Confederate partisans assumed that black troops would commit atrocities; in reality the black troops were more professional and far better behaved than the Unionist refugees, who were often in the game for a measure of revenge.[32]

In retaliation, Confederate guerillas launched a bitter campaign against civilians. Suspected Unionists around Fort Meade were harried, their property seized or burned. Almost a hundred people, mostly wom-

[30]Ibid., 329.

[31]Ibid., 329–30; Canter Brown, Jr., *Fort Meade, 1849–1900* (Tuscaloosa: University of Alabama Press, 1995) 47.

[32]Solomon, "Southern Extremities," 129, 133–34; Solomon and Erhart, "Race and Civil War in South Florida," 337–39.

en and children, were captured and imprisoned at Fort Meade. The Fort Myers soldiers responded with a vengeance. On May 14, they rode to the rescue, and their backwoods adventure concluded with the burning of Fort Meade on May 19. The Federals torched a number of Rebel homes, took Rebel prisoners, and liberated the Fort Meade captives, whom they claimed were "destitute of subsistence and subjected to most cruel treatment from the enemy." They also drove away a thousand head of cattle. The South Florida guerillas, and even the newly organized Cow Cavalry, were shown to be unable to defend the territory. The burning of Fort Meade infuriated many locals, leading to a "vary squally" time amid South Florida's pioneers.[33]

In late summer and fall 1864, the Cow Cavalry made progress in halting deprivations against the cattle herds and providing a measure of security to Confederates in the area. Meanwhile, a combination of heat, primitive sanitation, racism, and accusations of corruption made life miserable for both the refugees and the soldiers at Fort Myers. In late February 1865, the Cow Cavalry made a final attempt to dislodge the Union forces at Fort Myers, but the campaign turned into a soggy debacle. The Confederates returned, in the words of one veteran, "the most worn out and dilapidated looking set of soldiers you ever saw, horses jaded and men half starved." The Cow Cavalry had garnered only a few cattle, eleven prisoners, and one Union fatality. "The whole thing had been a failure," another veteran declared.[34]

No great invasion of Florida emerged from the fighting around Fort Myers. But as historian Rodney E. Dillon Jr. demonstrates, this small band of Union supporters changed the dynamic of the fighting: "In southwest Florida, the sometimes stagnant and often monotonous situation of Federal blockade and intermittent raids became an active struggle for vital supplies, territory, and the hearts and minds of the inhabitants."[35]

---

[33]Brown, *Fort Meade*, 46–48; Brown, *Florida's Peace River Frontier*, 169.
[34]Brown, *Florida's Peace River Frontier*, 169–75.
[35]Dillon, "The Little Affair," 330.

Chapter 11

A New Life

Late 1864 to Military Occupation

As 1865 approached, Florida was viciously divided. In the state's northeast corner, the Federals remained ensconced in Fernandina and St. Augustine. Having suffered through four invasions, Jacksonville was a tragic ruin although occupation by Federal forces was finally leading to new signs of life in the tortured city. Unionists of both political affiliation and impoverished affliction crossed picket lines almost daily, seeking protection and relief. "Everybody seemed tired of the war," Lincoln's agent John Hay had concluded, noting, "the spirit of the common people is broken."[1] Contrabands found freedom, and Northern investors greedily eyed post-war opportunities. Union troops rested and enjoyed the Florida weather. For all practical purposes, this section of Florida was now a Yankee state.

To the south and in the western reaches of the Panhandle, a true civil war was still being waged. Sporadic raids continued against salt workers and cattle herders. Union troops held a stalwart garrison in Fort Myers, but Cow Cavaliers lurked in the thickets and swamps. Neighbors quarreled, and even the most enthusiastic Confederate partisan would occasionally drive his herds to the Yankee market. In West Florida and around Pensacola, the Yanks and Rebs sparred and plundered, while deserter bands defiantly ruled their swampland fiefdoms. Almost everyone in West Florida was sick of the war and the anarchy that had come with it. Disloyalty was so strong that for over a year Governor Milton had feared a coalition of Yankees, Unionists, deserters, and slaves could "lay

---

[1]Reiger, "Florida after Secession," 141; Edward Marcus, ed., *A New Canaan Private in the Civil War: Letters of Justus M. Silliman, 17th Connecticut Volunteers* (New Canaan, CT: New Canaan Historical Society, 1984) 66.

waste, if not subjugate and occupy, all of Florida west of the Apalachicola River."[2]

Only Middle Florida remained Confederate Florida. Small towns were packed with refugees. Tallahassee was crowded with lawmakers incapable of solving the steadily mounting financial and legal crises. In the capital, Governor Milton's tragic depression was deepening, about to take a fatal turn. But through it all, Tallahassee's women maintained a feverish whirl of Confederate fund-raising: donating their jewelry, staging tableaux, performing concerts. Blissfully delusional, citizens of Middle Florida continued to sing "We Conquer or Die."[3]

* * *

Confederate victory at Olustee produced a euphoria that lingered in Middle Florida. Troops returning from the battlefield to Florida's small towns were treated to picnics, dances, and card parties. Madison responded with such generosity, and such memorable desserts, that the community was accused of feasting on sweets while other Floridians starved. A resident later defended her hometown, assuring detractors that the "delicacies" served to soldiers were cornmeal cakes sweetened with fruit and that the only thing truly plentiful in Madison in 1864 was Confederate money, which "represented nothing on God's earth."[4]

Another boost to Middle Florida's morale came via the exploits of Captain John Jackson (J. J.) Dickison. Leader of Company H, 2nd Florida Cavalry, Dickison won renown for his harassment of Union pickets and work details near St. Augustine. The dashing horseman also retrieved runaway slaves and annoyed Unionists and deserters, holding the Confederate interior line at Palatka through Green Cove Springs and along the St. Johns River. Floridians desperate for heroes endowed him

---

[2]Reiger, "Florida after Secession," 137; Rucker, "West Florida Unionists," 28.

[3]Long, *Florida Breezes*, 374.

[4]Mrs. Enoch Vann (Margaret Vann), "Reminiscences of the Battle of Olustee," United Daughters of the Confederacy Scrapbooks, vo. 1, State Archives of Florida.

with virtually supernatural powers, including the ability to walk disguised through the streets of St. Augustine, blithely chatting up the enemy. Dickison set so many hearts aflutter that the ladies of Orange Springs donated spoons to have ceremonial accoutrements crafted for their "Knight of the Silver Spurs."[5]

Dickison's great triumph came in August 1864 when he thwarted a Union raiding party determined to pillage Gainesville. The skirmish was quickly elevated to the status of an epic clash by reports of Gainesville women carrying water to their Rebel defenders and shouting "Charge!" from their doorsteps. "The ladies behaved with a good deal of composure, and in some cases even captured prisoners," the *Richmond Enquirer* boasted. If so, it was a rapid about-face for the Gainesville matrons, who (according to the *Philadelphia Inquirer*) had applauded the Yankees and cursed the Rebels as cowards during a similar skirmish in February. Though certainly distorted by the prejudices of the sectional journalists, both reports might still hold a grain of truth. By 1864, Floridians had learned the value of flexible loyalty over steadfast allegiance. They were becoming pragmatists and opportunists of the first order, not from any sense of craftiness, but strictly out of a struggle to survive.[6]

No matter how inspiring, Dickison could not be everywhere. In the wake of Olustee, General Beauregard developed a plan of "mobile defense" for the state. Florida's Confederates were to avoid any aggressive action. Federal forces could land uncontested for their raids and foraging. If a significant body of troops invaded, Florida's defenders would lure them inland along a scorched-earth trail, waiting for a confrontation until Union supply lines were extended and significant Confederate reinforcements had arrived. This strategy was an attempt to capitalize on Florida's geography, but to support it Florida would need more domestic troops, which the Confederacy could not spare. Governor Milton issued a proclamation on July 30 summoning all men capable of bearing arms—

[5]Brown, "The Civil War," 242–43; East and Jenckes, "St. Augustine during the Civil War," 88–89; Dickison, *Dickison and His Men*, 133–34, 217–21.

[6]Brown, "The Civil War," 243; F. W. Buchholz, *History of Alachua County, Florida: Narrative and Biographical* (St. Augustine: Record, 1929) 116–18, 127; *Richmond Enquirer*, 13 September 1864; *Philadelphia Inquirer*, 1 March 1864.

regardless of age or occupation—to organize militia companies. The proclamation was of dubious constitutionality, but few frightened Floridians cared. By November, more than three thousand men of all ages had formed forty-two companies. As Milton told the General Assembly, "the times did not admit of legal scruples when the safety of the State and its citizens was in hazard." The legislature quickly wrote the governor's actions into law.[7]

West Florida presented a special threat in the person of a Yankee commander itching for a fight. In October 1863 Hungarian-born Brigadier General Alexander Asboth took command of the Federal Military District of West Florida. Union authority was limited to the area around Pensacola, but Asboth was eager for action. His superiors vetoed two raids, but on September 12, 1864, apparently acting on his own initiative and perhaps goaded by information from deserter spies, he set out on a cavalry raid across the northeastern portion of West Florida. His goals were to capture Rebel forces in Washington and Jackson counties, liberate Federal prisoners held at Marianna, and collect recruits, horses, and mules.[8]

Marianna was a tiny village of approximately 500 residents, the seat of Jackson County but remote from the railhead at Quincy and some twenty miles from the Apalachicola River. It was guarded by an assortment of militia and patrols, and contained a Confederate hospital and stable. Asboth led some 700 men, a force that included West Florida Unionists and black soldiers, from Pensacola toward Marianna, surprising residents, liberating slaves, and taking prisoners as they went.

The Battle of Marianna is steeped in local legend and historical confusion. When the town's defender, Colonel A. B. Montgomery, somehow learned of the Yankee movements on September 26, a town meeting was hastily called and word sent out to scattered militia units to reassemble. A motley guard of about 100 boys, old men, and regulars

---

[7]Johns, *Florida during the Civil War*, 202–203.

[8]Mark F. Boyd, "The Battle of Marianna," *Florida Historical Quarterly* 29 (April 1951): 225–26; Charlotte Corley Farley, *Florida's Alamo: The Battle of Marianna as 'Twas Said to Me*, bound manuscript (State Library of Florida, 1980) 10.

home on sick leave shouldered shotguns, pistols, and antique flintlocks. They elected Jesse J. Norwood, a prominent Unionist, as their captain. Other Unionists, including some who had communicated with blockading vessels in the past, joined up as well. Hometown loyalty apparently trumped national partisanship. Whatever Marianna's "Cradle and Grave" Company lacked in terms of training or discipline, they made up for in belligerency.[9]

A barricade was erected across the central street and on the morning of September 27 the Yankee cavalry attempted to charge it, but withdrew under hot fire from buildings on each side. Asboth sent men to flank the town and charged again. Seeing his men were outnumbered, Montgomery ordered a retreat, forcing the mounted Confederates in the town to fight their way through the Yankees. While approximately thirty escaped, Montgomery was taken prisoner. The Home Guard had either not received or had ignored the order to withdraw and valiantly attempted to defend the town. Homes and a church were soon ablaze, and the guardsmen who had literally fought door to door were forced to surrender. Ten members of the guard were killed or died of wounds. Four of these bodies were discovered charred in the wreckage of the sanctuary, leading to accusations that Union troops had driven them into flaming church. More than fifty people, some of them noncombatants, were held prisoner. Asboth did not report his casualties, though a Northern newspaper put them at thirty-two and a Southern paper at fifty-five. Wounded in the face and left arm, Asboth decided that a quick return to Pensacola was in order. His force was back in its barracks before any Confederate revenge could be exacted.[10]

Asboth's attack accomplished relatively little. His men scooped up supplies, including 200 mules and horses and 400 head of cattle, as well as eighty-one prisoners of war. Some of these unfortunates would later die in Northern prisons. Though the town was not completely burned, it was thoroughly plundered because many of its residents had fled before hostilities erupted. The Battle of Marianna became a source of pride for

---

[9]Buker, *Blockaders, Refugees, and Contrabands*, 164–65; Boyd, "The Battle of Marianna," 226–31.

[10]Boyd, "The Battle of Marianna," 232–37.

its survivors. The Bible that had been rescued from the burning church was viewed as a relic, and family stories related how feisty grandmothers intimidated rowdy raiders and preserved households. While the battle may have made little difference in the outcome of the war (beyond demonstrating Florida's complete inability to defend her citizens), "Florida's Alamo" has been long remembered.[11]

The final significant Union offensive came not from occupied East Florida but from the contested region below Tampa. It reflected events outside the state as well as conditions within it. On January 15, 1865, Fort Fisher was battered into submission by the Federals, who closed the port of Wilmington, North Carolina, a popular destination for blockade runners. Union strategists feared that illegal vessels would now seek sanctuary at St. Marks and other more isolated areas on the Florida Gulf Coast. In February, a Federal raiding party out of Cedar Key met with unexpectedly fierce resistance from Dickison and his men, who crossed the peninsula to put up a stiff fight (until they ran out of ammunition). Cow Cavalry units demanded the surrender of Fort Myers but were easily repulsed. These actions convinced Brigadier General John Newton, in Key West, that Florida troops were being shifted to the south, leaving Middle Florida vulnerable to attack. A strong foothold just below Tallahassee would further discourage blockade running, and if things went well, the capital could be seized.[12]

General Newton was not one to waste time. He collected a force of approximately 1,000 men from the 2nd Florida Cavalry and the 2nd United States Colored Infantry and embarked from Cedar Key on February 27. The two transport vessels needed to rendezvous with blockading vessels, and a thick fog delayed this gathering and cost them the element of surprise. On March 2 six gunboats and three schooners joined Newton's two armed transports. A revised plan was made: a small party of raiders would go ashore to cut the bridge across the East River, and once that bridge was secured, the remaining troops would land and cap-

[11]Ibid., 236–40.
[12]Brown, "The Civil War, 1861–1865," 243; Edwin C. Bearss, "Federal Expedition against Saint Marks Ends at Natural Bridge," *Florida Historical Quarterly* (April 1967): 369–78.

ture Newport. The soldiers would then press forward, either to St. Marks or to the railroad that connected St. Marks to Tallahassee. While men marched, the gunboats would ascend the St. Marks River and cause damage along it banks. The warships would seize Port Leon.[13]

The expedition seemed ill-fated from the start. Bad weather slowed deployment and caused miscues. At 9:00 p.m. on March 4, the whistle of an unannounced train on the St. Marks railroad alerted Tallahassee residents to their peril. Word of the Union landing at the St. Marks lighthouse launched an immediate call to arms. Terrified citizens hurried to their city's defense and constructed a wall of earthworks they dubbed Fort Hudson. Major General Samuel Jones, the newly appointed Confederate commander in Florida, summoned reinforcements from across the state. Brigadier General William Miller, commander of the reserves, gathered all the local militia he could find. A last, heartbreaking addition to the troops was a company of young cadets from the West Florida Seminary.[14] In their ranks was John Milton IV, the governor's namesake. The governor's eyes filled with tears as he begged their commander to "take care of our boys." The train whistle blew, and on March 5 Tallahassee's "Cradle and Grave" company was off to war.[15]

Stumbling through the dense woods, General Newton decided to cross the St. Marks River at Natural Bridge, a place where the river descends and disappears into the earth. Early on March 6, the two forces met at this formation. The Federals tried twice to cross, but were held back. During the afternoon, Confederate reinforcements arrived, forcing the Union troops to retreat and seek the safety of their warships' guns. In a side action, William Strickland, the leader of the most dangerous deserter band in Taylor County, was captured and executed by the Confederates. Overall, the invasion was a small but embarrassing failure for the Union, with twenty-one killed, eighty-nine wounded, and thirty-eight missing. The Confederates reported three killed and twenty-two wound-

---

[13]Bearss, "Federal Expedition against Saint Marks," 378–81.

[14]Ibid., 382–84; David J. Coles, "Florida's Seed Corn: The History of the West Florida Seminary during the Civil War," *Florida Historical Quarterly* 77 (Winter 1999): 295; Johns, *Florida during the Civil War*, 203.

[15]Revels, *Grander in Her Daughters*, 72.

ed. The cadets had taken little part in the fighting and suffered no casualties, but they would forever be hailed as Florida's child heroes of the Lost Cause. As historian David Coles notes, "the mere participation in battle of such young combatants provided a sobering indication of the impending southern collapse."[16]

Relieved mothers, grateful citizens, and giggling girls met the returning train, where the victors were serenaded and the cadets' caps were topped with victory wreaths of wild olive branches. The next day, ghoulish souvenir hunters descended on the battlefield, collecting shell fragments and balls, and hoping for a glimpse of black troops floating dead in the river. On March 15, Tallahassee hosted a banquet for the city's defenders, complete with yet another flag presentation to the cadets. Newspapers boasted of the heroic feats of the boys and old men, distorting the "battle" until it had no resemblance to the haphazard affair in which luck, timing, and Florida's tangled swampland played a significant part. "If the people of Georgia had turned out to oppose Sherman as the Floridians have in the battle fought at Natural Bridge he would never have reached Savannah," one editor crowed. That was a grossly unfair comparison, and sensible Floridians knew it. They also knew, even if unwilling to express it in words, that the war was almost over.[17]

Reporting to his superiors, Newton noted that while his expedition had not achieved its central goals, it had not been a complete waste: two bridges, one foundry, two large mills, and a sizable saltworks had been destroyed in the raid. Union forces had also gained better knowledge of the St. Marks River and where to position their blockading vessels should this become a more likely route for blockade runners. And despite the celebrations in Tallahassee, not every resident of Middle Florida was convinced the danger was past. Alice Chaires had fled her plantation at the first alarm. In the wake of the battle she wrote to her friend Susan Bradford that she was packed up and ready to run again because she had learned from "deserters wives" that the Union forces would return, in

---

[16]Johns, *Florida during the Civil War*, 203–205; David Coles, "Florida's Seed Corn," 283.

[17]Revels, *Grander in Her Daughters*, 132; Johns, *Florida during the Civil War*, 205.

larger numbers. General Jones also did not share the city's faith that its old men and boys had whipped the Yankees. He fully expected another visit, along the same pathway.[18]

Time and events far from the swamps of Leon County prevented a second incursion and allowed Tallahassee to retain her small fame as the only Confederate capital east of the Mississippi not to fall to the Yankees. Lee and his Army of Northern Virginia finally broke out of their fortifications around Petersburg, ordering the evacuation of Petersburg and Richmond on April 2. Lee's only chance of survival was to link his troops with those of General Joseph E. Johnston, who was fighting in North Carolina. Sick, starved, and weary, Lee's men lasted for only a few days, being harassed and bloodied by the Yankees at every turn. On April 9, Lee could take the punishment no longer. Meeting with General Ulysses S. Grant in Wilmer McLean's house in the tiny village of Appomattox, Lee brought the madness to a close. Grant offered generous terms, including complete paroles and allowing the men to keep their horses. Rations were distributed to emaciated Confederates. Other commanders would surrender their scattered armies in the weeks to come, but this was the true end of the war.[19]

Floridians endured a series of shocks in that cruelest of all Aprils. On April 1, Governor Milton was at his Sylvania plantation. He had been ill for several days—the cause of his malady uncertain—but during that day he took a gun and ended his own life. His suicide horrified Floridians. Some who had admired him now changed their opinion, presuming he had taken the coward's way out.[20] But one of Milton's acquaintances could sympathize with his devastating mental imbalance. "The present condition of the country seems enough to drive all mad who had aught to do in producing this state of affairs," Ellen Call Long confided to her diary. "I do get out of patience with that class who in

---

[18]Bearss, "Federal Operations against Saint Marks," 389–90; Ellis and Rogers, *Tallahassee and Leon County*, 14.

[19]Masur, *The Civil War*, 78–79.

[20]Brown, "The Civil War, 1861–1865," 244. While most historians attribute Milton's death to suicide, his family members argued that the governor accidentally shot himself while trying to clean his gun.

answer to all argument cry out 'we must succeed for Providence is on our side.' I am inclined to think that Providence had nothing to do with the diabolical war."[21] Milton's death was a tragic loss; Florida could have used his "calm and steady hand" in the adjustment it was facing. Milton's death elevated Senate president A. K. Allison to the governor's chair. A political veteran, he quickly assured President Davis that he planned no changes and would try to continue Milton's policies of "cordial and earnest cooperation" with the Confederate government. Allison, however, had no opportunity to prove either his sincerity or his leadership potential.[22]

On April 9, as Lee was signing the surrender at Appomattox, the ladies of Tallahassee were preparing for yet another fund-raising concert to be given in the capitol building that evening. News of Lee's surrender did not arrive in Florida immediately, but when it did, many Floridians felt "the heavens had fallen." Poor communication and downed telegraph wires meant that some people heard it through word of mouth or read it in Northern newspapers. In Madison, the messenger who brought the news was nearly lynched as a "lying deserter." Floridians reacted to this dramatic turn of events in a variety of ways, and many simply refused to believe it.[23] Delusion remained strong, especially once the news of Lincoln's assassination by Southern sympathizer John Wilkes Booth followed news of Confederate surrender. Sarah Fletcher expressed the thoughts of many simple folks in her letter to her soldier son Malcolm: "is true that ol Lincoln is dead if that is so we may have some chance yet." Some Floridians continued to hope that France would intervene and negotiate a settlement recognizing Confederate independence, or that the confusion following Lincoln's murder would cause the North to let the South depart. Others called for a campaign of guerilla warfare and bushwhacking. Ellen Call Long must have rolled her eyes. Just before Lincoln's death, she confided to her diary that the Yankees would write

[21]Ellen Call Long Diary, 2 April 1865, State Archives of Florida.
[22]Parker, "John Milton," 360–62; Johns, *Florida during the Civil War*, 205.
[23]Denham and Brown, *Cracker Times*, 122; Enoch J. Vann, *Reminiscences of a Georgia-Florida-Pinewoods-Cracker Lawyer* (Privately printed, 1937) 39; Graham, *The Awakening of St. Augustine*, 130.

the history of the war and "we shall appear to succeeding generations as a nation of the most egregious fools—and I am no means sure but what we shall deserve it."[24]

Federal forces and Unionists in Florida received the news of Lee's surrender with delirious delight. Justus Silliman, a Connecticut volunteer, recorded that the men from his regiment returned to Jacksonville from a patrol on April 17 and assumed the cheering they heard signaled a street fight—"a common occurrence here." They soon learned the news from an April 10 edition of the *New York Times*, which had arrived on a boat from Fernandina. By the light of a tar barrel bonfire, the Federals "shook hands together, hugged each other and cut up all sorts of antics" in celebration. The revelation of Lincoln's assassination followed a short time later. Silliman was deeply suspicious of the Confederates in Florida: "woe to the traitor in our midst who shall dare to exhibit the feelings of his heart at this time."[25]

For every Floridian as distraught as Francis P. Fleming, who wrote, "I don't think I can live under Yankee rule," there was another Floridian who was simply relieved. Davis Bryant reported that when the news reached troops at Camp Baker the majority "seems rejoiced and do not hesitate to express themselves to that effect," even giving out a "hearty yell" that Bryant found disgraceful. Cow Cavalry Captain Francis A. Hendry spoke for most when he opined, "Thank God it is over with one way or the other."[26]

On April 30, General Johnston informed Governor Allison that he had surrendered to Major General William T. Sherman: "I made this convention to spare the blood of the gallant little army committed to me and to avoid the crime of waging hopeless war." Alerted to this surrender, General Jones met with Brigadier General Israel Vogdes, command-

---

[24]Sarah Ann Fletcher to Malcolm Fletcher, 29 April 1865, Zabud Fletcher family papers, State Archives of Florida; Johns, *Florida during the Civil War*, 206; Ellen Call Long Diary, 13 April 1865.

[25]Marcus, ed., *A New Canaan Private*, 100.

[26]Edward C. Williamson, "Francis P. Fleming in the War for Southern Independence: Letters from the Front, Part III," *Florida Historical Quarterly* 28 (January 1950): 209; Blakely, et al., *Rose Cottage Chronicles*, 365; Brown, "The Civil War, 1861–1865," 246.

ing in Jacksonville, to plan for peace-keeping in Florida. Vogdes received orders from General Gillmore on accepting the surrender of Florida troops. Gillmore insisted that Federal forces in the state remember "that while we are to be humane toward surrendered enemies, these men are still rebels to whom any forgiveness is an act of grace and not of justice." But a miscommunication robbed Vogdes of a central honor. Brigadier General Edward McCook was ordered down from Macon to accept Tallahassee's surrender. Leaving his 500 troops just outside of town, McCook rode in with a small group of officers and was received by city officials on May 10. The next day, McCook raised the Union flag over St. Marks, and on May 20 the Stars and Stripes were hoisted above the Florida capitol building. There was little ceremony—gone were the cheering crowds, the fluttering handkerchiefs, the hats tossed in the air. The great Republic of Florida was dead.[27]

"To be a conquered people is a novel experience, and we have daily both amusing and mortifying incidents in our unadaptedness to the change," Ellen Call Long wrote. "The women are especially cantankerous," she confided, but General Vogdes seemed to "think a few fashionable bonnets will subdue them." Floridians were uneasy, and about far graver issues than attractive millinery. Many families worried about reprisals against their sons who had worn the gray. "Do not tell them that you killed a Yankee for they might want to kill you for it," one mother warned. Slaveholders, especially in Middle Florida, were uncertain of the status of their bondsmen and hoped they could keep them enslaved through the fall harvest season. By late April, slaves on many plantations were becoming unmanageable, breaking into storehouses and smokehouses, stealing food but generally offering no violence to their owners. Soldiers returned to ruined farms and demoralized families. Refugees from coastal cities were shocked to find that their property had been confiscated and sold off for back taxes. Homes where generations of a family had grown up now belonged to Yankee strangers or even to former slaves.[28]

---

[27]Johns, *Florida during the Civil War*, 206–209.

[28]Long, *Florida Breezes*, 381; Sarah Ann Fletcher to Malcolm Fletcher, 29 April 1865, Zabud Fletcher family papers, State Archives of Florida; Johns,

Governor Allison presumed that political life would have to continue and that he was responsible for restoring civil stability. But on May 19 the state was placed within the Federal Department of the South and a military occupation was ordered. On May 24 General Vogdes declared martial law in Florida. David Yulee, Stephen Mallory, and Governor Allison were arrested. All persons of prominence and leadership in Florida, including doctors, lawyers, and ministers, were required to take an oath of allegiance to the United States. On July 23 President Andrew Johnson appointed William Marvin of Key West, a moderate Unionist who was well-known and generally acceptable even to former Confederates, as provisional governor of the state. The long and turbulent process of Reconstruction was about to begin.[29]

The Federal occupation in 1865 was not a reign of terror, despite white Floridians' distaste for the black troops sent to enforce military rule. Confederate soldiers were quickly paroled, some 7,200 in Tallahassee and 800 more around the state. Most of these parolees were quiet and orderly, content to sign their names and go home. Rations were generously distributed. Mules and horses were loaned to needy farmers to help work their fields. Most men went back to work, eager to repair their lives and their fortunes, and many women began careers born of necessity rather than choice, opening boardinghouses and teaching school.[30]

Beginning on May 21, slaves were systemically informed of their freedom, told that no one could force them to stay on their plantations. By the end of the month, virtually every slave in Florida, however remote his home, had been liberated. The legends of a slave "jubilee" upon emancipation are largely unfounded. Most Florida slaves accepted the news with restrained dignity, though scattered incidents of joyful celebration, such as the "great saturnalia" that inspired a vindictive tirade in Ellen Call Long's journal, are certainly creditable. Overall reactions to

Florida during the Civil War, 212; Revels, *Grander in Her Daughters*, 137–39; Shofner, *Nor Is It Over Yet*, 7.

[29]Johns, *Florida during the Civil War*, 209–11; Tebeau, *A History of Florida*, 241.

[30]Johns, *Florida during the Civil War*, 209–11; Coles, "They Fought Like Devils," 41; Revels, *Grander in Her Daughter*, 139.

emancipation were mixed; some freedmen opted to stay on their plantations and began working out agreements as to how crops would be divided or wages paid. This was the option that Federal forces and the Freedmen's Bureau actively encouraged, and the 1865 crops were not neglected. Other former bondsmen departed from places where their enslavement had been especially cruel. Many went in search of lost family members, reuniting with spouses and children. No significant acts of retribution against former owners were recorded, and by October 1866 a Freedman's Bureau inspector reported from East Florida that the "condition of the Freedmen is generally better than expected. Instead of finding them wandering from place to place, or idling, they were generally employed on the plantations, in mechanical labor or as house Servants."[31]

Florida's freedmen and women demonstrated remarkable empathy and compassion to their former owners, and many were glad to swap the designation of slave for the title of friend. Princess Murat, who had lost everything in the war, was maintained for a time by donations from her former slaves. Mary Brown Archer noted that an impoverished woman was receiving advice and support from a former slave who "acts more like a *brother* than a servant." It would not be a perfect readjustment between blacks and whites, however. Gone was the deference, the doffing of hats, but true freedom—including the right to express one's opinion—was still elusive. In Quincy, a freedwoman named Sarah Ann "got right unmanageable and had an overgrown idea of her own importance and privileges" to the point that her former owner called in a Union officer, who arrested her. On January 15, 1866, the Florida legislature made it a crime for a former slave or person of color to "intrude himself" into any gathering of whites, including worship services. This was a pointed and bitter rejection of all black religious communicants, who during slavery had often attended church with their masters. During that same year, Florida would draft the infamous "black codes" which recreated in spirit, if not

---

[31]Johns, *Florida during the Civil War*, 211–12; Mormino, "Florida Slave Narratives," 415; Ellen Call Long Diary, 23 May 1865, State Archives of Florida; Jerrell H. Shofner, "Reconstruction and Renewal, 1865–1877," in Gannon, *The New History of Florida*, 249–50; Joe M. Richardson, "A Northerner Reports on Florida: 1866," *Florida Historical Quarterly* 40 (April 1962): 382.

exact letter, the old ways of slavery. The Freedman's Bureau would work hard in Florida, but ultimately it would fail to break the power of white supremacy, or alter the way most white Floridians looked contemptuously at their black neighbors. Racism was deeply and tragically rooted in the state, with far too many white residents eager to "hug the ghost of slavery" and pretend that little had changed.[32]

Paperwork filed in 1865 and 1866 paints an intriguing picture of a conquered state. General McCook reported that the only men who gave him any trouble about taking the oath of allegiance were the ministers. Many had taken it "with mental reservation" when they were threatened with the closing of their churches. Reports filed with Reconstruction Committees by Freedmen's Bureau agents claimed the "old women and silly girls," along with men who had never served, were the least willing to submit to the occupation. Irascible as ever, Florida's crackers formed the largest and most pitied body of the Unreconstructed Rebels. One inspector described them as "too poor...to purchase the habiliments of mourning—too proud to confess the guilt that caused their grief, too hateful to love what they can not possess." Despite their poverty and ignorance, they wished "to be let alone": monetary and religious assistance were equally unwelcome. Crackers were determined to live unfettered by any superior, and despite their many hardships they were "not poor in Spirit!"[33]

---

[32]Long, "Princesse Achille Murat," 36; Bertram H. Groene, "A Letter from Occupied Tallahassee," *Florida Historical Quarterly* 48 (July 1969): 72; Stowe, *Southern Practice*, 612; Ellen Call Long Diary, 27 June 1865; State Archives of Florida; Revels, *Grander in Her Daughters*, 137–39; Hall, "'Yonder Come Day,'" 415–16, 419. For an overview of the work of the Freedmen's Bureau, see Joe M. Richardson, "An Evaluation of the Freedmen's Bureau in Florida," *Florida Historical Quarterly* 41 (January 1963): 223–38, and for a discussion of the new rules that governed African-American life in the immediate aftermath of the war, see Joe M. Richardson, "Florida Black Codes," *Florida Historical Quarterly* 47 (April 1969): 365–79.

[33]Johns, *Florida during the Civil War*, 211; Joe M. Richardson, *The Negro in the Reconstruction of Florida*, 1865–1877; Richardson, "A Northerner Reports on Florida," 388–89.

The final tally of Florida's losses presents an even more sobering view. Between 14,000 to 15,000 men entered Confederate service, and some 1200 white Floridians and approximately 1000 freedmen joined the Union forces. At least 5,000 Floridians died in battle or from their wounds and camp diseases. Floridians fought at almost every major battle in Virginia, Tennessee, and Kentucky, often with distinction and always with great sacrifice. Two Florida Regiments that furled their flags at Appomattox each did so with less than a company's strength. Five thousand men returned home with some type of injury, many of them with permanent disabilities. Though approximately a third of Florida's veterans returned unscathed, modern insight into post-traumatic stress disorder suggests that many of those men never truly came home from the war, at least within their minds. What percentage of survivors became alcoholics, or grew addicted to opiates, or manifested shocking personality changes that their families could not understand? We will never know.[34]

Florida's total loss in property, including the value of her slaves, was estimated at $44,669,302. These figures cannot include the unknown amount of damage caused by raids, scorched-earth policies, and simple deterioration in property. Compared to larger states, where long campaigns were fought, Florida's losses might seem insignificant, yet an economic historian argues that invasions, raids, and disruption caused a "percentage decline in property values greater even than that suffered by war-torn Virginia." Cold calculations tell little to nothing of the intensity of human suffering or the bitterness of generational memory. At the end of the war, Florida's citizens were left with stacks of worthless currency, deteriorating or ruined homes, and far too many freshly dug graves. Slaves had their freedom, but that was all they had, and bold promises of land, tools, and education often turned into sad, unfulfilled dreams.

---

[34]Johns, *Florida during the Civil War*, 213. The exact number of Floridians who entered military service is impossible to calculate, and statistics vary, but most agree that Florida made an exceptional sacrifice of manpower. For more discussion of military contributions and casualty rates, see Dodd, *Florida in the War*; Gannon, *A Short History of Florida*; and Wynne and Taylor, *Florida in the Civil War*.

Those who had endured the Civil War, no matter which side they espoused, would not forget Florida's terrible sacrifices.[35]

Florida had entered the war as a frontier; at war's end, it was even more of a wilderness than it had been before. Frontiers dealt harshly with weakness and rewarded strength. Before the war, Floridians were known for their courage and determination in facing both human enemies and the unpredictable elements. These inner resources would be called upon once more. Floridians surely echoed the prayer of newly widowed Octavia Stephens: "I now begin as it were a new life and I pray that the Lord will give me the strength to bear up under the great affliction...."[36]

---

[35]C. A. Haulman, "Changes in the Economic Power Structure in Duval County, Florida, during the Civil War and Reconstruction," *Florida Historical Quarterly* 52 (October 1973): 175; Johns, *Florida during the Civil War*, 213–24.

[36]Blakey, et al., *Rose Cottage Chronicles*, 329.

Epilogue

The Lonesome Soldiers

With eyes of stone, they stare sightless across the state. Some shoulder their rifles while others stand at ease. One goes off to war with confidence, then returns broken and bandaged, lucky to be alive. A Confederate mother, her children pensive at her side, reads from a book of gallant deeds. A Union soldier in an unseasonable overcoat guards a plot of veterans' graves. Cast in zinc, he is leaning backward, in danger of toppling to the ground.

These are some of Florida's Civil War monuments.[1] Most were erected in the late 1800s and in the first twenty years of the 1900s. Reconstruction had passed, leaving native Southerners to "redeem" their states. A "New South" was rising, one that emphasized modern industry and economics, embracing Yankee entrepreneurial energy while seeking to maintain Southern "values": these included hospitality, family unity, conservative religion, and unquestioned maintenance of white supremacy. Southerners might have lost the war, but they were in the process of winning the history. Northern writers conceded the field, leaving a Columbia University historian named William Archibald Dunning to lead a vanguard of students in crafting Civil War and Reconstruction histories sympathetic to white Southerners, caustic to blacks, and critical of Federal actions. The brief and glorious Spanish-American War of 1898 rehabilitated white Southerners in the eyes of other Americans, thanks to their fiery resolve for "Cuba Libre." Confederate memorials and general Civil War commemorations became more prevalent as death thinned the

---

[1]To take a photographic tour of Florida's Civil War monuments, consult the Florida Public Archeology Network online at http://www.flpublic-archaeology.org/civilwar/monuments. For a complete history of Florida's war memorials, see William B. Lees and Frederick P. Gaske, *Recalling Deeds Immortal: Florida Monuments to the Civil War* (Gainesville: University Press of Florida, 2014).

ranks of veterans. With every year, fewer graybeards gathered to camp and swap lies about their days in blue and gray. Stone monuments, especially those with human figures at their zeniths, were seen by Southern communities as a way of keeping alive the memory of the men who fought for "Southern Rights."[2] Town by town, the unveiling rituals were the same: there was a parade, perhaps led by aged veterans, welcoming remarks by local dignitaries, musical selections and the reading of a poem, followed inevitably by a pompous oration. The draperies would be lifted and a photograph might be made, then the stone soldier would be left on guard for eternity. But Florida was not entirely Southern, despite her location on the map. Members of the Grand Army of the Republic succeeded in erecting monuments to their fellows in places where they had either served during the war or retired in their dotage: Jacksonville, Key West, Lynn Haven, and Miami.[3]

How often do modern Floridians study these monuments or ponder their meaning? How many of Florida's tourists—97.3 million in 2014, with numbers projected to climb—even realize that Florida was once a part of the Confederacy? Who remembers that there were 140 military events in Florida—skirmishes, raids, evacuations, engagements, and one disproportionately bloody battle—at eighty different locations on the peninsula?[4] Who has time for the granite man on a pillar when he's in a big hurry to see Mickey Mouse?

In the second half of the nineteenth century, as tourism became an even more lucrative industry, Floridians never tried to remind visitors

---

[2]For a thoughtful consideration of the Lost Cause myth and Confederate memory, see Gaines Foster, *Ghosts of the Confederacy: Defeat, the Lost Cause, and the Emergence of the New South, 1865 to 1913* (New York: Oxford University Press, 1987).

[3]W. Stuart Towns, "Honoring the Confederacy in Northwest Florida: The Confederate Monument Ritual," *Florida Historical Quarterly* 57 (October 1978): 205.

[4]Florida most likely passed the 100 million tourist mark in 2015, but as of this writing the figures were not available. Therefore, I have chosen to use 2014, which was a record-setting year (*Tampa Bay Times*, 16 February 2015); Allen W. Jones, "Military Events in Florida during the Civil War, 1861–1865," *Florida Historical Quarterly* 39 (July 1960): 42.

that the state had been the third to secede. Doors were thrown open to Yankee investors, and suddenly "every third man you meet from the North is arranging to build a hotel." About the only connection to the war that Floridians readily promoted was a rather odd one. Harriet Beecher Stowe, who had taken up residence along the St. Johns River, became a living tourist attraction, paid to sit in her yard by steamboat captains who would then point her out to their passengers. In the 1950s, the Lewis Plantation near Brooksville made a short-lived experiment in romanticizing slavery, hauling visitors around an old farm in a wagon and engaging black children to pretend to be playful pickaninnies. It soon closed. As historian Lamar York writes, "the tourist economy of Florida probably would not rise significantly from an enhancement of the state's regional character." As the twenty-first century dawned, Florida's antebellum history was largely confined to isolated historical markers and nostalgic dioramas in the museum at the Stephen Foster Folk Culture Center State Park in White Springs. Even the famous "Southern belles" in Cypress Gardens disappeared when the park closed in 2009.[5]

In the 150 years since its conclusion, more than 50,000 books have been written about the Civil War, yet Florida is generally fortunate to rate a footnote in major works.[6] A quick mention of Fort Pickens, a word or two about the blockade, a peek at Olustee, a snide comment about the cadets at Natural Bridge, and the job is done. Slaves worked, women made bandages, many people were ragged and hungry; what more is there to be said?

There is so much more. Florida has been blessed over the last century with a number of gifted historians. Starting with the work of William Watson Davis, a member of the Dunning school of historians who sympathized with the South, through the many contributions in the *Florida Historical Quarterly* and John E. Johns's more balanced interpretation in 1963's *Florida during the Civil War*, Florida's academics, historians, writers, archivists, and archeologists have been diligently reclaiming a history

---

[5]Tracy J. Revels, *Sunshine Paradise: A History of Florida Tourism* (Gainesville: University Press of Florida, 2011) 21–24, 101, 104.
[6]David J. Eicher, *The Civil War in Books: An Analytical Bibliography* (Urbana: University of Illinois Press, 1997) xxi.

that was sealed away in the tomb of the Lost Cause. Over time, Florida's searchers have found the Civil War story of its Unionists, its slaves, and its women. Other stories wait to be told, of foreigners, of Seminoles, of free persons of color. The tale is far from complete.

The story of Florida during the Civil War is a story worth heeding; it is a story filled with questions that could lead to valuable modern lessons. How does a radical minority lead a silent majority into danger? How can morale be maintained among a divided populace in a time of crisis? What is the duty of a state to its most imperiled citizens? What is the meaning of nationalism, of patriotism, of opportunism? Whose beliefs are worth fighting for?

In Fort Myers there are two Civil War memorials. One is a bust of Robert E. Lee, honoring the naming of Lee County for the Confederate commander. In Centennial Park, a statue of a sergeant of the 2nd United States Colored Troops looks out over the waterfront, a reminder of the Union presence and the military service of African Americans. Lee is stern and traditional, the very embodiment of the Old South. The sergeant is watchful, with just a hint of a smile on his face, as if thinking of better days to come.

Bibliography

Articles

"At the Dry Tortugas During the Civil War: A Lady's Journal." *Californian Illustrated* (January 1892): 87–93; (February 1892): 179–89; (March 1892): 274–82; (April 1892): 397–403; (May 1892): 585–89; (June 1892): 206–10; (August 1892): 388–95; (September 1892): 557–60.

Baltzell, George F. "The Battle of Olustee (Ocean Pond), Florida." *Florida Historical Quarterly* 9 (April 1931): 199–223.

Baptist, Edward E. "The Migration of Planters to Antebellum Florida: Kinship and Power." *Journal of Southern History* 62 (August 1996): 527–54.

Bearss, Edwin C. "Civil War Operations in and around Pensacola, Part I." *Florida Historical Quarterly* 36 (October 1957): 125–65.

———. "Civil War Operations in and around Pensacola, Part II." *Florida Historical Quarterly* 39 (January 1961): 231–55.

———. "Civil War Operations in and around Pensacola, Part III." *Florida Historical Quarterly* 39 (April 1961): 330–53.

———. "Federal Expedition against Saint Marks Ends at Natural Bridge." *Florida Historical Quarterly* 45 (April 1967): 369–90.

Bickel, Karl A. "Robert E. Lee in Florida." *Florida Historical Quarterly* 27 (July 1948): 59–66.

Bingham, Millicent Todd, ed. "Key West in the Summer of 1864." *Florida Historical Quarterly* 43 (January 1965): 262–65.

Bittle, George C. "Fighting Men View the Western War, 1862–1864." *Florida Historical Quarterly* 47 (July 1968): 25–33.

———. "Florida Prepares for War, 1860–1861." *Florida Historical Quarterly* 51 (October 1972): 143–52.

Bornet, Vaugh D., and Milton M. Woodford. "A Connecticut Yankee Fights at Olustee: Letters From the Front." *Florida Historical Quarterly* 27 (January 1949): 237–59.

Boyd, Mark F. "The Battle of Marianna." *Florida Historical Quarterly* 29 (April 1951): 225–42.

Brevard, Caroline Mays. "Richard Keith Call." *Florida Historical Quarterly* 1 (October 1908): 8–20.

Brown, Canter, Jr. "Tampa's James McKay and the Frustration of Confederate Cattle-Supply Operations in South Florida." *Florida Historical Quarterly* 70 (April 1992): 409–33.

Cash, W. T. "Taylor County History and Civil War Deserters." *Florida Historical Quarterly* 27 (July 1948): 28–58.

Chamberlain, Valentine. "A Letter of Captain V. Chamberlain 7th Connecticut Volunteers." *Florida Historical Quarterly* 15 (October 1936): 85–95.

———. "'Southern Rights' and Yankee Humor: A Confederate-Federal Jacksonville Newspaper." *Florida Historical Quarterly* 34 (July 1955): 30–35.

Clarke, Robert L. "Northern Plans for the Economic Invasion of Florida, 1862–1865." *Florida Historical Quarterly* 28 (April 1950): 262–70.

Clubbs, Occie. "Stephen Russell Mallory: United States Senator From Florida and Confederate Secretary of the Navy." *Florida Historical Quarterly* 25 (January 1947): 221–45.

Coles, David J. "Florida's Seed Corn: The History of the West Florida Seminary during the Civil War." *Florida Historical Quarterly* 77 (Winter 1999): 283– 319.

———. "Southern Hospitality: A Yankee Prisoner at Olustee, Tallahassee, and Andersonville." *Apalachee* 10 (1984–1990): 12–31.

———. "Unpretending Service: The James L. Davis, the Tahoma, and the East Gulf Blockading Squadron." *Florida Historical Quarterly* 71 (July 1992): 41–62.

Cushman, Joseph D., Jr. "The Blockade and Fall of Apalachicola, 1861–1862." *Florida Historical Quarterly* 41 (July 1962): 38–46.

———. "The Episcopal Church in Florida During the Civil War." *Florida Historical Quarterly* 38 (April 1960): 294–301.

Denham, James M. "The Florida Cracker before the Civil War as Seen through Travelers' Accounts." *Florida Historical Quarterly* 72 (April 1994): 453–68.

Dibble, Ernest F. "War Averters: Seward, Mallory, and Fort Pickens." *Florida Historical Quarterly* 49 (January 1971): 232–44.

Dillon, Rodney E., Jr. "'A Gang of Pirates': Confederate Lighthouse Raids in Southeast Florida, 1861." *Florida Historical Quarterly* 67 (April 1989): 441–57.

———. "South Florida in 1860." *Florida Historical Quarterly* 60 (April 1982): 440–54.

———. "'The Little Affair': The Southwest Florida Campaign, 1863–1864." *Florida Historical Quarterly* 62 (January 1984): 314–31.

Dodd, Dorothy. "The Manufacture of Cotton in Florida before and during the Civil War." *Florida Historical Quarterly* 13 (July 1934): 3–15.

———. "The Secession Movement in Florida, 1850–1861, Part I." *Florida Historical Quarterly* 12 (July 1933): 3–24.

———. "The Secession Movement in Florida, 1850–1861, Part II." *Florida Historical Quarterly* 12 (October 1933): 45–66.

Doherty, Herbert J., Jr. "Code Duello in Florida." *Florida Historical Quarterly* 29 (April 1951): 243–52.

————. "Florida in 1856." *Florida Historical Quarterly* 35 (July 1956): 60–70.

————. "Union Nationalism in Florida." *Florida Historical Quarterly* 29 (October 1950): 83–95.

Doty, Franklin A. "The Civil War Letters of Augustus Henry Mathers, Assistant Surgeon, Fourth Florida Regiment, C.S.A." *Florida Historical Quarterly* 36 (October 1957): 94–124.

Duren, C. M. "The Occupation of Jacksonville, February 1864 and the Battle of Olustee: Letters of Lt. C. M. Duren, 54th Massachusetts Regiment, U.S.A." *Florida Historical Quarterly* 32 (April 1954): 262–87.

East, Omega G., and H. J. Jenckes. "St. Augustine during the Civil War." *Florida Historical Quarterly* 31 (October 1952): 75–91.

Edwards, Helen M. "Memoirs." *Keystone Kin* 11 (December 1997): 1–6.

Ely, Robert B. "This Filthy Ironpot." *American Heritage* 19 (February 1968): 46–51, 198–211.

Falero, Frank, Jr. "Naval Engagements in Tampa Bay, 1862." *Florida Historical Quarterly* 46 (October 1967): 134–40.

Foster, Sarah Whitmer, and John T. Foster, Jr. "Chloe Merrick Reed: Freedom's First Lady." *Florida Historical Quarterly* 71 (January 1993): 279–99.

————. "Historic Notes and Documents: Harriet Ward Foote Hawley: Civil War Journalist." *Florida Historical Quarterly* 83 (Spring 2005): 448–67.

Garvin, Russell. "The Free Negro in Florida before the Civil War." *Florida Historical Quarterly* 46 (July 1967): 1–17.

Graham, Thomas. "Florida Politics and the Tallahassee Press, 1845–1861." *Florida Historical Quarterly* 46 (January 1968): 234–42.

————. "Letters from a Journey through the Federal Blockade, 1861–1862." *Florida Historical Quarterly* 55 (April 1977): 439–56.

Granade, Ray. "Slave Unrest in Florida." *Florida Historical Quarterly* 55 (July 1976): 18–36.

Groene, Bertram H. "A Letter from Occupied Tallahassee." *Florida Historical Quarterly* 48 (July 1969): 70–75.

————. "Civil War Letters of Colonel David Lang." *Florida Historical Quarterly* 54 (January 1976): 340–66.

Hadd, Donald R. "The Irony of Secession." *Florida Historical Quarterly* 41 (July 1962): 22–28.

Hall, Robert L. "'Yonder Come Day': Religious Dimensions of the Transition from Slavery to Freedom in Florida." *Florida Historical Quarterly* 65 (April 1987): 411–32.

Harper, Roland M. "Ante-bellum Census Enumerations in Florida." *Florida Historical Quarterly* 6 (July 1927): 42–52.

Haulman, C. A. "Changes in the Economic Power Structure in Duval County, Florida, during the Civil War and Reconstruction." *Florida Historical Quarterly* 52 (October 1973): 175–84.

Havard, William C. "The Florida Executive Council: An Experiment in Civil War Administration." *Florida Historical Quarterly* 33 (October 1954): 77–96.

Hodges, Ellen E., and Stephen Kerber. "'Rogues and Black Hearted Scamps': Civil War Letters of Winston and Octavia Stephens, 1862–1863." *Florida Historical Quarterly* 57 (July 1978): 54–82.

Ingle, John P., Jr. "Soldiering with the Second Florida Regiment." *Florida Historical Quarterly* 59 (January 1981): 335–39.

Jones, Allen. "Military Events in Florida during the Civil War, 1861–1865." *Florida Historical Quarterly* 39 (July 1960): 42–45.

Jones, Sarah L. "Governor Milton and His Family: A Contemporary Picture of Life in Florida during the War, by an English Tutor." *Florida Historical Quarterly* 2 (July 1909): 42–50.

Kearney, Kevin E. "The Autobiography of William Marvin." *Florida Historical Quarterly* 36 (January 1958): 179–222.

Keene, Otis L. "Jacksonville, Fifty-Three Years Ago: Recollections of a Veteran." *Florida Historical Quarterly* 1 (January 1909): 9–15.

Kimball, Winifred. "Reminiscences of Alvan Wentworth Chapman." *New York Botanical Garden Journal* 22 (January 1921): 4.

Kokomoor, Kevin. "A Re-assessment of Seminoles, Africans, and Slavery on the Florida Frontier." *Florida Historical Quarterly* 88 (Fall 2009): 209–36.

Linsin, Christopher E. "Skilled Slave Labor in Florida: 1850–1860." *Florida Historical Quarterly* 75 (Fall 1996): 183–96.

Long, Ellen Call. "Princesse Achille Murat: A Biographical Sketch." *Florida Historical Quarterly* 2 (April 1909): 27–38.

Lonn, Ella. "The Extent and Importance of Federal Naval Raids on Salt-Making in Florida, 1862–1865." *Florida Historical Quarterly* 10 (April 1932): 167–84.

Lucas, Marion B. "Civil War Career of Colonel George Washington Scott." *Florida Historical Quarterly* 58 (October 1979): 129–49.

Martin, Richard A. "Defeat in Victory: Yankee Experience in Early Civil War Jacksonville." *Florida Historical Quarterly* 53 (July 1974): 1–32.

————. "The '*New York Times*' Views Civil War Jacksonville." *Florida Historical Quarterly* 53 (April 1975): 409–27.

McGuire, William. "A Connecticut Yankee in St. Augustine, 1863." *El Escribano* 28 (1991): 56–80.

Mellon, Knox, Jr. "A Florida Soldier in the Army of Northern Virginia: The Hosford Letters." *Florida Historical Quarterly* 46 (January 1968): 243–71.

Mormino, Gary R. "Florida Slave Narratives." *Florida Historical Quarterly* 66 (April 1988): 399–419.

Mueller, E. A. "Suwannee River Steamboating." *Florida Historical Quarterly* 45 (January 1967): 270–88.

Nest, John F. Van. "Yellow Fever on the Blockade of Indian River: A Tragedy of 1864, Letters of Acting Master's Mate John F. Van Nest." *Florida Historical Quarterly* 21 (April 1943): 352–57.

"Notes on Secession in Tallahassee and Leon County." *Florida Historical Quarterly* 4 (October 1925): 61–67.

Nulty, William H. "The Seymour Decision: An Appraisal of the Olustee Campaign." *Florida Historical Quarterly* 65 (January 1987): 298–316.

Ordonez, Margaret T. "Plantation Self-Sufficiency in Leon County, Florida: 1824–1860." *Florida Historical Quarterly* 60 (April 1982): 428–39.

Otto, John S. "Florida's Cattle-Ranching Frontier: Hillsborough County (1860)." *Florida Historical Quarterly* 63 (July 1984): 71–83.

———. "Florida's Cattle-Ranching Frontier: Manatee and Brevard Counties (1860)." *Florida Historical Quarterly* 64 (July 1985): 48–61.

———. "Hillsborough County (1850): A Community in the South Florida Flatwoods." *Florida Historical Quarterly* 62 (October 1983): 180–93.

———. "Open-Range Cattle-Herding in Southern Florida." *Florida Historical Quarterly* 65 (January 1987): 317–34.

Paisley, Clifton. "How to Escape the Yankees: Major Scott's Letter to his Wife at Tallahassee." *Florida Historical Quarterly* 50 (July 1971): 53–61.

———. "Tallahassee through the Storebooks: War Clouds and War, 1860–1863." *Florida Historical Quarterly* 51 (July 1972): 37–51.

Parker, Daisy. "Battle Flags of the Florida Troops." *Apalachee* 1 (1948–50): 1–10.

———. "John Milton, Governor of Florida: A Loyal Confederate." *Florida Historical Quarterly* 20 (April 1942): 346–61.

Prince, Sigsbee C., Jr. "Edward A. Perry, Yankee General of the Florida Brigade." *Florida Historical Quarterly* 29 (January 1951): 197–205.

Proctor, Samuel. "Jacksonville during the Civil War." *Florida Historical Quarterly* 41 (April 1963): 343–55.

———. "The Call to Arms: Secession From a Feminine Point of View." *Florida Historical Quarterly* 35 (January 1957): 266–70.

Rayburn, Larry. "'Wherever the Fight is Thickest': General James Patton Anderson of Florida." *Florida Historical Quarterly* 60 (January 1982): 313–36.

Reaver, J. Russell. "Letters of Joel C. Blake." *Apalachee* 5 (1962): 5–25.

Reiger, John F. "Deprivation, Disaffection and Desertion in Confederate Florida." *Florida Historical Quarterly* 48 (January 1970): 279–98.

———. "Florida after Secession: Abandonment by the Confederacy and Its Consequences." *Florida Historical Quarterly* 50 (October 1971): 128–42.

———. "Secession of Florida from the Union: A Minority Decision?" *Florida Historical Quarterly* 46 (April 1968): 358–68.

Richardson, Joe M. "A Northerner Reports on Florida: 1866." *Florida Historical Quarterly* 40 (April 1962): 381–90.

———. "An Evaluation of the Freedmen's Bureau in Florida." *Florida Historical Quarterly* 1 (January 1963): 223–38.

———. "Florida Black Codes." *Florida Historical Quarterly* 47 (April 1969): 365–79.

Rivers, Larry. "Dignity and Importance: Slavery in Jefferson County, Florida 1827–1860." *Florida Historical Quarterly* 61 (April 1983): 404–30.

———. "Slavery and the Political Economy of Gadsden County, Florida: 1823–1861." *Florida Historical Quarterly* 70 (July 1991): 1–19.

Rogers, William Warren. "A Great Stirring in the Land: Tallahassee and Leon County in 1860." *Florida Historical Quarterly* 64 (October 1985): 148–80.

———. "Florida on the Eve of the Civil War as Seen by a Southern Reporter." *Florida Historical Quarterly* 39 (October 1960): 145–58.

———. "Newspaper Mottoes in Ante-bellum Florida." *Florida Historical Quarterly* 42 (October 1963): 154–58.

Rucker, Brian R. "Bad Day at Blackwater: Confederate Scorched Earth Policy in West Florida." *Pensacola History Illustrated* 6 (Summer 2002): 3–13.

———. "West Florida's Unionists." *Pensacola History Illustrated* 2 (Winter 2012): 21–30.

Ruffin, Edmund. "Edmund Ruffin's Account of the Florida Secession Convention: A Diary." *Florida Historical Quarterly* 12 (October 1933): 67–76.

Schellings, William J., ed. "On Blockade Duty in Florida Waters." *Tequesta: The Journal of the Historical Association of Southern Florida* 15 (1955): 55–72.

Schwartz, Gerald. "An Integrated Free School in Civil War Florida." *Florida Historical Quarterly* 61 (October 1982): 155–61.

Sharp, Helen R. "Samuel A. Swann and the Development of Florida, 1855–1900." *Florida Historical Quarterly* 20 (October 1941): 169–96.

Sheehan-Dean, Aaron. "'If It Was Not for You I Would Be Willing to Die': The Civil War Correspondence of Michael and Sallie Raysor." *Florida Historical Quarterly* 86 (Winter 2008): 390–405.

Sheppard, Jonathan C. "'This Seems To Be Our Darkest Times': The Florida Brigade in Mississippi, June–July, 1863." *Florida Historical Quarterly* 85 (Summer 2006): 64–90.

Slavin, Jessica. "'Everyone Is Tired of this War': An Examination of Desertion and Confederate Florida." *Apalachee* 11 (1991–1996): 16–24.

Smith, Julia F. "Slavetrading in Antebellum Florida." *Florida Historical Quarterly* 50 (January 1972): 252–61.

Smith, Marion O. "Confederate Nitre Bureau Operations in Florida." *Florida Historical Quarterly* 74 (Summer 1995): 40–46.

Solomon, Irvin D. "Southern Extremities: The Significance of Fort Myers in the Civil War." *Florida Historical Quarterly* 72 (October 1993): 129–52.

Solomon, Irvin D., and Grace Erhart. "Race and Civil War in South Florida." *Florida Historical Quarterly* (Winter 1999): 320–41.

Staudenraus, P. J. "A War Correspondent's View of St. Augustine and Fernandina: 1863." *Florida Historical Quarterly* 41 (July 1962): 60–65.

Sterkx, Henry Eugene, and Brooks Thompson. "Letters of a Teenage Confederate." *Florida Historical Quarterly* 38 (April 1960): 339–46.

Summerall, Charles P. "Soldiers Connected with Florida History since 1812." *Florida Historical Quarterly* 9 (April 1931): 242–58.

Taylor, Robert A. "Cow Cavalry: Munnerlyn's Battalion in Florida, 1864–1865." *Florida Historical Quarterly* 65 (October 1986): 196–214.

———. "Rebel Beef: Florida Cattle and the Confederate Army, 1862–1864." *Florida Historical Quarterly* 67 (July 1988): 15–31.

———. "Unforgotten Threat: Florida Seminoles in the Civil War." *Florida Historical Quarterly* 69 (January 1991): 300–314.

Thomas, David Y. "The Free Negro in Florida before 1865." *South Atlantic Quarterly* 10 (October 1911): 335–45.

Thompson, Joseph Conan. "Toward a More Humane Oppression: Florida's Slave Codes, 1821–1861." *Florida Historical Quarterly* 71 (January 1993): 324–38.

Towns, W. Stuart. "Honoring the Confederacy in Northwest Florida: The Confederate Monument Ritual." *Florida Historical Quarterly* 57 (October 1978): 205–212.

Uhler, Margaret. "Civil War Letters of Major General James Patton Anderson." *Florida Historical Quarterly* 56 (October 1977): 150–75.

Waters, Zack C. "Florida's Confederate Guerillas: John W. Pearson and the Oklawaha Rangers." *Florida Historical Quarterly* 70 (October 1991): 133–49.

Williams, Edwin L., Jr. "Negro Slavery in Florida, Part I." *Florida Historical Quarterly* 28 (October 1949): 93–110.

———. "Negro Slavery in Florida, Part II." *Florida Historical Quarterly* 28 (January 1950): 182–204.

Williamson, Edward C. "Francis P. Fleming in the War for Southern Independence: Letters from the Front, Part I." *Florida Historical Quarterly* 28 (July 1949): 38–52.

———. "Francis P. Fleming in the War for Southern Independence: Letters from the Front, Part II." *Florida Historical Quarterly* 28 (October 1949): 143–55.

———. "Francis P. Fleming in the War for Southern Independence: Letters from the Front, Part III." *Florida Historical Quarterly* 28 (January 1950): 205–10.

Wooster, Ralph A. "The Florida Secession Convention." *Florida Historical Quarterly* 36 (April 1958): 373–85.

Willis, Lee L., III. "Secession Sanctified: Bishop Francis Huger Rutledge and the Coming of the Civil War in Florida." *Florida Historical Quarterly* 82 (Spring 2004): 421–37.

Yonge, Julien C. "Pensacola in the War for Southern Independence." *Florida Historical Quarterly* 37 (January 1959): 357–71.

Yulee, C. Wicliffe. "Senator David L. Yulee." *Florida Historical Quarterly* 2 (July 1909): 3–22.

Zornow, William Frank. "State Aid of Indigent Soldiers and Their Families in Florida, 1861–65." *Florida Historical Quarterly* 34 (January 1956): 259–65.

Books

Abbey, Kathryn Trimmer. *Florida: Land of Change*. Chapel Hill: University of North Carolina Press, 1941.

Akerman, Joe A., Jr. *Florida Cowman: A History of Florida Cattle Raising*. Kissimmee: Florida Cattleman's Association, 1976.

Akerman, Joe A., Jr., and J. Mark Akerman. *Jacob Summerlin: King of the Crackers*. Cocoa: Florida Historical Society Press, 2004.

Avant, David A. *J. Randall Stanley's History of Gadsden County 1948*. Tallahassee: L'Avant Studios, 1985.

Baptist, Edward E. *Creating an Old South: Middle Florida's Plantation Frontier before the Civil War*. Chapel Hill: University of North Carolina Press, 2002.

Berlin, Ira, Barbara J. Fields, Thavolia Glymph, Joseph Reidy, and Leslie S. Rowland. *Freedom: A Documentary History of Emancipation, 1861–1867*. Series 1, vol. 1, *The Destruction of Slavery*. Cambridge: Cambridge University Press, 1985.

Blakey, Arch Frederic, Ann Smith Lainhard, and Winston Bryant Stephens, Jr. *Rose Cottage Chronicles: Civil War Letters of the Bryant-Stephens Families of North Florida*. Gainesville: University Press of Florida, 1998.

Board of State Institutions. 1903. *Soldiers of Florida in the Seminole Indian, Civil, and Spanish-American Wars*. Reprint edition. Macclenny, FL: Richard J. Ferry, 1983.

Bobbit, Mary Reed. *With Dearest Love to All: The Life and Letters of Lady Jeb*. Chicago: Regnery, 1960.

Bragg, Jefferson Davis. *Louisiana in the Confederacy*. Baton Rouge: Louisiana State University Press, 1941.

Brevard, Caroline Mays. *A History of Florida*. Vol. 2, *Florida as a State*. Deland: Florida State Historical Society, 1925.

Broadwater, Robert P. *The Battle of Olustee: The Final Union Attempt to Seize Florida*. Jefferson, NC: McFarland & Company, 2006.

Brown, Canter, Jr. *Florida's Peace River Frontier*. Orlando: University of Central Florida Press, 1991.

———. *Fort Meade, 1849–1900*. Tuscaloosa: University of Alabama Press, 1995.

Browne, Jefferson B. *Key West: The Old and the New*. St. Augustine: The Record Company, 1912.

Buchholz, F. W. *History of Alachua County, Florida: Narrative and Biographical*. St. Augustine: Record, 1929.

Buker, George E. *Blockaders, Refugees, and Contrabands: Civil War on Florida's Gulf Coast, 1861–1865*. Tuscaloosa: University of Alabama Press, 1993.

Cabaniss, Jim R., ed. *Civil War Journal and Letters of Serg. Washington Ives, 4th Florida C.S.A.* Tallahassee: Jim R. Cabaniss, 1987.

Campbell, R. Thomas, ed. *Southern Service on Land and Sea: The Wartime Journal of Robert Watson, CSA/CSN*. Knoxville: University of Tennessee Press, 2002.

Cashin, Joan E. *A Family Venture: Men and Women on the Southern Frontier*. New York: Oxford University Press, 1991.

Civil War Letters of Edmund C. Lee. Jacksonville: Historical Records Survey, 1937.

Colburn, David R., and Jane L. Landers, eds. *The African American Heritage of Florida*. Gainesville: University Press of Florida, 1995.

Crary, John Williamson, Sr. *Reminiscences of the Old South from 1834 to 1866 and a Biographical Sketch of John Williamson Crary, Sr. by May Crary Weller*. Pensacola: Perdido Bay Press, 1984.

Davis, William Watson. *The Civil War and Reconstruction in Florida*. 1913 facsimile ed. Gainesville: University of Florida Press, 1964.

Denham, James M. *"A Rogue's Paradise": Crime and Punishment in Antebellum Florida, 1821–1861*. Tuscaloosa: University of Alabama Press, 1997.

Denham, James M., and Canter Brown, Jr., eds. *Cracker Times and Pioneer Lives: The Florida Reminiscences of George Gillett Keen and Sarah Pamela Williams*. Columbia: University of South Carolina Press, 2003.

Dennett, Tyler, ed. *Lincoln and the Civil War in the Diaries and Letters of John Hay*. New York: Dodd Mead, 1939.

Dickison, Mary Elizabeth. *Dickson and His Men*. 1890 facsimile ed. Gainesville: University of Florida Press, 1962.

Dodd, Dorothy. *Florida in the War, 1861–1865*. Tallahassee: Peninsular Publishing, 1959.

Doherty, Herbert J., Jr. *Richard Keith Call: Southern Unionist*. Gainesville: University of Florida Press, 1961.

Dorman, G. H. *Fifty Years Ago: Reminiscences of 61–65*. Tallahassee: T. J. Appleyard, 1912.

Durkin, Joseph T. *Stephen R. Mallory: Confederate Navy Chief.* Chapel Hill: University of North Carolina Press, 1954.

Egan, Patrick. *The Florida Campaign with Light Battery C, Third Rhode Island Heavy Artillery.* Providence: Soldiers and Sailors Historical Society of Rhode Island, 1905.

Eicher, David J. *The Civil War in Books: An Analytical Bibliography.* Urbana: University of Illinois Press, 1997.

Ellis, Mary Louise, and William Warren Rogers. *Tallahassee and Leon County: A History and Bibliography.* Tallahassee: Historic Tallahassee Preservation Board, 1986.

Eppes, Susan Bradford. *The Negro of the Old South: A Bit of Period History.* Chicago: Joseph G. Branch Publishing, 1925.

———. *Through Some Eventful Years.* 1926 facsimile ed. Gainesville: University of Florida Press, 1968.

Escott, Paul D. *After Secession: Jefferson Davis and the Failure of Confederate Nationalism.* Baton Rouge: Louisiana State University Press, 1978.

Evans, Clement A., ed. *Confederate Military History.* Vol. 11. Atlanta: Confederate Publishing Company, 1899.

Farley, Charlotte Corley. *Florida's Alamo: The Battle of Marianna as 'Twas Said to Me.* Bound manuscript: State Library of Florida, 1980.

Farr, Cynthia. *A Sketch From the Life of Mrs. Nancy Jackson.* Tampa: 1900.

Faust, Drew Gilpin. *Mothers of Invention: Women of the Slaveholding South and the American Civil War.* Chapel Hill: University of North Carolina Press, 1996.

———. *This Republic of Suffering: Death and the American Civil War.* New York: Alfred A. Knopf, 2008.

Fleming, Francis P. *A Memoir of Capt. C. Seton Fleming of the Second Florida Infantry, C.S.A.* Jacksonville: Times-Union Publishing House, 1884.

Foster, Gaines M. *Ghosts of the Confederacy: Defeat, the Lost Cause, and the Emergence of the New South, 1865 to 1913.* New York: Oxford University Press, 1987.

Franco, Elizabeth Coldwell, ed. *Letters of Captain Hugh Black to His Family in Florida during the War between the States, 1862–1864.* Evansville, IN: Evansville Bindery, Inc., 1998.

Franklin, John Hope, and Alfred A. Moss, Jr. *From Slavery to Freedom: A History of Negro Americans.* 6th ed. New York: Alfred A. Knopf, 1988.

Fretwell, Jacqueline K., ed. *Civil War Times in St. Augustine.* St Augustine: St. Augustine Historical Society, 1988.

Gannon, Michael. *Florida: A Short History.* Gainesville: University Press of Florida, 1993.

———, ed. *The New History of Florida.* Gainesville: University Press of Florida, 1996.

Gordon, George H. *A War Diary of Events in the War of the Great Rebellion, 1863–1865.* Boston: James R. Osgood, 1970.

Graham, Thomas. *The Awakening of St. Augustine: The Anderson Family and the Oldest City, 1821–1924.* St. Augustine: St. Augustine Historical Society, 1978.

Greenburg, Mark I., William Warren Rogers, and Canter Brown, Jr., eds. *Florida's Heritage of Diversity: Essays in Honor of Samuel Proctor.* Tallahassee: Sentry Press, 1997.

Grismer, Karl H. *Tampa: A History of the City of Tampa and the Tampa Bay Region of Florida.* St. Petersburg, FL: St. Petersburg Publishing, 1950.

Hayes, John D. *Samuel Francis Dupont: Selections from His Civil War Letters.* 3 vols. Ithaca: Cornell University Press, 1969.

Hebel, Ianthe Bond, ed. *Centennial History of Volusia County, Florida, 1854–1954.* Daytona Beach: College Publishing, 1955.

Higginson, Thomas Wentworth. *Letters of Major Seth Rogers, MD., Surgeon of the First South Carolina Volunteers.* Boston: John Wilson and Son, 1910.

Hopley, Catherin Cooper [Sarah L. Jones]. *Life in the South.* 2 vols. London: Chapman and Hall, 1863.

Johns, John E. *Florida During the Civil War.* Gainesville: University of Florida Press, 1963.

Lees, William B., and Frederick P. Gaske. *Recalling Deeds Immortal: Florida Monuments to the Civil War.* Gainesville: University Press of Florida, 2014.

Little, Henry F. W. *The Seventh Regiment New Hampshire Volunteers in the War of the Rebellion.* Concord, NH: Ira C. Evans, 1896.

Long, Ellen Call. *Florida Breezes: or, Florida New and Old.* 1883 facsimile ed. Gainesville: University of Florida Press, 1962.

Lonn, Ella. *Desertion during the Civil War.* New York: Century, 1928.

———. *Salt as a Factor in the Confederacy.* Tuscaloosa: University of Alabama Press, 1965.

Luraghi, Raimondo. *A History of the Confederate Navy.* Paolo E. Coletta, trans. Annapolis: Naval Institute Press, 1996.

Marcus, Edward, ed. *A New Canaan Private in the Civil War: Letters of Justus M. Silliman, 17th Connecticut Volunteers.* New Canaan, CT: New Canaan Historical Society, 1984.

Marten, James. *The Children's Civil War.* Chapel Hill: University of North Carolina Press, 1998.

Martin, Richard A. *The City Makers.* Jacksonville: Convention Press, 1972.

Martin, Richard, and Daniel L. Schafer. *Jacksonville's Ordeal by Fire: A Civil War History.* Jacksonville: Florida Publishing, 1964.

Massey, Mary Elizabeth. *Bonnet Brigades.* New York: Alfred A. Knopf, 1966.

———. *Refugee Life in the Confederacy.* Baton Rouge: Louisiana State University Press, 1964.

Masur, Louis P. *The Civil War: A Concise History*. New York: Oxford University Press, 2011.

McDuffee, Lillie B. *The Lures of Manatee: A True Story of South Florida's Glamorous Past*. 2nd ed. Atlanta: Foote & Davies, 1961.

McPherson, James M. *Battle Cry of Freedom: The Civil War Era*. New York: Oxford University Press, 1988.

Mitchel, Cora. *Reminiscences of the Civil War*. Providence: Snow & Farnham Co., Printers, 1916.

Mitchell, Reid. *Civil War Soldiers*. New York: Viking Penguin, 1988.

Moore, Albert Burton. *Conscription and Conflict in the Confederacy*. New York: The MacMillan Company, 1924.

Nichols, James M. *Perry's Saints: or, the Fighting Parson's Regiment in the War of the Rebellion*. Boston: D. Lothrop, 1886.

Nulty, William H. *Confederate Florida: The Road to Olustee*. Tuscaloosa: University of Alabama Press, 1990.

Owsley, Frank L. *Plain Folk of the Old South*. Baton Rouge: Louisiana State University Press, 1949.

Paisley, Clifton. *The Red Hills of Florida, 1528–1865*. Tuscaloosa: University of Alabama Press, 1989.

Parks, Joseph Howard. *General Edmund Kirby Smith, C.S.A.* Baton Rouge: Louisiana State University Press, 1954.

Parks, Virginia, and Sandra Johnson, eds. *Civil War Views of Pensacola*. Pensacola: Pensacola Historical Society, 1993.

Patrick, Rembert. *Jefferson Davis and His Cabinet*. Baton Rouge: Louisiana State University Press, 1944.

Pearce, George F. *Pensacola during the Civil War: A Thorn in the Side of the Confederacy*. Gainesville: University Press of Florida, 2000.

Proctor, Samuel, ed. *Florida a Hundred Years Ago*. Tallahassee: Florida Civil War Centennial Committee, 1963.

Rawick, George P., ed. *The American Slave: A Composite Autobiography*. Vol. 17: *Florida Narratives*. Westport, CT: Greenwood Publishing, 1972.

Reddick, H. W. *Seventy-seven Years in Dixie: The Boys in Gray of 61–65*. H. W. Reddick: Washington County, Florida, 1910.

Reid, Mary Martha. *What I Know of the Travers Family*. Jacksonville: Historic Records Survey, 1937.

Revels, Tracy J. *Grander in Her Daughters: Florida's Women during the Civil War*. Columbia: University of South Carolina Press, 2004.

———. *Sunshine Paradise: A History of Florida Tourism*. Gainesville: University Press of Florida, 2011.

Richardson, Joe M. *The Negro in the Reconstruction of Florida, 1865–1877*. Tampa: Trend House, 1973.

Rivers, Larry Eugene. *Slavery in Florida: Territorial Days to Emancipation.* Gainesville: University Press of Florida, 2000.

Rogers, William Warren. *Outposts on the Gulf: Saint George Island and Apalachicola from Early Exploration to World War II.* Pensacola: University of West Florida Press, 1986.

Schafer, Daniel L. *Thunder on the River: The Civil War in Northeast Florida.* Gainesville: University Press of Florida, 2010.

Schwab, John Christopher. *The Confederate States of America 1861–1865: A Financial and Industrial History of the South during the Civil War.* New York: Yale University Press, 1904.

Schwartz, Gerald A., ed. *A Woman Doctor's Civil War: Esther Hill Hawks' Diary.* Columbia: University of South Carolina Press, 1984.

Sheppard, Jonathan C. *By the Noble Daring of Her Sons: The Florida Brigade of the Army of Tennessee.* Tuscaloosa: University of Alabama Press, 2012.

Shofner, Jerrell H. *History of Jefferson County.* Tallahassee: Sentry Press, 1976.

———. *Nor Is It over Yet: Florida in the Era of Reconstruction, 1863–1877.* Gainesville: University Press of Florida, 1974.

Sims, Elizabeth H. *A History of Madison County, Florida.* Madison, FL: Jimbob Printing, 1986.

Smith, Julia Floyd. *Slavery and Plantation Growth in Antebellum Florida, 1821–1860.* Gainesville: University of Florida Press, 1973.

Stampp, Kenneth M. *The Peculiar Institution: Slavery in the Ante-bellum South.* New York: Alfred A. Knopf, 1956.

Sternhell, Yael A. *Routes of War: The World of Movement in the Confederate South.* Cambridge: Harvard University Press, 2012.

Stowe, Steven M., ed. *A Southern Practice: The Diary and Autobiography of Charles A. Hentz, M.D.* Charlottesville: University Press of Virginia, 2000.

Taylor, Lou. *Mourning Dress: A Costume and Social History.* London: George Allen and Unwin, 1983.

Taylor, Robert A. *Rebel Storehouse: Florida in the Confederate Economy.* Tuscaloosa: University of Alabama Press, 1995.

Teabeau, Charlton W. *A History of Florida.* Coral Gables: University of Miami Press, 1971.

Ulmer, Herman, Jr., ed. *The Correspondence of Will and Ju Stockton 1845–1869.* Bound manuscript. State Library of Florida, 1984.

Vann, Enoch J. *Reminiscences of a Georgia-Florida-Pinewoods-Cracker Lawyer.* N.p.: privately printed, 1937.

Waterbury, Jean Parker. *The Treasurer's House.* St. Augustine: St. Augustine Historical Society, 1994.

———, ed. *The Oldest City: St. Augustine, Saga of Survival.* St. Augustine: St. Augustine Historical Society, 1983.

Waters, Zack C., and James C. Edmonds. *A Small but Spartan Band: The Florida Brigade in Lee's Army of Northern Virginia.* Tuscaloosa: University of Alabama Press, 2010.

Weitz, Mark A. *More Damning Than Slaughter: Desertion in the Confederate Army.* Lincoln: University of Nebraska Press, 2005.

White, Deborah Gray. *Ar'n't I a Woman? Female Slaves in the Plantation South.* New York: W. W. Norton, 1985.

Wiley, Bell Irvin. *Southern Negroes, 1861–1865.* New York: Rinehart, 1938.

———. *The Life of Johnny Reb: The Common Soldier of the Confederacy.* New York: Bobbs-Merrill, 1943.

Windhorn, Stan, and Wright Langley. *Yesterday's Key West.* Miami: E. A. Seeman, 1973.

Wooster, Ralph A. *The Secession Conventions of the South.* Princeton: Princeton University Press, 1962.

Work Progress Administration. *Slave Narratives: A Folk History of Slavery in the United States, from Interviews with Former Slaves.* Vol. 17. *Florida Narratives.* St. Clair Shores, MI: Scholarly Press, 1976.

Wynne, Lewis N., and Robert A. Taylor. *Florida in the Civil War.* Charleston: Arcadia Printing, 2001.

Yearns, W. Buck, ed. *The Confederate Governors.* Athens: University of Georgia Press, 1985.

Dissertations

Rucker, Brian R. "Blackwater and Yellow Pine: The Development of Santa Rosa County, 1821–1865." 2 vols. Ph.D. diss., Florida State University, 1990.

Archival Material

Auld Family Letters, State Archives of Florida

Council A. Bryan Papers, State Archives of Florida

Capo Family Biographical File, St. Augustine Historical Society

Eighth Census: Population, 1860.

Zabud Fletcher Family Papers, State Archives of Florida

Gibbs Family Biographical File, St. Augustine Historical Society

Hanna Family Papers, State Archives of Florida

William Burr Jones Biographical File, St. Augustine Historical Society

Ellen Call Long Diary, State Archives of Florida

John Milton Letterbook, State Archives of Florida

Palmer Family Letters, State Archives of Florida

George Washington Parkhill Letters, Florida State University Special Collections

Raysor Family Letters, University of Florida, P. K. Yonge Library

Reid Family Letters, transcripts, University of Florida, P. K. Yonge Library
Lewis G. Schmidt Collection, State Archives of Florida
Dena E. Snodgrass Collection, University of Florida, P. K. Yonge Library
United Daughters of the Confederacy Scrapbooks, State Archives of Florida
Washington Waters Papers, State Archives of Florida
Dallas Wood Letter, Florida State University Special Collections

Newspapers

Charleston Daily Courier
Fernandina Peninsula
Florida Sentinel (Tallahassee)
Gainesville Cotton States
Key West New Era
New York Herald
New York Times
New York Daily Tribune
Pensacola Weekly Observer
Philadelphia Inquirer
Quincy Dispatch
Quincy Republic
Richmond Enquirer
St. Augustine Examiner
St. John's Mirror (Jacksonville)
Sunbury American
Tallahassee Floridian and Journal
Tampa Bay Times
Tampa Tribune

Website
http://www.flpublicarchaeology.org/civilwar/monuments

Index

Cedar Key, 43, 85, 98, 159
Central Florida, 97
Chaires, Alice, 161
Chamberlin, Valentine, 45
Chapman, Alvan Wentworth, 110
Charlotte Harbor, 150, 151
Chase, Salmon P., 115-117, 119, 140
Chase, William H., 23-26
Chattahoochee Arsenal, 14, 15, 39, 50
Choctawhatchee 86
Choctawhatchee Bay, 96
Citrus fruit, 95
Clay County, 114
Confederacy, 1, 15, 33, 37, 52, 55, 63,
    72, 81, 104, 106, 123, 125, 131,
    133, 139, 141, 143, 149, 155;
    abandonment of Florida, 33, 38,
    46, 85, 29, 107, 108, 113, 142, 150;
    Florida as part of 1, 15, 33, 35, 36,
    148, 172; Florida contributions to
    47, 92-106; Florida soldiers in, 47-
    62
Confederate government, 21, 23, 35-
    37, 92, 103, 124, 133, 147, 163
Confederate taxes, 112, 131, 132, 138,
    150
Conscription, 35, 47, 97, 112, 131,
    133, 134, 138, 139, 149
Conscription dodging, 76, 97, 103,
    133, 134, 136, 150
Constitutional Union party, 9, 11
Contrabands, 84-88, 143, 150, 154,
    155
Corn production, 94, 94, 97, 124, 132
Cow Cavalry (1st Battalion, Florida
    Special Cavalry), 103, 105, 153,
    154, 159, 164
Cowmen, 100-106, 133
Crackers, 4, 7, 63, 67, 103, 123, 127,
    168

Daniels, Enoch, 150, 151
Davis, Jefferson, 21, 27, 28, 36, 37, 46,
    60, 61, 105, 108, 133, 163
Davis, William Watson, 173

Democratic party, 8, 9, 11, 36, 140
Deserters, 76, 103, 128, 134, 136, 141,
    150, 154, 155, 157, 160, 161, 163
Dickison, Charlie, 137
Dickison, John J., 66, 112, 137, 155,
    156, 159
Distilling, 95
Douglas, Stephen, 11
Dry Tortugas, 15
Dunning, William Archibald, 171
DuPont, Samuel F., 40
Duren, C.M., 117
Duval County, 64, 88

East Florida, 74, 85, 107, 112, 113,
    116, 118, 139, 143, 144, 159, 167
East River, 159
Egan, Patrick, 144, 145
Egmont Key, 87
Eighth Florida Infantry Regiment, 49
Eleventh Florida Infantry Regiment,
    50
Ellis, W. J. 10
Emancipation Proclamation, 77, 85
Eppes, Elizabeth, 14
Eppes, Susan Bradford (Susan Brad-
    ford), 8, 67, 90, 161
Erban, Henry, 16, 17
Escambia River, 85
Eucheeanna, 65
Executive Council, 36

Fernandina, 6, 37, 39-42, 46, 70, 74,
    85, 88, 89, 117, 154, 164
Fifth Florida Infantry Regiment, 49, 53
Fifty-fifth Massachusetts Infantry Reg-
    iment, 90, 140
Fifty-fourth Massachusetts Infantry
    Regiment, 140, 141, 145
Finegan, Joseph J., 50, 88, 142, 143,
    144 147
First Florida Infantry Regiment, 19, 50
Fisheries, 95
Fleming, C. Seaton, 65